MAKING MANAGED CARE WORK

MAKING MANAGED CARE WORK

Strategies for Local Market Dominance

GENIE JAMES

IRWIN
Professional Publishing®
Chicago • London • Singapore

Times Mirror
Higher Education Group

Library of Congress Cataloging-in-Publication Data

James, Genie.
Making managed care work: strategies for local market dominance / Genie James.
p. cm.
Includes index.
ISBN 0-7863-1012-X
1. Medical care—Marketing. 2. Health service administration. 3. Medical care, Cost of. I. Title.
RA410.5.J36 1997
362.1'068'8—dc20 96–20990

Printed in the United States of America
1 2 3 4 5 6 7 8 9 0 DO 3 2 1 0 9 8 7

This book is dedicated to my mother, Betty Frank Sandusky Williams (1929–1995). I thank you for always believing in my abilities, inspiring me towards excellence, and, finally, seeing my vision and believing my dream. I miss you, yet you are with me still.

PREFACE

The good news is that if you're reading this book, you still have a job in healthcare. Even better, you may be one of those business forerunners who has already survived one industry upheaval—like banking or the automobile industry—and you recognize a new industry swiveling on the pinhead of financial disaster as an opportunity to translate your successful survival strategies to another market arena. The reality is as the bottom falls out of healthcare only a few leaders will remain standing. But what will differentiate those individuals and systems that emerge as the heirs apparent in the new business of healthcare from those that fall by the wayside?

My answer calls for strategic transformation across our industry. It is obvious that the tried-and-true competitive strategies of the last two decades are no longer sufficient to win market share and profits. The essence of the healthcare business has changed. Before, individual hospitals and providers could function autonomously and duplicate services, and still enjoy a ringing cash register. Today, we must coalesce, integrate functions, share control, synchronize systems and divvy up the profits in order to remain viable. Innovation will require leaders who understand the power of a fast, multifunctional, parallel team approach to new business development, in order to give the healthcare industry fresh force. The solutions that work will be organized locally and rooted in fundamental business disciplines.

This book is organized to address the primary and critical questions that will frame your future (see Figure A), namely:

- What *business am I in?*
- Within that business framework, how do I *define my mission, vision, and purpose?*
- How do I *get prepared and organized* for what is coming?
- What can I do today to *"build a bridge" into the future,* that is, to contribute to the growth of a new industry and to ensure that I still *have a job and a role to play?*

First, tactics for uncovering marketplace needs are discussed. Next, I outline methodologies for conducting an internal diagnosis and evaluating the financial impact of current operational structures. Also included is a matrix that may assist you in analyzing how the relationship between market

FIGURE A

Managing Care and Staying in Business

Defining Your Business

- Alignment of competitive financial strategies with organizational mission/vision/purpose
- Analysis of managed care market and self-pay
- Evaluation of market factors posing immediate financial tension/risk
- Analysis of large employers' and local business coalitions' health care services purchasing trends and benefits designs
- Analysis/negotiation of managed care contracts
- Profile of provider performance: cost, quality, patient satisfaction
- Development of pricing strategies
- Development of managed care "shelf products" to be rolled out as reimbursement structures shift

Getting Prepared

- Building provider networks across regions and states
- Re-engineering health care services so that the patient is the "driver," and education and informed decision making become the central theme
- Designing spectrums of care that bring services to the patients
- Restructuring the hospital environment to reflect a focus on "healing" vs. "sickness"
- Shifting from a high-tech focus on treatment to one that emphasizes a multi-disciplinary and complementary approach to well-being
- Incorporating of complementary therapies into traditional medical model
- Fostering of new partnerships, joint ventures as needed
- Collapsing of boundaries between public/private service providers
- Design of interdisciplinary processes across a continuum of care
- Developing systems for outcomes tracking and monitoring

Bridging into the Future

- Create the environment for a "new business": establish vision/mission/purpose
- Analyze population's health-care spending patterns
- Identify/define "population or community"
- Prepare for managing a capitated population base
- Establish baseline health status and current utilization profile
- Assess degree of financial tension associated with population health status utilization patterns
- Assess communication climate and impact on health practices
- Use utilization and health status data to impact benefit plan design
- Design health education, prevention, behavioral lifestyle change incentive programs and materials
- Integrate health promotion and disease prevention with medical and personnel benefits
- Measure impact
- Evaluate, educate, communicate, modify, implement improvements
- Act as liaison between business and managed care groups

dynamics and corporate culture can affect organizational readiness for revolutionary change.

Economic competition—in the form of managed care—is driving a new industrial order. As a consultant, my role is to understand what is happening in the marketplace and proactively respond to the needs of my clients. Over the last three years, I have received an increasing number of calls from healthcare business decision makers who tell me that they feel as if they are "drowning in the quagmire of new managed care reimbursement scenarios, combustible and toxic organizational dynamics, physician tensions, and the pressures to be all things to all people at the community level." Watching peers lose jobs while a few monoliths appear to be gobbling up market share has intensified these cries for real-life pragmatic solutions.

As a purveyor of new products and services, I am called upon to synthesize ideas, assess the opportunities and barriers for market entry, anticipate market threats, and, ultimately, use financial projections to drive the implementation plan. Before the advent of managed care, one didn't have to be a genius to be successful in developing profit-centered strategies. Everybody was a winner. In today's competitive environment, however, the rules of the market are dynamic and treacherous in their impact. Healthcare leaders must be equipped with sophisticated business acumen and risk-taking abilities. However, the government's role in shaping a model that will finance that reform is questionable. "Capitation is coming" is a cry that portends doom and gloom, yet there is no real evidence that capitation works or that it can successfully supersede all other existing reimbursement strategies. Instead of trying to support key players as they grapple with controversial issues associated with access and cost and attempt to find common ground on complex issues—coverage for the uninsured, entitlement for graying America, rationing, medical specialty imbalance—politicians have used the idea of managed care to play up conflicts and cross-fires in a quest to enter the fray and capture the votes of a confused public. The truth as I see it is that managed care is not about managing health at all. It is simply an economic approach to decreasing cost and utilization via economic controls.

At least our industry is consistent in its mistakes: Just as we have been guilty of treating episodes of sickness rather than addressing the risk factors associated with community health concerns, our current efforts at organizational change too often address the symptoms rather than the root causes of the performance malaise. Unfortunately, there are many management consulting firms (and books) cashing in on the immediate opportunities created by industry-wide panic by touting cookie-cutter solutions and slash-and-burn strategies. The answer to healthcare reform will not begin with another physician-hospital organization (PHO) or a new management services organization (MSO).

I do not recommend investing any more financial or intellectual capital in attempting to maintain the status quo. Already the healthcare industry bears too close a resemblance to a war gone sour. We don't need a little more time and one more battle to recapitulate what has already been lost. Instead, we need a fresh beginning to concede the war and start over. We must first reformulate our system and return to the local market to create a framework for profiting from the new realities of managed care.

At the risk of being redundant, I must underscore that we need to realize that what worked before will not work now. The issue for those in the business of healthcare is literally one of survival. The reflux of managed care is a new world of intensifying competition. Providers—both physicians and hospitals—are caught in a vise. There are no pat solutions; there is no primer or handbook that has the answers. We must all learn in the streets.

I believe that this book is germaine to today's tumultuous industry because it challenges many of the myths associated with managed care. We know that the old system has not effectively impacted the root causes of illnesses and injury. It remains to be seen if a financial vehicle such as managed care will prove to be a market-driven impetus for health status improvement. In examining the underpinnings of managed care, I feel justified in somewhat pessimistically pointing out the frequency with which I view a lot of new "stuff" frantically being plugged into old boxes. Still, a select few innovators offering pragmatic ideas and creative solutions derived from real-life scenarios are infusing the industry with a degree of cautious optimism. This book tells some of their stories.

The scope and approach to the strategic transformation I recommend has been shaped by my experiences in the field. The revolution in my own mind began in 1990 when I served on HealthTrust, Inc.'s Managed Care Task Force. At that time, Clayton McWhorter (then CEO of HealthTrust, Inc., and former Chairman of Columbia/HCA) challenged me to "get out of my box" when analyzing the business of healthcare services delivery. Before paradigm shifting was a buzz phrase, Mr. McWhorter looked to the models of other industries to discern translatable strategies for growth and market dominance.

Using organizations like Chrysler Manufacturing and Texas Instruments as templates, HealthTrust removed the multiple layers from the organizational hierarchy typical of healthcare companies. They switched to a lean, mean system of macro-management. Within the corporate office, top executives set overall goals and objectives but it was the regional vice-presidents (RVPs) and local hospital CEOs who functioned as independent business unit managers with profit and loss responsibility. The result was some very entrepreneurial solutions to local market dilemmas. Once considered to be the rural "dog hospitals" of HCA, HealthTrust emerged as the industry's pygmalion when Columbia/HCA orchestrated a $5.6 billion merger of the two investor-owned hospital chains in 1995.

Obviously the HealthTrust story is one to be more deeply examined, understood, and emulated. The intent of this book is to take examples like HealthTrust and build a case for returning to the basics of business development, common sense approaches, market-driven strategies, and locally derived solutions as a means of confronting the ricochet effect of healthcare reform. Even Lee Kaiser devotees don't have the time to read another rhetorical book on how "sick" the industry is today. Consequently, the text of this book is a practical scheme demonstrating how to move from philosophy into action. Clear, real-world examples from inside and outside the healthcare arena, as well as from other industries, are analyzed to show how to achieve success in a new economic world order.

Recognizing that community health is becoming an issue with political, social, and marketplace leverage, this book aligns pragmatic solutions for market-driven change with the new political realities and shifting social contexts. Community health sounds inviting but still looks idealistic when providers begin to examine their bottom lines. Altruism does not show up immediately in bank accounts or financial reports. Goodwill efforts do not protect against pink slips or acquisitions. Even those providers contending for market share in the most mature managed care markets realize that they have never before been in the *business of managing health.* The fiscal realities associated with capitation do not often afford more than one bite of the apple.

Community health initiatives have substance when they operate within a framework of shared visions, joint ownership, and collective responsibility. Hospitals can elect to play a key role in enacting the public health principles of linking medical care to community factors such as socioeconomic status, unemployment rules, environmental concerns, housing, and education. Why? Because in the future being at risk for utilization means being invested in anything impacting the health status of a base of covered lives.

What I recommend will set many providers on their ears (see Figure A). I have stopped listening to my colleagues and clients who continue to whine and wail about managed care as if it is the Grinch stealing Christmas. Instead, I am observing those leaders within our industry who are already shifting into a new mode of doing business. Although the cacophony of despair seems almost overwhelming, this book heralds those voices that can be heard through the din, defining the new themes for an emerging industry. A healthcare system that is both socially responsible and financially solvent will construct a service delivery that is:

- relational
- non-institutional
- mobile
- primary-care driven
- localized to the patient consumer
- linked across a continuum
- responsive to cultural diversity

Furthermore, health systems searching for any format [*replacement revenue*] should follow the healthcare dollar to identify new opportunities in:

- worksite wellness
- senior care
- women's health services
- complementary therapies

Investors need to forego the information systems realm for telecommunications. We are in a new game now!

Within the text of this book, you will find case studies that include what may still be considered radical techniques for winning and maintaining market share. For instance, I profile real-life examples where the definition of primary care has been expanded to include a tithing approach to community health services, nurse practitioner clinics, naturopathic triage, and computer programs/telecommunications systems that enable the patient to participate more fully in the process of care. I feature those innovative health systems that are using new techniques and approaches to restructure their delivery systems in ways that will satisfy real marketplace needs and address changing customer expectations.

Although I am not without personal bias, my goal here is to serve you as a professional. The intent of this book *is not* to champion a certain technique or approach. Even if I wanted to, I can not provide you with a magic bullet because it doesn't exist. My goal *is* to assist you in initiating a process of inquiry that will translate what healthcare reform can mean to you and to your business.

This book will bring value to the reader because it crosses over a spectrum of interrelated variables that are converging to define comprehensive change for the healthcare industry. I believe that the base nature of healthcare as it will be known in the new millennium will be determined by leaders committing to *integrity of purpose.* As a new economic order forces us to centralize resources while we localize functions, it will be the *congruency between intentions and actions* that will be measured against the bottom line.

As important as the outlined business principles will be to the future, I contend that it will be a commitment to *principled business* that will be the most critical dimension responsible for our industry's future.

This book's recurring message underscores an acute need to develop a multifaceted strategy. Marketplace success will be defined by the intersection of strategic principles, core competencies and new organizational structures. Interconnected processes will be required to address both the immediate financial tension of staying in business and the long-term challenge of making substantive changes at the operational level.

Medical scientists will identify with the hologamous nature of the unfolding process. If the mission statement is regarded as the germ cell, then it should morphologically resemble any somatic cell that is subsequently developed, that is, the business plan, the technology plan, or the outlined approach for re-engineering. In other words, one should be able to pick up any internal planning document and infer its originating premise. It should be the *definition of mission, vision and purpose that informs all subsequent business activities.*

Within this context, I use the framework of this book to intertwine three critical dimensions that, I believe, will differentiate the winners from the losers:

1. The need for strategic organizational transformation that will *centralize the resources for operational excellence*—that is, capital, information systems, network development, and contract negotiations—and *localize the responsibility for customer-intimate responses*—that is, product/service lines, distribution systems, and community health initiatives.
2. The importance of *understanding the marketplace* and *identifying the new hierarchy of customer groups* in order to develop a multifaceted approach to change the core competencies of business operations.
3. A need to *look to other industries* that have cycled through similar stages of market chaos and *identify the winners* in order to derive strategies that provide the substance for dealing with change and profiting in a new era.

In the past we built an industry around *creating demand;* now we must develop an operating model vested in *managing demand.* A new economic order is creating new forms of competition. Coping with this reality and learning to thrive in an environment of constant, unpredictable change will require a whole new set of core values and processes. I believe it will be this

FIGURE B

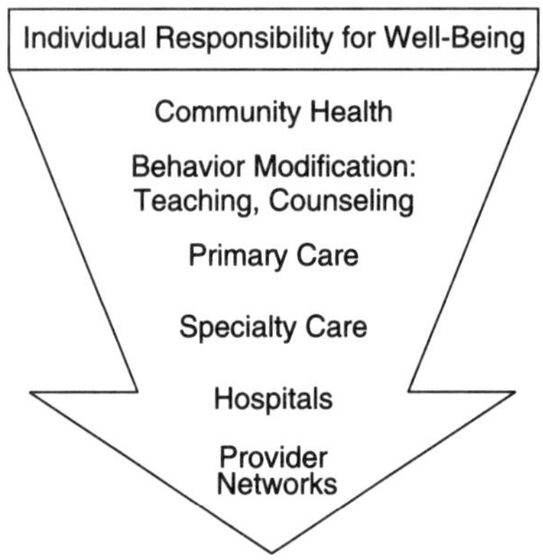

commitment to true transformation which will make or break providers as they transition into the future. (See Figure B.)

Those of us in the healthcare industry who sense the challenge of transforming our industry recognize that we need more leaders who respond with a reasoned and concerted strategy for pragmatic change. As you sit in what probably looks like a worsening situation, facing a future in which the professional options for success appear to be minimal, I hope to stimulate your imagination in such a way that you will feel summoned into new action. As bad as it seems today, I believe we have a unique opportunity to bridge the hiatus between sick-care and well-care, and build an equitable and humane system of healthcare delivery.

ACKNOWLEDGMENTS

Three years ago, when my heart first led me from the managed care businesses of IPA and PHO development to community health and integrated models of care, most of my colleagues thought I had gone crazy (or was suffering from early menopause or late divorce depression). Undaunted, I began to research "who was doing what" and determine for myself if any viable models existed. I found lots of models that were philosophically intact but financially flakey; still my search did not end in disillusionment.

This book has not been produced on the power of *one*—its existence is derived from the energies of *many* others who contributed time, input and written materials. I consider it my honor to have the opportunity to use this forum to highlight the real-life work of those creating new ways of being in the business of healthcare. I feel privileged to cite the names of my colleagues and mentors who overtly contributed their thoughts, ideas and testimonies to the content of this book: Tom Andrews, Dir. Managed Care, DeKalb Regional Healthcare System, Inc.; Donnie Belangia, Dir. Financial Management Systems, Sentara Health System; Richard Bressler, CEO, Bressler & Yauger; Kathy Bushnell, RNC, EDD, MPH; Charles Carlstrom, Research Dept., Federal Reserve Bank of Cleveland; Yonnie Chesley, President and CEO, Gordian Health Solutions, Inc.; Richard M. Cooper, M.D.; Roger Conant, Source Capital; Tom Cook, Ph.D., Vanderbilt University; Ed Day, Managed Care Consulting Associates; Brandon Dyson, Dir. Human Resources & Administration, PhyCor, Inc.; Michael Felix and James Burdine, Felix, Burdine & Assoc.; David Fine, President New Orleans Division, Columbia/HCA Healthcare Corporation, Tulane University; Elsbeth Freeman, Ph.D.; Peggy Garrett, Dir. Consulting Services, Harris Kovacs Alderman; Joane Goodroe, R.N., MBA, President, Goodroe & Co. Inc.; Michael Heard, Child Welfare Consultant; M. K. Key, Ph.D., Senior Vice President, Center for Quality Improvement, Quorum Health Resources; Susan McBroom, President, *HealthLINX*; Clayton McWhorter, former Chairman, Columbia/HCA Healthcare Corporation; Nancy Paris, President, Saint Joseph's Mercy Care Services; Kenneth Pelletier, Ph.D., M.D. Clinical Associate Professor of Medicine, Stanford University School of Medicine; Lillian Pfaff, Marketing Consultant; Joe Pizzorno, President, Bastyr University; Joanne Pulles, Exec. Director, Nashville Healthcare Partnership; Burt Reese, Corporate Dir. Information Systems, Sentara Health System; Debbie Sampsel, Catholic Hospital Association; Robert Sandler,

Assoc. V. P. Shared Services, Connecticut Healthcare Research & Education Foundation, Inc.; Sally Sjobeck, Principal, SIDUS, LLC; Diane Sollee, MSW, Director, The Collaborative Family Health Care Coalition; Roxanne Spitzer, Ph.D., R.N., MBA, Professor and Assoc. Dean/Practice Management, Vanderbilt University School of Nursing; Bruce White, J.D., D.O., Director Clinical Ethics Center, St. Thomas Hospital; and John Yauger, MBA, Principal, Bressler & Yauger. Michael Felix, of Felix, Burdine & Assoc., has made community health a critical variable in the fiscal reality of health system survival. His work is manifesting across the nation in medicaid HMOs, health and human services risk-sharing models and pragmatic systems for information sharing that begins with health status measurement. Michael taught me and told me I could write. This work began with our knowing one another and I am grateful.

I also extend my heartfelt thanks to my own team that came together—mostly after hours—to provide needed organizational and technical support. I regard Judy McCaskill as the true midwife for this book's production. Her positive attitude, encouraging words and honest feedback were as important as her abilities to format, cut, paste and re-order. Susan McBroom spent many Sunday mornings and long distance phone calls helping think out loud to find words to describe a new organizational order. Rebecca Smith also played a key role in managing the process and attending to the day-to-day mechanics of production.

Because this book is much more than a theoretical treatise and is intended to be a framework for principled and intentional action, it is important for me to acknowledge those who shaped me both personally and professionally. My grandfather, Doug Williams, Sr., was an early real-life model who showed me that social responsibility and financial viability can be successfully intertwined. My sister-in-spirit Sue Fort White lives her mission as a community leader, a social change agent/activist, a wife, a mother and friend. She has shown me that we all don't need to be Mother Theresa to do our work in this world. My friend Pat Glaser has taught me about integrity and tenacity. Through her example I have realized that caring enough to confront is even more important in the business world.

I also humbly express my deepest gratitude to those who have willingly been of service to me and with me. It is from those listed below that I have taken strength and found illumination. From them came the light to define my vision and to see my place within it. The first image of my holograph—my mission—was conceived within this community: Gayle Alexander; Stacey Graham, Marketing Strategist; Suzee Waters Benjamin; Julie Bresciani, Ph.D.; Jan Shepard, JHS Consultants; Elizabeth Fontana; Nan Allison, Allison & Beck Nutrition Consultants, Inc.; Ann Vincent; Gail Catlin; Diane

Bush; Wendy Silverthorn, Silverthorn Studios; Donna Stoneham, Stoneham Associates; Leah Hall; Stephen Hines, M.D.; Michelle Molden, Vice President of Planning and Marketing, Saint Joseph's Health Systems; Laurie Jewett; Kay Bawart, R.N., BSN, Assistant Administrator, Marshall Hospital; Robin Growden; Sister Catherine Hellman, President, St. Charles Medical Center; Marlene Von Friedrich Fitzwater, Founder/President, Health Communications Research Center; Pam Baggett, Managed Care Associates; Jean Marie Stalma; Cammie Claybrook; Shirley Serena, R.N.; Sheryl Dalton; Harry Owens, M.D.; Beverly Doggrell; Lauren James; Don Flint, Commonweal; Sharon Reidell; Annie Freeman; Cathy Hoot; Aleene Day; Fran Wade Harris; Bill Adamsky, Ph.D., Art of Living Institute, Marshall Hospital; Bonnie Manson; Corrine Matthews; Andrew Marks, Vice President, Miller & Schroeder Financial, Inc.; Therese Gauguin; Susan Galey; and all my brothers at the Hermitage Camaldolese Monastery, particularly Brother David Stendahl-Rast, Fr. Arthur Poulin and Fr. John Powell, Marilyn Berman, Ph.D., John Tonkovich, Ph.D., Connie Tatgenhorst, Linda Anderson Slovic, Cliff Adlerz, Gregg Lehman, Cliff Meador, M.D., Edna Kleinbaum, Sister Michelle Carroll, Sister Anne Lutz, David Koontz, Wynne Bailey, John Shea, Wynne James and Dean Dyanne Affonso.

I must express my appreciation to the members of my family who stood by me and believed in my ability to create even in a time of loss: my father, Doug Williams, Jr.; my sister, Sheila Hardeman; and my nephew and niece, Terry and Shelley Hardeman.

I will always be indebted to Bill Danaher for believing this book would be written, for editing my "garbage drafts," for holding my hand and for encouraging me to keep at it when I felt I no longer could. The words of a critic are never harsh when spoken with the voice of a friend. Thank you for the many ways you continue to teach and guide me. I pray you always will.

Finally, the inception and the creation always begin in Spirit. Thank you, God, for Your merciful grace and indwelling love.

TABLE OF CONTENTS

PART ONE

ECONOMIC COMPETITION AND THE NEW ORGANIZATIONAL ORDER

1

CHAPTER

Internalizing Mandates for Change

THE JUXTAPOSITION OF DOLLARS AND HEALTH

Mention the words "managed care" and your audience—whether it is composed of physicians, healthcare business executives, social activists, or confused consumers—will usually groan and shrink away. Few individuals make a living as healthcare futurists. Managed care is not yet synonymous with an evolving construct of a new industry vested in health and well-being rather than disease. The reality is that most markets are in an evolutionary stage where cost, chaos, and competition continue to camouflage a true system of care.

Before the industrial age, physical labor often defined an individual's livelihood; consequently, individuals understood the value of their health. Since there was no insurance, the cost of medical care also had a very personal translation. If cash was short, the doctor was often paid with a local currency from crops or livestock. Finally, the definition of health was not confined to the physical body and a "healing experience" was not a consequence of biomedical technology. A peaceful state of mind, good relationships with family and friends, and a sense of satisfaction regarding this life's work often differentiated the body that had been "healed" from one that had not.

Prior to World War II, healthcare providers were as close to the patient-customer as their own breath. Physicians were regarded as god-like personas and no wonder—in their day-to-day responsibilities of birthing and burying, they actually wielded the force of life with their own hands. The physician carried a black bag in his hand and the Hippocratic oath in his heart.

What happened to displace both individual responsibility for well-being and the patient-caregiver relationship from the center of the healthcare system? How did we arrive at this junction with such a fragmented, disease-oriented, episodic, subspecialty-focused model of care? I suggest that first we follow the dollar across history to find the answer to "how we got here from there." Our critical challenge will then be to anticipate the path of the dollar over the next few decades in order to understand the scope of the complex restructuring of finance and delivery that will be required for the future.

THE AGE OF TECHNOLOGY

The disparity of the current situation that the healthcare industry is facing can be traced back to a basic tenet of our capitalistic society: how we make money! The economic impact of the technological age on the practice of medicine is analogous to the consequence of the industrial age on craft-based production. In the 18th century, industry and science fostered the development of factories that began to challenge the dominance of the individual craftsman. The economies of scale that could be achieved via mechanisms of mass production drastically altered the critical variables in the supply and demand equation, that is, cost and access displaced quality and individuation. With more products available to more people at prices they could afford to pay, a new industrial order arose in the wake of a dollar-rich market opportunity. The economics of the industrial age spawned a new set of rules for production, distribution, and consumption while the once revered craftsman became almost passe. Sound familiar?

In the 1960s and 1970s, our society entered a new age of technology. Advances within the electronics, telecommunications, and defense industries soon became transferable to the world of medical diagnostics. The prevalence of infectious disease defined a ready-made market base for products like X-rays, computerized axial tomography (CT scanners) and magnetic resonance imaging (MRI).

Because health is a universal and emotionally laden concern, there is always a customer with a heightened motivation to buy products and/or services with a known or perceived positive benefit. Once questions of safety and accuracy were addressed, expensive technologies faced relatively few barriers to new market entry. Technological advances exploded into the world of medicine and drastically altered the political, legal, social, and economic context of its practice. The modus operandi of the healthcare system was revolutionized almost overnight.

Commercial success for advanced medical technologies created a surplus of profit centers. The technology age fostered a biomedical model of care in which the physician often assumed the role of broker and the hands-on caregiver was considered obsolete. As a result, the individual relationship between the producer, the receiver, and the desired product or service was lost. New delivery systems thwarted previous standards of quality and customization; *more* was automatically regarded as *better*.

In the 1970s and 1980s, the business of healthcare evolved around the treatment of symptoms, with individuals and communities increasingly regarded only as market opportunities. Because of the high cost of care, the distribution system required a new customer with deeper pockets. The government and the insurance company became the payor, thereby displacing the individual patient in the buyer–seller equation. With someone else picking up the tab, it was easy for a sense of individual responsibility for health and well-being to be diffused. The cash register rang every time someone got sick and continued to ring at every point of access. The dollar drove duplication of services and fragmented delivery of care.

The irony of our current industry situation is that despite such a high level of investment, it doesn't look as if there has been a good return on the dollar. As healthcare became more technology-driven, industry leaders excitedly exploited the commercial value of medical products and services. An awareness of the primary and secondary customer, that is, the payor and the patient, was lost as healthcare entrepreneurs excitedly cashed their checks and built more big buildings. Today we are paying the price for an exponential growth that was driven by competition—not marketplace forces. Healthcare reform has its genesis in two marketplace realities: (1) the soaring cost of healthcare and (2) the increasing prevalence of chronic disease.

THE CUSTOMER HAS EMPTY POCKETS

In 1991, the United States government's running tab for healthcare services totaled out at a sum greater than 12 percent of the Gross National Product (GNP)—more than $900 billion or $2,700 for every person.[1]

Healthcare reform has become such a political football because the government is out of money. The Clinton health reform efforts have engendered a passionate debate and a renewed sense of urgency regarding what Americans should do about the following facts:

- 16 percent of all Americans (almost 40 million) have no health insurance.
- 25 percent of those who have health insurance have only partial coverage.

- The so-called safety health insurance net for the poor is riddled with barriers to needed care.
- Healthcare costs are projected to consume almost 20 percent of America's GNP by 2010. Today it is more than 10 percent and it is one-half to two-thirds this amount in Great Britain and Canada, a typical figure in the industrialized world.

Large industry is a major payor for healthcare services. Between 1988 and 1991, annual healthcare costs per employee increased from $2,354 to $3,605.[2]

In another survey, the healthcare costs of 120 of the nation's biggest companies were projected to rise 3 percent in 1996, Towers Perrin, also a benefits consulting firm, said. These companies foresaw no change for 1996 in the costs of covering employees in health maintenance organizations and a 4 percent increase, on average, for employees covered by traditional benefits or other types of managed care. Healthcare analysts say the increases reflect continued demand for expensive new tests and procedures as well as the medical needs of the growing numbers of older or retired employees.[3] With sources predicting that the United States could spend up to $1.6 trillion on healthcare by 2000, the force of the payor is moving the concepts of healthcare reform and managed care from rhetoric to market reality.

One of the reasons for rising costs is the fact that advancements in technology have helped to create specialties—and the pressurized industry has quickly spread out horizontally. In 1940, fewer than 20 percent of all U.S. physicians were specialists. Today, that number has jumped to more than 60 percent, the highest percentage worldwide. With each specialist group battling to gain a market niche, the healthcare system has become increasingly stratified and segmented. Jurisdictional disputes became more important than seamless delivery of healthcare services. While free-market competition usually drives prices down, among medical providers it seems to operate in an inverse fashion: The more specialists there are, the higher the utilization, and thus the higher the costs. The benefit of increased competition has been lost in the helter-skelter horizontal expansion of expensive facilities, services, technologies, specialties, and sub-specialties.[4]

THE PATIENT IS STILL SICK

Although the technology incumbent in the biomedical model has been successful in the identifying and controling of infectious diseases, a new set of problems has emerged to take their place: chronic, degenerative diseases. Whereas acute, infectious diseases accounted for almost 700 deaths per 100,000 population in 1900, they accounted for fewer than 20 in 1970. Conversly, in 1900, chronic disease accounted for fewer than 400 deaths per 100,000 population; in 1970, they accounted for more than 700. Glazier predicts that of every 100 males now born in the United States, 83 are likely to suffer and eventually die of a chronic disease (see Figure 1–1).[5]

The ten most prevalent causes of death in the United States in 1900, 1970 and 1988–90 are as shown in Table 1–1 on page 7.

Death rates from heart disease and cancer have risen more than 250 percent since 1900. But these rates tell only part of the story. Infectious diseases usually appear rapidly and have fairly short and measurable life spans. They are generally cured, heal naturally, or result in death within a relatively short time. Chronic diseases, on the other hand, appear slowly, cause gradual dysfunction or disability, persist after protracted treatments, and cause continuing hardship, both in terms of personal suffering and cost of treatment and care.

We see from the *Historical Abstracts of the United States,* that during the time that deaths from infectious diseases have fallen and deaths from chronic disease have risen, *private and public expenditures for healthcare have grown logarithmically.*[6] Physicians and hospitals have "hit the wall" regarding what to do in the treatment of chronic diseases. Consequently, chronic disease care is a *real* driver for healthcare reform. Providers are now challenged to identify modalities of care that are both more efficacious and cost efficient.

Some experts allege that medical intervention significantly impacts outcomc in only about one-tenth of all diseases and that up to 70 percent of

FIGURE 1–1

Comparison of Deaths per 100,000 Population: 1900–1970

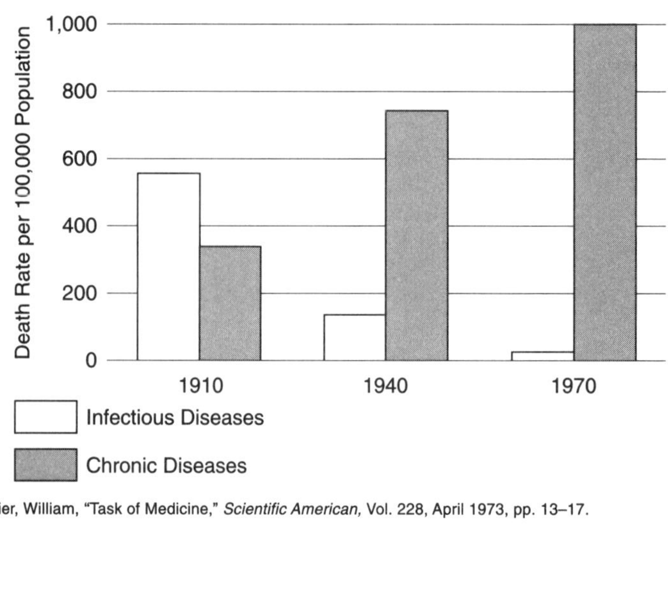

Source: Glazier, William, "Task of Medicine," *Scientific American,* Vol. 228, April 1973, pp. 13–17.

TABLE 1–1

Most Prevalent Causes of Death in the United States

Cause 1900	Deaths/ 100,000	Cause 1970	Deaths/ 100,000	Cause 1988–1990	Deaths/ 100,000
Influenza & pneumonia	201	Heart Disease	360	Cardivascular disease	194.2
Tuberculosis	198	Cancer	175	Heart disease	155.9
Gastroenteritis	145	Cerebrovascular lesions	105	Lung cancer	38.8
Heart disease	135	Accident	54	Stroke	28
Cerebrovascular lesions	105	Circulatory diseases	31	Female breast cancer	23
Chronic nephritis	80	Influenza & pneumonia	30	Syphilis (reported)	20.2
Accident	72	Diseases of infancy	21	Motor vehicle crash	18.9
Cancer	63	Diabetes mellitus	18	AIDS (reported)	16.7
Diseases of infancy	62	Cirrhosis of the liver	15	Suicide	11.3
Diphtheria	40	Bronchitis, emphysema, asthma	13	Work-related injury	2.3

Source: Compiled from *Historical Abstracts of the United States* and *The Quality Letter for Healthcare Leaders.*

physician services are for conditions that could be managed without professional care. But in this regard, consumers must share some culpability.[7]

MANAGED CARE: BAND-AID OR TOURNIQUET?

From 1960 to the late 1980s, providers adhering to a technological model of care found the world of healthcare to be a competitive lotto in which everybody won. Today, however, economic realities and the overcapacity within the healthcare system are causing providers to humbly reassess the value of the services they deliver.

The centerpiece of this managed care movement requires the shifting of economic incentives in order to control utilization and expenses. Paramount to President Clinton's intentions is that the growth of healthcare, as a percentage of GNP shall be arrested. At a minimum, this ambition would require hospital budgets to grow no faster than the economy as a whole—roughly half the rate of annual budget increases of the past. The larger concern, however, is of zero or negative growth. The principal opportunity for savings among health plans—themselves under serious constraint—is to purge hospital inpatient days. Already the major integrated systems in California have reduced inpatient days per 1,000 enrollees by over half. All hospital planning should at least consider budget scenarios with 20 percent, 30 percent, 40 percent fewer inpatient days.[8]

In a managed care environment, hospitals are the first to be hit. Immediate cost swings are achieved by reducing the average length of stay and resource demand. Nevertheless, this quick fix does not guarantee an increase in health status or a decrease in the growth of costs over time.

The irony of the current crisis facing providers is that no one can really be sure that managed care will last. Put simply, managed care is being heralded as an approach to both health status improvement and cost containment, with very little data to substantiate its effectiveness. To risk the pun, managed care may simply be a Band-Aid for a gushing wound. Because capitation merely inverts the incentives to encourage underutilization, the danger is that—by 2005—the healthcare industry will seem an even bigger ogre than it does today. When the rewards are tied to *not* providing services, then managed care becomes a tourniquet.

While the evolving construct of health status management versus episodic disease treatment is becoming an increasingly popular theoretical debate, political hype and touchy-feely public relations lingo are not effectively assuaging industry chaos. Most CEOs are not yet running down hospital halls elated to see empty beds. Even with the awareness that new business principles associated with consolidation and leading to collaboration can be valuable tools for moving into the future, most healthcare decision makers have little time or energy to commit to new total quality management (TQM) programs or to the exercise of becoming a "learning organization."[9] Survival is the immediate all-consuming issue for these decision makers. They recognize that being fit for the current transitional environment may mean being unfit—or at risk—for the future. Today's and tomorrow's financial incentives are perversely related.

For the provider community, the urgent issue is financial risk. With managed care contracting, the price war has become so competitive that getting the business may be more perilous than losing the contract. The combination of low admissions and shorter lengths of stay has reduced average occupancy to around 60 percent, which means that in highly competitive markets such as Southern California, average occupancy in some locales has dropped to below 50 percent. At that level, hospitals are so hungry for patients that they will agree to any contract which promises additional admissions.[10] The bottom line must be this: costs cannot exceed revenues. Forced to contract at prices that cover marginal operating costs, hospitals and physicians are on a short leash to control utilization and expenses.

I believe it is a serious mistake to regard capitation as an end-all solution in this reform movement. With capitation, the provider's equation for profit is simply reversed. Success continues to pivot on utilization and cost-containment, not health status indicators. For-profit managed care companies are manipulating financial incentives in order to restructure the delivery of healthcare services. Capitation is not a formula that supports long-term investments in the health of a community. It is simply an aggressive contracting device for controlling the cost of purchasing services from hospitals and physicians. Capitation may prove to be an interim financial strategy for incenting providers to begin to manage health.

Although the debate about policy decisions is increasingly volatile, those providers in the midst of the crises have to be concerned with the immediate issue of surviving managed care's economic pressures. When forced to operate at prices that minimally cover the costs of opening the doors, the day-to-day challenges of major restructuring use up all available resources. Simply staying in business can suck dry all available time, money, and intellectual capital. Any investment in the future is usually spent on costly information systems that often are as fragmented as the provider communities they serve. In the marketplace today, there is little energy left and few resources remaining to grapple with questions regarding healthcare's overall mission to serve individuals and society. With the flow of needed services unduly restricted, the odds are that the health of a population will suffer rather than improve.

The daunting challenge facing the healthcare industry today is to manage the transition while staying financially viable. Even if managed care is simply an interim economic solution, it should serve as a catalyst for a new organizational order. The winners will quickly become efficient at operating within a managed care framework, but will also remain flexible enough in structure to respond to changing market forces. Deterioration will not be reversed by looking to changes in reimbursement and incentives, that is, capitation, or by relying on federal and state public policy mandates. When the definition of managed care expands beyond a cost-cutting approach and entwines local strategies for managing health, then it will become the impetus for creating a new system for healthcare services delivery.

STRATEGIC TRANSFORMATION

The problem with reform is that, by definition, the goal is to "improve social or economic conditions without radical or revolutionary change".[11] In the last couple of decades, healthcare has experienced several waves of reform movements—total quality management, conflict resolution/collaborative management, business re-engineering—that have been tactical responses to marketplace pressures.

Even those who recognize the perverse relationship between incentives will need to do more than reform by espousing a commitment to a healthy community while they continue to play an internal game of "who's on first." No one can deny that, for the hospital administrator, keeping the doors open in a time of declining census and decreasing reimbursement has become a daunting challenge. Those who are paralyzed by fear are being easily cannibalized by aggressive market feeders. Others who have invested in the status quo or adopted a wait-and-see approach, their inertia and passive resistance has become an organizational cancer which is mestatisizing systemically. Everyone realizes that they must do something but they are not sure *what* or *how*.

Reform management is often the path of least resistance because it protects the existing organizational structure. Reform management—or phased product development—is seductively pleasant. All the functional areas have their jobs to do, one after the other, and senior management thinks everything is going well.[12] The problem is, while everyone is busy cosmetically attending to the status quo the industry begins to die from systemic toxins.

Other industries have made the mistake of investing in reform management and, in doing so, have set the stage for their own suicide. "Too bad the railroad magnates forgot they were in the transportation business" is the example that rings through a lot of recent keynote speeches to the healthcare industry leaders. While the railroad industry was putting down more tracks and improving the capacity of its freight cars, the transportation industry was redefined by aerospace engineers.

The saga of the first giants of the computer industry is also rife with application. As far back as the early 1960s, IBM serviced a lion's share of the business machine market selling computer hardware. IBM lost its place as an industry leader because it got so caught up in the momentum of selling business machines that it failed to expand its niche in the computer-based information market. Companies like Unisys and Electronic Data Systems were able to establish market dominance quickly because they recognized they were not in the hardware/software business, they were in the information-based solutions business. Although IBM woke up in the early 1990s and began to commit extensive resources to shifting its foundation from selling computer hardware to selling management information services, it is still playing catch-up as an information vendor .

Reform management is magnified to crisis management any time an industry is guilty of believing that it has the right—or power—to manipulate its customers. For example, Kraft General Foods took its consumers for granted and cheapened the beans it used in its Maxwell House coffee. As a result, many once-loyal customers looked elsewhere for their coffee fix and abandoned Maxwell House down to the last drop.[13] (Thank God for Starbucks!)

The healthcare industry should examine the examples of IBM and Kraft General Foods to avoid the same mistakes. Without a doubt, there are now those healthcare industry leaders who are already studying the examples of Unisys and Starbucks because they want to better understand what went right!

There is no doubt that healthcare is reorganizing. However, reorganization alone will not define success. The question that has yet to be answered is, Do the strategists for the new business structures recognize that they are in the *healthcare business* or are they stuck in the misconception that they are in the *biomedical technology business*? Furthermore, are they so busy wrestling with cost concerns that they are circumventing the importance of developing concurrent strategies for market-based, customer-configured continuums of care? If so, they are making costly investments in reform movements that have little likelihood of paying off in long-term profitability.

Vertical integration is a common phenomenon that is making an impact on the local market. The consolidation of health systems and the development of regional provider networks are mobilizing new, larger players. Medical monoliths like Columbia/HCA and PhyCor, Inc. are capitalizing on economies of scale and developing competitive advantages that are simply beyond the reach of an autonomous hospital or solo provider. These large players are aggressively responding to marketplace forces. Their tack for staying in business is to keep the inflationary cost of healthcare delivery in check by merging ailing hospitals, consolidating purchasing and slashing personnel. Undoubtedly, large-scale operations and vertical integration promise dramatic economies and high profits.[14]

This marketplace reorganization is vested in the benefits of scale. Here again we can learn from other industries. In the 20th century, the model has been provided by companies such as Swift Meat Packing Company, Standard Oil of New Jersey, U.S. Steel, General Electric, Dupont, and the Ford Motor Company. Each of these companies redefined the terms of industrial competition through a distinctive synthesis of existing technologies and a novel corporate organizational structure—vertically integrated, hierarchically organized, and centrally administered.[15] As a result, each came to dominate its industry.

The current evolution of the healthcare industry is analogous; the benefits of scale are already resulting in the emergence of a small number of dominant players. Still, all we are witnessing is a reform movement in which mass production is being combined with streamlined systems for delivery. Centralizing resources of capital, information, and technologies is certain to be advantageous and can increase the efficiency of seamless processes. But this methodology has questionable long-term viability if the continuum of care is not tailored to the needs of the local marketplace.

What is occurring in Minneapolis/St. Paul, Minnesota, one of the most mature managed care markets in the United States, is a good example. The large provider networks are facing a new form of competition and this time the one(s) that "win" will be determined by customer choice *not* cost. The Business Healthcare Action Plan Group (BHCAG), an influential purchasing coalition of large employers in the Twin Cities area, said on February 2, 1995, that it would restructure the health plan it offers to employees of its 22 member companies to *broaden the choices* of medical clinics. Although changes would not go into effect for two years, the announcement by BHCAG could extend beyond BHCAG plan members and affect the entire local healthcare industry. Indeed, the effect could be felt nationally.

"This new approach is very compatible with where MinnesotaCare [the state reform program] was going. It allows care systems to compete without having to be absorbed in a merger," said George Halverson, CEO of HealthPartners. "By creating that sort of competition, we ensure that the system focuses on the consumer and doesn't become complacent."[16] Healthcare systems that feel that size and cost efficiency will be their security blankets for long-term market dominance should not get too comfortable. We should watch closely what happens in the Twin Cities and hopefully, in the process, learn from those who are recognizing the need to *view the patient as customer* and to *earn the right to be a consumer choice* instead of getting the business by default.

For the healthcare industry, reformation is not enough. Although reform efforts can be appropriate and valuable, they reflect an acceptance of the status quo, rather than a recognition of the need to confront a new competitive reality, one that challenges what organizations *ought* to be doing, not just how they can do a better job of what they are already doing.[17] What our industry needs is *strategic transformation.*

By definition, to transform means "to change the base nature, function, condition and form of".[18] The current economic pressures within the marketplace are mandating fundamental change for the healthcare industry. Structural change, or transformation, is needed for any initiative to have lasting impact. Prevailing system paradigms must be discarded. Innovative tactics will always be short-lived unless they are embedded in comprehensive organizational change that is in turn anchored in new strategic goals.[19]

FIGURE 1–2

Managed Care: The Evolution

- Capitation drives the fiscal reality of managing the health of a population
- Boundaries collapse between public and private health sectors
- Service delivery characterized by a continuum of care, ease of access, seamless processes
- Patient care begins to be characterized by a blending of mainstream medical and complementary approaches to address both the bio-medical and psycho-social factors impacting health
- Impact measurements: "what works/what doesn't" is analyzed and reported
- Communication, dissemination and social marketing become critical strategies
- Consolidation of provider systems and payor partners

- Independent Hospitals
- Autonomous Physicians
- Full beds; long waits in physicians' offices
- Unsophisticated consumers
- Fee-for-service

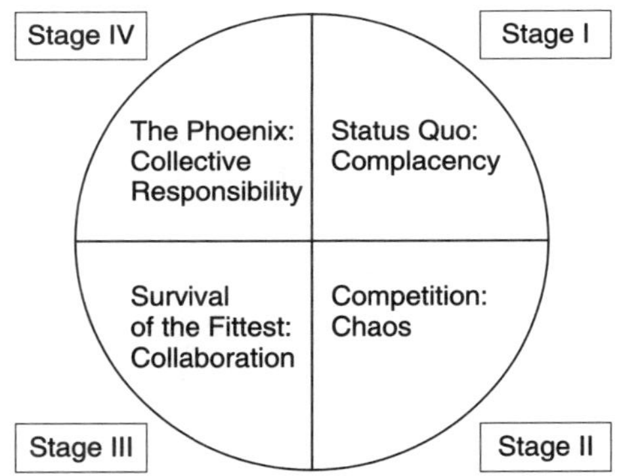

- HMO/PPO(s) consolidate
- Providers rapidly merging, acquiring, organizing, and looking at systems for integration
- The price window narrows
- "Report Cards" emphasize quality and patient satisfaction, not just cost
- Reimbursement continues to shift; primary care services capitate, pricing more common
- Information technology is recognized as a cornerstone for designing continuums of care
- Organizational structure begins to try new ways for building consensus, committing to action
- Private and public health sectors come to the table to address primary care access, prevention, and education issues
- Physicians and clinical caregivers begin to look beyond the medical model for non-traditional approaches to patient-centered care to enhance cost efficiency and clinical efficacy

- HMO/PPO/POS(s) enter the market like popping popcorn
- Alphabet soup: PHO, MCO, MSO, IPA, etc.
- Reimbursement shifts from FFS to per diem to global pricing
- Profit margins erode
- Organizational re-design: hospitals "slash and burn"
- Physicians begin to meet in groups, call lawyers
- Loose networks form
- Managed care emerges as a replacement product
- Consumer choice is restricted

Source: © Copyright 1995. Genie James, Integrated Healthcare Consultant/*Ausculta*

A NEW ORGANIZATIONAL ORDER

What will it take for healthcare providers to survive and grow in the next decade and beyond? The answer is clear. They will have to *forget the status quo, move through the chaos, organize for survival and define a new way of being in business* (see Figure 1–2).

Providers will have to grasp the importance of understanding the customer in order to effectively interconnect systems of care. The continuum of care must intrinsically be defined by new relationships. Instead of fighting to maintain some degree of profitability, new partners will find that the relationship framework allows them to tap into the power of synergy. Old, ineffective management styles will have to be abandoned. Centralized resources and localized action will be the dynamic for the new organizational order for healthcare systems.

Who will take the lead? The boundaries between provider, payor and consumer are becoming increasingly blurred. With capitation, managed care is demanding that the provider community become accountable not for a single episode of care, but for the health status management of a base of covered lives. The need to own a continuum of care in order to remain competitive is driving comprehensive change in the prevailing healthcare delivery system.

Market dominance will ultimately be determined at the local level of operation. It will be the scope—not the scale—of services individualized to the needs of the customer that will define the system that wins out over time. The parts must be considered in the context of the whole. Emerging healthcare systems must adopt a holistic methodology which integrates evolving customer requirements, existing resources, and operational functions. In contrast to the business approach of the 1970s and 1980s, healthcare providers that survive the 1990s will be required to configure an array of services that *begin with the patient* and *end with technology*.

Once again, transformation across the industry will occur through a distinctive synthesis of available talent and existing technologies. While there may be a centralized location for resources of capital and the hub of information systems, it will be the innovative crafting of local solutions that will ultimately differentiate the winners from the losers. Customer choice, marketplace economics, and new competitive forces are converging to foster nubile forms of strategic transformation and a new organizational order.

ENDNOTES

1. Alternative and the Law, 1994.
2. Foster Higgings & Co., Benefits Consultants.

3. Freudenheim, Milt. "Health Costs for Workers in U.S. Rose Last Year, Reversing '94 Dip," *The New York Times* (Jan. 20, 1996).
4. Dauner, C. Duane, with Michael Bowker. *Understanding the Crisis and the Cure: The Healthcare Solution* (Sacramento: Vision Publishing, 1994), pp. 18–20.
5. Kaslow, Arthur L., M.D. and Richard B. Miles, *Freedom From Chronic Disease: A Drug-Free Nutritional Program for Managing Your Health Problems.* (1984), p. 40.
6. ibid., pp. 41–42.
7. Cooper, Richard M. "Buyer Beware: A No-Nonsense Guide to Health Care Cost Containment," (Brentwood, TN: Richard M. Cooper, M.D., 1998), p. 17.
8. McWhorter, R. Clayton. "U.S. Health Care in Transition: A Response to the Health Security Act of 1993." *Health Care Management: State of the Art Reviews,* vol. 1, No. 1 (August, 1994), p. 59.
9. Senge, Peter M. *The Fifth Discipline: Mastering the Five Practices of the Learning Organization* (New York: Doubleday, 1990).
10. "Hospitals Use Community Needs Assessment as Tool to Focus Upon Healthier Communitites," *Change* (December 1, 1995).
11. *The American Heritage Dictionary,* 1992.
12. Himmelfarb, Philip A. *Survival of the Fittest: New Product Development in the 90s* (Englewood Cliffs, NJ: Prentice-Hall, 1992), p. 10.
13. Treacy, Michael and Fred Wiersma. *The Discipline of Market Leaders: Choose Your Customers, Narrow Your Focus, Dominate Your Market,* (Pennsylvania: Addison Wesley, 1995) p. 9.
14. Goldman, Steven L., Roger N. Nagel, and Kenneth Preiss. *Agile Competitors and Virtual Organizations: Strategies for Enriching the Customer* (New York: Van Nostrand Reinhold, 1995), p. 9.
15. ibid., pp. 51–52.
16. Howatt, Glen. "Business Health Care Action Group Alters Plan," *Minneapolis Star Tribune,* (February 3, 1995).
17. Goldman, Steven L., Roger N. Nagel, and Kenneth Preiss. *Agile Competitors and Virtual Organizations: Strategies for Enriching the Customer,* (New York: Van Nostrand Reinhold, 1995), p. 4.
18. *American Heritage Dictionary,* 1992.
19. Goldman, Steven L., Roger N. Nagel, and Kenneth Preiss. *Agile Competitors and Virtual Organizations: Strategies for Enriching the Customer,* (New York: Van Nostrand Reinhold, 1995), p. 45.

PART TWO

UNDERSTANDING MARKETPLACE FORCES

Marketplace forces determine the operating environment. The hospital's operating environment is defined by several sets of factors. The first set includes both the regulators that play a heavy hand in setting the parameters for doing business and the customers who pay the bill. The second set of factors are the forces or trends that can affect the hospital's competitive position. These forces include the economic trends that can affect purchasing behaviors and the relative influence of customer groups; the technological trends that affect the availability, usefulness, and cost effectiveness of specific products and services; and the demographic/psychographic trends that affect the composition of the customer base. A third set of factors is the basic competitive structure in which a hospital exists. The relevant factors here are the rate of industry consolidation and the rate of hospital closings in this time of market decline.

For those who would be industry leaders, understanding the power of marketplace forces is an important first step for both the situational diagnosis and the business planning process. With an adequate understanding of its environment, a hospital—or health system—will be able to focus its analyses on those factors that most significantly affect its ability to be successful. Because in today's healthcare environment the marketplace forces are so volatile, all business strategies must be based on both the expected benefits of the strategy and the expected risks associated with moving in new directions.

2 CHAPTER

The Health Policy Debate

THE ROLE OF GOVERNMENT

Depending on where you stand, you are probably giving Hillary Clinton the finger or a standing ovation. Regardless of your politics, you should at least be able to acknowledge that the Clinton administration has tackled an incredibly complex issue and entered into the fray with an agenda to put the problems on the table. It is also notable to recognize that by addressing issues associated with efficiency, fairness, and inflationary budgets, the government has angered several weighty constituent groups: the American Medical Association (AMA), the American Hospital Association (AHA), the insurance industry, the labor movement, employers, and special advocacy groups like the American Association of Retired Persons (AARP).

Healthcare industry leaders engage in contentious debates regarding the federal government's role in establishing health policy. For instance, Clayton McWhorter, former Chairman of Columbia/HCA, and former Chairman and CEO of HealthTrust, Inc., states:

> President Clinton's leadership in healthcare reform is admirable. Although I believe that businesses and providers can work together to develop a cost-efficient healthcare system without government intervention, government has an important role in this process. As both provider and purchaser of healthcare, I challenge Washington to remove the obstacles to a truly cost-effective healthcare system. Government should revise medical liability laws, exercise flexibility in regard to anti-trust laws, help to reform private insurance, reduce

> paperwork and administrative costs, and support collaborative efforts. Many of these concrete steps have been taken in President's Clinton's plan, but they may be offset by its reliance on government controls.[1]

Mr. McWhorter continues:

> The danger inherent in granting such power to Congress is illustrated by the government's disastrous track record in managing expenses for Medicaid, Medicare, Social Security, the military, and the welfare system. During the healthcare debate, voters must continually ask themselves whether or not they want to give the federal government complete control of a healthcare system, which represents one-seventh of the national economy and touches everyone's personal and family lives, as well as jobs and retirement. My answer is obvious: No.[2]

While the government may not complete the final script for healthcare reform, the President's Health Security Act of 1993 has impacted two very important areas. First, it has engendered a grassroots awareness of and a consumer demand for the need to integrate six essential components of healthcare delivery, that is, security, quality, choice, responsibility, simplicity, and savings. Secondly, it has served as a potent catalyst for local activity that is now translating to market-based reform. State governments, large employers, HMOs, insurers, hospitals, physicians, and vendors have taken action to reposition for survival. Successful politics of health reform financing will correspond closely to the three basic reasons why healthcare became intensely politicized in the early 1990s:[3]

1. A sizeable portion of the public grew upset over the uncertain availability of health insurance coverage.
2. A range of interested parties—business, labor, providers, and even insurers—discovered that weak government involvement allowed each to shift costs to others.
3. Political leaders themselves increasingly deplored the strong-standing claims of healthcare on public budgets.

As I began to research the history of governmental policy and healthcare, it became obvious that I was attempting to logically map a phenomenon that has had as many twists, turns and about-faces as a 16 year old with a crush. The obvious lack of focus and consistency has continuously created more problems than solutions. In fact, it has been something of a catastrophe whenever the government has gotten involved in the healthcare business: The ineffectiveness of government intervention has been documented over history and there are other market forces—like employer-based health insurance—that are already playing signature roles in healthcare reform.

The government will continue to fumble with cost containment strategies. Moving Medicaid into managed care is a strategy that is already underway in several states. However, big savings from managed care won't be so easy to gain. The fallacy in this approach exists because some 50 percent of Medicaid spending actually goes to pay for nursing home care of the elderly and care for the blind and disabled. An analysis by the Kaiser Family Foundation's Commission on the Future of Medicaid projected overall national savings in the range of only 2 to 3 percent per year over the next seven years from moving most poor, non-disabled adults and children into managed care. The Congressional Budget Office projects a 5 percent savings.[4]

With the Medicaid program—serving some 34 million low-income Americans—undergoing intense scrutiny, two recent studies looked closely at the potential of managed care to cover more uninsured Americans and save money. One study, published in the Spring 1995 issue of *Health Affairs,* analyzed what would happen if all 50 states were to adopt Medicaid waivers like those in Tennessee, Oregon, and Rhode Island, which seek to place beneficiaries in managed care and use the savings to expand coverage to the working uninsured. The researchers concluded that if families with incomes below 200 percent of poverty level were made eligible, about 12.7 million people would gain coverage and another 4.8 million who had other coverage would switch to Medicaid. The expansion would add $27.4 billion to the program's present $67.8 billion cost. In all likelihood, less than one-third of that could be funded by managed care savings, and possibly as little as 15 percent.[5]

In sum, the government is a market force that can immediately impact the provider's profitability and operational structure. Even more ominous, the government has a track record of screwing up when creating health policies or regulations that are intended to control the costs of healthcare. With the government adopting managed care as its system of choice, we will be face-to-face with its associated myth of cost containment.

A QUESTION OF ENTITLEMENT

During the recent recession, already disturbing trends in health insurance coverage got even worse. Since economic growth slowed down in 1988 until the recession bottomed out in 1991, the share of the nonelderly population covered by health insurance fell from 84.7 percent to 84.1 percent.[6] This modest decline in overall coverage masks a more substantial decline (2.7 percent points) in the share of individuals covered by employer-sponsored insurance (ESI). Indeed, fewer people have health insurance, and coverage is shifting away from traditional, private-sector employment-based plans to public insurance under Medicaid.[7]

Let's examine this health insurance trend more closely. You might have heard that 38 million people in the U.S. are uninsured today. In fact President Clinton, in his 1996 State of the Union address, said 58 million people will be uninsured at some point during the year. Let's look at these numbers in a little more detail: 50 percent are uninsured for under 5 months and only about 24 percent were uninsured for the entire year. Most people without coverage have low incomes by U.S. standards; almost 30 percent are below the U.S. government's definition of the poverty level (about $15,000 for a family of four in 1993). Another one-third are between the poverty level and two times the poverty level. Why aren't those who live below poverty level receiving government assistance? The answer is that Medicaid, the U.S. government program designed to help these individuals, only covers 47 percent of those who live below the poverty level.[8]

The contest between the Clinton administration and the GOP has centered around the dollars budgeted for Medicaid, Medicare, and tax cuts. Clinton's goal to preserve healthcare for the poor and uninsured as a federal guarantee has been the deal-buster. Republicans want states to take over Medicaid. The question of whether to retain Medicaid as an entitlement program affects coverage for 7.7 million people but it *impacts* every taxpayer. Clinton's plan would slow spending on Medicaid by about $54 billion; the GOP plan by $163 billion.

Mainstreaming Medicaid

Medicaid is the principal payer for healthcare services for the economically poor. Since its enactment in 1965 as companion legislation to Medicare, Medicaid has evolved from a program providing financing to states for health coverage of their welfare population to a program that now finances health and long-term services for one in eight Americans. Although less central than Medicare to the political debate in 1965 and again in 1995, Medicaid nonetheless plays a major role as a health insurer and safety net for vulnerable Americans throughout the healthcare system.[9]

Today, Medicaid finances care for one in four American children, pays for one-third of the nation's births, assists 60 percent of people living in poverty, pays for half of all nursing home care for frail elderly and disabled Americans, and accounts for 13 percent of all U.S. healthcare spending.[10] It is the source of insurance for 13 percent of the nonelderly population and supplements Medicare by paying premiums and cost sharing for one in 10 elderly and disabled Medicare beneficiaries.[11] Its funding is the major source of federal financial assistance to the states, accounting for 40 percent of all federal grant-in-aid payments to states.[12]

As it enters its 30th year, Medicaid is at a critical juncture. At a cost of $158 billion to federal and state governments in 1995, Medicaid is the mainstay of financing for health insurance and long-term care for 37 million low-income and aged and disabled Americans. It is also a substantial and growing federal and state budgetary commitment.[13] Shifting federal social program funding to states in the form of block grants could harm major urban centers' health services and devastate public hospitals, according to *Urban Social Health,* a report released by the National Public Health and Hospital Institute.[14] The rising cost of maintaining the Medicaid safety net underlies a growing tension in the federal and state partnership for Medicaid and the debate over new approaches for the future.

The actual benefits provided by Medicaid are quite variable across states although, in general, they have become more restrictive in an effort to contain the accelerating costs of medical care. Today, managed care has redefined the Medicaid population as an identifiable base of covered lives. The result is that both for-profit and not-for-profit providers view the Medicaid business as a potential revenue stream and as a means for capturing a market share in a managed care environment. In many states, it is Medicaid that is ushering in capitation as a marketplace reality. Arizona Healthcare Cost Containment System (AHCCCS), a managed care system in which healthcare providers enter an intensely competitive auction to win state contracts, serves some 455,000 patients, almost all of whom would be eligible for Medicaid. (Total budget for 1995: $1.9 billion, of which $1.2 billion comes from the federal government.) Thanks to the program's emphasis on primary care physicians and preventive medicine, the percentage of AHCCCS patients since 1989 who receive most of their treatment in emergency rooms has dropped from 18 percent to 8 percent, while those seeing regular doctors has jumped from 18 percent to 36 percent.[15]

In Tennessee, TennCare has not entered the market as smoothly. Perhaps the most ambitious state-waiver program in the nation, this managed care system provides coverage to the one in four state residents who have enrolled in TennCare. That number includes 877,000 former Medicaid beneficiaries and 418,000 previously uninsured residents. An estimated 250,000 people in the state, about 5 percent of the population, still lack coverage.[16]

Patients and providers alike have had to bear the brunt of a plan that was launched abruptly and haphazardly. From the moment TennCare was law, its opponents had much to grouse about. The speed of the transition from a fee-for-service Medicaid plan to the new system—in which the state takes $2.9 billion in federal and state funds and contracts with 12 privately run managed care organizations—wreaked havoc on doctors and patients. The chaos that even a small private business often undergoes when switching medical plans was multiplied a thousandfold. Many patients did not know which managed care group they had been assigned to, and in the early days it could take hours to get through to TennCare's phone lines. The managed care groups were sometimes four or five months late reimbursing doctors and other providers, who were unhappy already with TennCare's lower fee schedule.

TennCare catapulted the percent of managed care business from 7–8 percent to 18–20 percent almost overnight. The private sector health marketplace quickly jumped on the bandwagon and began aggressively contracting with managed care organizations (MCOs). The reality was that TennCare caught even the state's biggest hospital players unaware. Medicaid reform was the catalyst for a major market shakeup.

Baby Boomers Really Bounce the Check

Medicare and Medicaid pay for most of the health expenses for 67 million—one in four—Americans. The programs are projected to cost $273 billion in the current fiscal year. That's 18 percent of the $1.5 trillion federal budget and 27 percent of all health spending in the nation. At current trends, the programs will cost an estimated $684 billion in 2004, 28 percent of the federal budget.[17]

By 2000, the number of persons 65 and over in the U.S. is expected to double, to some 45 million; the number of those over 85 will triple. And by 2030, the over-65 group will make up 21 percent of our population. The rapid aging of our society is already placing great stress on our healthcare system: Although the over-65 group made up only 12 percent of the population in 1984, they accounted for 31 percent of the nation's total healthcare expenditures.[18]

The real problem will start around 2014, when the Baby Boomers begin to reach 65. Seventy-five million strong, they will flood into Medicare and qualify for Social Security at the same time. If nothing is done, the health and retirement needs of this group would consume almost every tax dollar collected by the federal government by 2030, according to calculations made by the President's Commission on Entitlement and Tax Reform.[19]

Compounding the issue is the fact that, according to the American Hospital Association's report, *Hospitals and Older Adults,* eighty percent of individuals over 75 years of age have a chronic health condition with many experiencing four to five different problems.[20] Poverty expedites the age of disease onset and increases the incidence of multiple health problems. With an increased incidence of chronic disease, there is a greater likelihood that hospitals could be deluged with demands to care for the catastrophic and unpredictable health needs of the aging population. The question becomes,

How do we establish the ratio between the provider's financial risk and the government's burden of social responsibility?

The impending cost of caring for the Baby Boomers is the fodder for some very loaded political debates in Washington, D.C. The American Association of Retired Persons (AARP) has a very loud lobbying voice and controls a lot of votes. Topics like raising the retirement age to 70, reducing Social Security benefits, or the scaling back of retiree health programs are explosive. Still, because low payments to providers cost-shifts tens of billions of dollars every year in healthcare costs to the employer community, politicians won't be able to avoid the pressure to restructure the government's own health programs much past the election year.

In the end, Medicare will follow the suit of Medicaid managed care. The government has already designed demonstration projects with this in mind and is sifting through provider candidates. However, health systems do not have to be identified as a demonstration project to begin to get prepared. Providers are challenged to stay in business while the government attempts to balance its budget and experiments with new forms of Medicaid and Medicare reimbursement. The budget cuts of the magnitude proposed by Congress would swallow most hospitals' bottom lines and cripple future investments.

The GOP wants to trim $250 billion from Medicare spending over the next seven years. A significant portion of these dollars will come from the nation's small community hospitals, which tend to be more reliant on Medicare and Medicaid than their big-city counterparts because they have disproportionately large elderly and poor populations. Most rural hospitals are already struggling financially because of low occupancy rates. Community hospitals will be very much in danger if they do not strategically spread their risk across a regional provider network. As Joseph A. Parker, president of the Georgia Hospital Association recently remarked, "Every community in this state cannot afford a free-standing inpatient facility like we have always had since the early 1950s and '60s. But I would hope there will be efforts at the local level to plan what *will* be there. If you don't have accessible healthcare that is planned in some way, then you don't have quality of life in that community."[21]

Over the next three to five years, the government will play a major role in defining which providers are the winners and losers. Very simply, those that survive the cuts in Medicaid and Medicare reimbursement will have to have very deep pockets. Consequently, for the next several years, size and capital resources may be the primary determinants of market strength.

The government is forcing the healthcare industry into a cycle that has definitive features akin to the precepts of lean manufacturing. Providers are responding to the pressure, banding together, and striving for cost efficiency.

The strategies that are working today involve centralizing authority, standardizing processes, and slashing unit costs of service delivery. In a sense, the government is birthing a few dominant market players who will achieve their market position and prosperity via economies of scale. Those providers who become proficient at learning how to run a lean and mean operational unit will most likely be the ones who survive the first cut of healthcare reform.

HEALTH STATUS BECOMES REAL BUSINESS

It seems that the healthcare reform movement is bringing the importance of improving the health status of the community into the spotlight. Managed care is forcing hospitals and health systems to shift their focus from planning service delivery to population-based community health planning. In part, these efforts reflect the rediscovery of a basic *public health principle,* enunciated two decades ago by visionaries such as Henrik Blum, M.D., Emeritus Professor at the University of California—Berkeley School of Public Health. Dr. Blum counseled students that health and well-being products are not only of medical care, they are "closely linked" with community factors such as "financial resources, health manpower, socioeconomic status, education, and housing."[22]

The daunting challenge facing the healthcare industry today is to identify the means to manage the transition and stay financially viable while creating a new system for health services delivery. Deterioration will not be reversed by looking to changes in reimbursement and incentives, that is, capitation, or by relying on federal and state public policy initiatives. Managed care must become a local reality. Organizations and caregivers committed to survival and vested in the business of health must fundamentally realign efforts and direct resources in order to foster community-based solutions. If community health is defined as population-based health status, then the juxtaposition of managed care and community health is an unexpected pairing of previously unlikely partners.

As the payors empty their pockets, the providers are recognizing a need for a radically different focus. Dwindling resources require entrepreneurial approaches and collaborative efforts. The market shift from a reimbursement scenario characterized by fee-for-service rates to one driven by capitation is moving the pendulum from a service delivery model to one vested in decreased service utilization. In 1993, John F. Fries, M.D., of Stanford University School of Medicine, stated that "by emphasizing both disease prevention and individual responsibility, we can reduce yearly healthcare costs by $200 billion."

According to Robert L. Sandler, Vice President of Shared Services for Connecticut Health Institutional Services, "Most things that make people sick have nothing to do with hospitals and doctors. Successful providers of the future are already aware that *sickness* no longer defines their business. Most of all, as they ascertain the new parameters for managing health, they see *the hospital as simply a facility used by physicians to treat people."*[23]

Within this context, prevention, education, and health promotion are moving out of the goodwill column and into the research and development section of the balance sheet. From the bottom line perspective, investments in prevention, education, and health promotion programs will be justified if they correlate with negative utilization trends. Furthermore, it is critical that substantial resources of manpower and dollars be put into moving beyond the hospital walls. Outpatient services and primary care delivery will need to expand to include a means of identifying and addressing the root causes of illness and injury within a community. Obviously, healthcare factors impact utilization and should drive the re-engineering of acute care services to a full continuum of care. Already proactive hospitals are beginning to incorporate home health, pharmacy, and sub-acute care services into seamless case management delivery systems.

Regional health systems may take a corporate stance on the community health issue but *the approach and solutions must be locally driven.* Industry leaders must share cost effective strategies for:

1. Demand management and preventive healthcare.
2. Patient education.
3. Self-care models.
4. Risk assessment.
5. Intervention techniques.

HEALTHCARE DOLLARS FUND SOCIETAL SOLUTIONS

Healthcare reform is emerging as a critical social issue in America. Escalating medical costs, a sluggish economy, increasing insurance burdens on employers, and the growing number of uninsured have created a national mandate for change.[24] Because of the dollars attached to this service industry, healthcare reform can undoubtedly be an incredibly potent wedge for social reform at the local level.

When the financial incentives are tied to decreased utilization, a health system may consider outreach programs, public health services, health education activities, immunization programs, nutrition services, and other social benefits programs to be loss leader investments. In many markets, the debate regarding the provider's responsibility for community benefit is highly charged with emotion. In the past, there was a direct correlation between a provider's willingness to commit dollars and staff to subsidize community service efforts and its not-for-profit status. In the future, whether or not a provider will invest resources in services targeting community health improvement will depend on how rapidly a market is moving toward capitation.

Healthcare leaders embrace a formidable social mission. Societal responsibility requires actions and decisions that are not always pragmatic from an immediate business perspective. Health promotion activities and community service agendas are low-revenue services and may not seem to make budgetary sense until one considers the more long-term financial consequences of cost shifting and reimbursement structures that dis-incent for utilization. With healthcare reform, our industry has the opportunity to parallel fiduciary responsibility with community obligation. At the local market level, providers must determine their own equilibrium and invest accordingly.

ENDNOTES

1. McWhorter, R. Clayton. "U.S. Healthcare in Transition: A Response to the Health Security Act of 1993." *Health Care Management: State of the Art Reviews,* vol. 1, no. 1 (August 1994), p. 62.
2. ibid., p. 59.
3. Brown, Lawrence D. "Who Shall Pay? Politics, Money and Healthcare Reform." *Health Affairs,* vol. 13 (2) (Spring 1994), p. 175.
4. Carlstrom, Charles T. "The Government's Role in the Health Care Industry: Past, Present, and Future," *Economic Commentary.*
5. "News and Trends: Managed Care Can't Solve Everything for Medicaid," *Business & Health,* (July 1995), p. 9.
6. Winterbottom, 1993.
7. Acs, Gregory. "Explaining Trends in Health Insurance Coverage Between 1988 and 1991," *Inquiry* 32 (Spring 1995), p. 102.
8. Dovi, Dr. Sebastian F. and Dr. James M. Neil. "Total Cost Management of U.S. National Healthcare," *Cost Engineering,* vol. 36/no. 11 (November 1994), p. 10.
9. Tallon, James R. Jr. and Diane Rowland "Federal Dollars and State Flexibility: The Debate Over Medicaid's Future," *Inquiry* 32 (Fall 1995), p. 235.
10. Holahan, J., C. Winterbottom, and S. Rajan. *The Changing Composition of Health Insurance Coverage in the U.S.* (Washington, D.C.: Kaiser Commission on the Future of Medicaid, 1995); Levit, K., et al. "National Health Expenditures, 1993," *Health Care Financing Review* 16 (1994), pp. 247–294.
11. Employee Benefit Research Institute (EBRI). *Sources of Health Insurance and Characteristics of the Uninsured: Analysis of the March 1994 Current Population Survey* (Washington, D.C.: Employee Benefit Research Institute, 1995).
12. National Association of State Budget Officers. *1993 State Expenditure Report* (Washington, D.C.: National Association of State Budget Officers, 1994).

13. Holahan, J., and D. Liska. *The Impact of the Budget Resolution Conference Agreement on Medicaid Expenditures* (Washington, D.C.: The Urban Institute, 1995).

14. "Medicaid Plan Ignores Inner-City Needs," *Hospital and Health Networks* (Dec. 20, 1995) p. 17.

15. Glieck, E. "A Tale of Two States: Arizona and Tennessee Reinvent Medicaid," *Time* (December 18, 1995), p. 32.

16. Schear, Stuart. "Shock Treatment for a Sick System," *Business & Health* (March 1995), p. 31.

17. Findlay, Steven. "Entitlement Reform: The Time Has Come," *Business & Health,* (January 1995), p. 43.

18. Dimond, Margaret. "Health Care and the Aging Population," *Nursing Outlook,* vol. 37, no. 2, (March/April 1989), p. 76.

19. Findlay, Steven. "Entitlement Reform: The Time Has Come," *Business & Health,* (January 1995), p. 43.

20. AHA report on Hospitals & Older Adults.

21. Teegardin, Carrie. "On the Critical List," *Atlanta Journal,* (Oct. 22, 1995), p. 1.

22. "Measuring and Improving Community Health." *The Quality Letter for Healthcare Leaders,* vol. 6, no. 5 (June 1994).

23. *Healthcare Reform Journal,* Nov./Dec. 1993.

24. McWhorter, R. Clayton. "U.S. Health Care in Transition: A Response to the Health Security Act of 1993." *Health Care Management: State of the Art Reviews,* vol. 1, no. 1 (August 1994), p. 57. Philadelphia: Hanley & Belfus.

3 CHAPTER

Economic Trends and Purchasing Behaviors

COST SHIFTING ACTIVATES EMPLOYERS

The employee benefit of group health coverage has only come to pass in the last few decades. Employers are not required by law to provide any benefits to their employees, and many small employers cannot afford to do so.[1] Although some people advocate a system that divorces health insurance coverage from employment, the employer likely will continue to be the main source of health insurance. Currently, about 75 percent of the U.S. population has private health insurance, and about 80 percent of these persons are covered by employer-sponsored health insurance.[2]

Between 1988 and 1991, annual healthcare costs increased from $2,354 to $3,605 per employee. As a result of the astronomical rise in costs and the consequent impact on their bottom line, many small businesses decided they could no longer offer coverage. Others reported that the increased stress on their bottom line has caused them to lose all compunction regarding the need to continue to shoulder the healthcare cost for workers. The consequence? Three out of four small businesses no longer include healthcare coverage in their benefit plans.

In the early 1990s, while the government was beginning to scurry around and kick up dust around national health reform, large employers looked at their bottom lines and began taking stands to decrease their costs of healthcare. Their big-gun approach was to negotiate managed care contracts and shift employees into new benefit plans.

Large employers and business coalitions have become increasingly aggressive about demanding the best buy from the provider community. Large, self-insured employers have even gone so far as to bypass the intermediary and contract directly with local hospitals and regional provider panels. Small employers have banded together to form purchasing co-ops in order to put their companies in a better bargaining position when buying healthcare services. Both large and small employers have made significant changes in health benefit programs. Also, most have not been shy about using financial incentives to steer employees into new plans.

For *Health Benefits in 1994*, KPMG surveyed 1,037 human resources executives from companies with more than 200 employees to find out how they were spending their healthcare dollars. The results of the survey indicate that the market is reforming itself, despite the lack of legislation. With or without government-mandated reform of the healthcare system, the employer is leaning on managed care as a predominant cost-containment strategy.

Employee enrollment in HMOs, PPOs, and POS plans reached a combined 63 percent in 1994, 10 points higher than in 1993. In the same year, the annual Foster Higgins survey of employer costs showed a 1.1 percent decline in per-employee health expenditures. Employers got costs down by shifting millions of workers (about 10 percent of all employees) into cheaper plan types and by carving out some of the costliest parts of their benefit packages—covering such things as mental health care, prescription drugs, and substance abuse treatment—for separate, heavily discounted contracts.[3]

The problem is, while the employers finally reduced their per-employee expenditures for the first time in years, it appears that these cost savings may have been a one-time occurrence. The following clip appeared February 4, 1995, in *The New York Times:*

> The cost of employee health care climbed in 1995 and is continuing to rise this year, two surveys of businesses found, after a dip in 1994. The increase reflects the higher cost of traditional insurance, the increased demand for new and expensive tests and the number of older and retired employees. The cost of care provided by managed-care networks fell for the first time.[4]

The core unresolved issue is cost shifting. To the extent that states have been able to control Medicaid spending, they have done so by sharply limiting payments to providers. Some states pay doctors less than $10 for an office visit. And guess who makes up the difference? Employers and private insurers. This Medicaid shift has been estimated to add between 5 and 10 percent to the cost of healthcare for private payers.[5]

Similarly, a study published in 1995 by the California Business Roundtable calculates a 7 percent cost shift from Medi-Cal and uncompensated care to private industry. But the study, done by Lewin-VHI researcher and vice president Linda Bergthold, found an even larger cost shift—9 percent—from small employers to large. That is, large employers that cover spouses and dependents who work for small firms might trim their healthcare costs by 9 percent if those small employers provided coverage.[6]

Because they recognize how changes in legislation regarding coverage for the Medicaid and uninsured populations will impact their pockets, large employers are already mounting forces to lobby against block grants and the dissolution of the employers' entitlement status. In the meantime, they are attempting to counter the effects of cost shifting by looking closer to home. Large employers are controlling what they can: *provider contracts*. With reduced government reimbursement combined with aggressive employers driving managed care negotiations, providers are getting squeezed from both ends.

By increasing their demands at the negotiating table, employers are using managed care to force providers to come close to pricing at cost. As you might imagine, this is a big driving factor in the formation of networks because providers see that the cost savings they can achieve through economies of scale may be the only way to stay in business. In addition, once the price window has narrowed, employers will be closely scrutinizing what they are getting in return for their dollar; in other words, they will be paying close attention to measurements of quality and patient satisfaction. As a major purchaser of healthcare services, employers will use their marketplace clout to *demand value* for their money (see Figure 3–1).

Since 1991, the Washington-based National Committee for Quality Assurance has conducted detailed inspections and evaluations of HMOs, giving those that measured up an endorsement known as accreditation. The process, which is voluntary and funded largely through fees paid by the HMOs, is similar to the one hospitals have gone through for decades. A standardized report card is now available to consumers. The summaries rate each HMO on six broad areas: quality and improvement of care, member satisfaction, physician qualifications, preventative health services, prompt and fair approvals of medical treatment, and the accuracy of medical records.[7]

Consequently, the employer will play a big role in determining which providers survive the cost crunch and, as they become more informed purchasers, they will play an even more active role in determining which provider networks will be capable of managing the next market transition into an era of value purchasing. Providers who are now reeling from the first wave of government-induced market reform will have little time to get their balance before the employer community drives healthcare reform into the

FIGURE 3-1

Four Components of Value-Based Buying

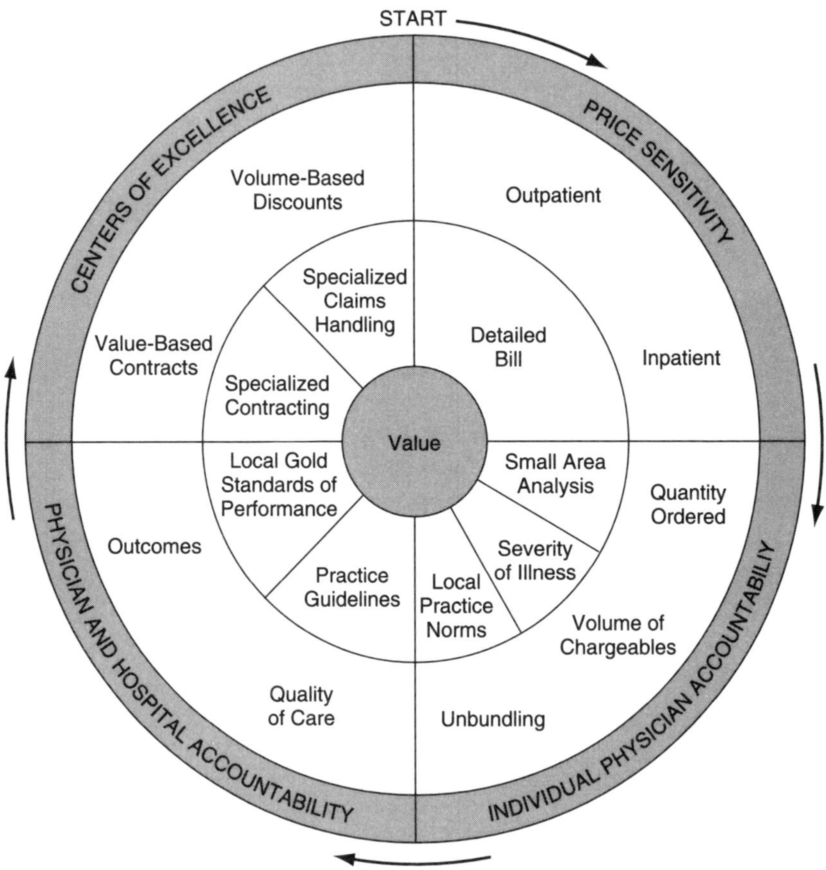

Source: Gregg Lehman, Ph.D.

next dimension. In order to secure a competitive advantage in the future, provider networks need to begin today to commit resources to the development of value-added service.

PUTTING TECHNOLOGY IN ITS PLACE

In *Future Edge: Discovering the New Paradigms of Success,* Joel Arthur Barker writes about the Swiss watch manufacturers who lost their dominent market share when the Japanese introduced the electronic quartz watch. The Swiss could not envision a watch made with electronic components instead of mechanical gears, bearings, and mainsprings. The Japanese eclipsed the Swiss by changing the rules of the game for watchmaking. Intel Corporation had a similar experience with its Pentium chip. After spending millions in advertising dollars touting the superiority of its microprocessors, Intel begrudgingly agreed to replace flawed Pentium chips after initially ignoring the problem. Preoccupied with creating faster, more powerful microprocessors and attaining a dominant market share for its market, Intel failed to understand that its *ultimate accountability was to customer, not technology.* Consumer expectations changed the ground rules for mighty Intel.[8]

As we examine our current system, we need to remember something very important: The system we currently have exists because of choices we as a nation have made. For example, we have chosen to guarantee emergency medical care and heroic measures to all citizens, while at the same time choosing not to fund preventative care that might have made emergency care unnecessary. We will spend thousands of dollars to care for a child who contracts measles and becomes acutely ill because we did not spend a few dollars to immunize that child against the disease.

Experts estimate that between 20 and 30 percent of all medicine practiced in this country is defensive; that is, it can be traced to physicians ordering extra tests and procedures as a precautionary measure in the very real event of a malpractice lawsuit. That does not even take into account the increased fees physicians must charge to cover their malpractice insurance fees, which average $22,000 per physician per year in this country.[9]

For instance, most anyone who is rushed from a car wreck to the emergency room with open wounds does not want to be seen by a hypnotherapist upon admission. Trauma care is an intensive, high-technology service that will continue to have its place in a continuum of care. Similarly, flow cytommetry will continue to be an asset in earlier diagnosis of cancer and immune deficient disorders. The demand for cardiovascular surgeries and transplant procedures will not be eradicated immediately (if ever) by an increasing emphasis on lifestyle changes and prevention. Not everyone will choose to take measures to prevent heart disease. Some people will still be "couch potatoes," eating chips, dips and cheeseburgers. These people will be likely candidates for invasive procedures if they develop heart disease. Such complex procedures will continue to require state-of-the-art technology.

"You will always have to have the larger hospitals to treat the acutely ill, but I don't think you are going to have as many of them," said M. Jo Edwards, professor and holder of the Adams Chair of Excellence in Health Care Services at Middle Tennessee State University. Edwards continues, "You will not have as many centers jumping in to do heart transplants or bypass surgery, for instance. In the past, hospitals got into it very quickly. That will decline. Technology is very expensive and research and development dollars are going to be reduced because of the emphasis on prevention." But at the same time, access to this technology will become harder to get and even harder to justify, especially when the health problems are avoidable or when the outcome doesn't guarantee what most Americans deem an acceptable quality of life. And the bottom line is dollars. Future forecasters predict that the health of our population 30 years from now will depend on the interplay of four factors: technology, human behavior, biological evolution, and economics. They don't specify in which order.[10]

In the future, investments in high technology should emphasize earlier diagnosis of chronic diseases such as cancer and cardiac concerns. In the cardiac communities, the value of investing in an ultra-fast CT scanner is getting new attention. In addition, chronic disease management, infertility, and Alzheimer treatments are predicted to continue as niche areas of growth for biotechnology and medical devices. When you look at managing the health of a population, it is sort of a matter of *pay me now or pay me later.*

In short, because of the cost, technological care will be configured into a continuum in a way that allows the physician to better serve the patient. Technology will continue to be an important component of the healthcare delivery system matrix. The difference is that it will not be the driver of care, it will simply be a tool.

NARROWING THE CUSTOMER FOCUS

Managed care has caused the provider community to truly re-think its definition of customer. In the initial stages of managed care market penetration, the paramount importance of cost containment makes the payor the most immediate customer. One has only to look at the volume of healthcare business that is funded by Medicare and Medicaid dollars to recognize the federal and state governments as major payors—and a major customer. With an intensive focus on strategies to trim the deficit and reduce the stress on the government system, Medicaid and Medicare managed care are new market realities. There is little doubt that the government will continue to be a major customer, however, with the introduction of a new competitive structure, the third-party payors—or managed care organization (MCO)—become the provider's primary customer.

When managed care enters a market, providers vie for contracts with MCOs. Often the negotiated rates are such that the providers are "damned if they do, and damned if they don't" win the contract. Consequently, as the market matures, it is characterized by consolidated provider groups who have survived the price wars by resorting to the use of economies of scale as ammunition.

Moreover, with the first thrust of managed care comes a horde of MCOs, all eager to enter the market. However, managing a base of covered lives means managing financial risk, and not all MCOs will have deep enough pockets to sustain the variable costs of insuring healthcare costs for a shifting base of covered lives. Thus, while many MCOs initially enter the market and pummel the providers with increasingly restrictive rates, not all are able to sustain a marketplace presence. Once again, a few dominate the market.

With MCOs come HMOs, PPOs, and POSs. The question for the provider becomes, How do you play the provider panel game and come out ahead? Contracting for volume business is one answer. Many providers have found that one of the best ways to reach a primary (and large) target market of middle-class, insured healthcare consumers is through the workplace, specifically large, self-insured employers. Direct contracts with employers bypass the intermediaries, that is, the third-party payors and MCOs. Price is a hook in getting the contract in the first place because employers realize how much they have been hurt by rising costs. Still, most employers continue to be very sensitive to issues like ease of access, communication, status of an employee once he or she has entered the system, and employee satisfaction with services.

It seems that once the market has managed the cost crisis, the definition of target customer begins to return to the patient–consumer. As was previously discussed, the Minneapolis Health Care Action Group is returning *choice to employees* by expanding options for selecting medical clinics and physicians. Similarly, in August of 1995, New York Governor George Pataki signed legislation requiring HMOs to offer policies allowing individuals to use doctors of their choice and not just those in the network.[11] Finally, for health plans trying to raise their enrollments, a strategic truth stands out: People want a choice of doctors and hospitals.

For no more money, subscribers can choose from Kaiser Foundation Health Plan's new network of 2,000 "community" doctors in Charlotte and the Research Triangle cities of Raleigh, Durham, and Chapel Hill, North Carolina, or they can stick with doctors who work in clinics run by Kaiser.[12] The physician or certified primary care health professional working most closely with the patient is the pivot of provider performance. Health systems and hospitals cannot afford to forget that their medical staff is their most obvious interface with the end-user, the patient. As a side note, in the role of patient advocate, the physician or other primary care health professional is a very important intermediary customer. Primary care providers can take the pulse of community health while they add the personalized touch to patient-centered care.

In the 1995 edition of *The Satisfaction Report,* information about trends and what influences patient choices of providers is outlined, based on Press,

Ganey Associates, Inc.'s national databases. As healthcare moves toward integrated delivery, patient satisfaction data take on increasing importance. Patients who are dissatisfied with one segment of a healthcare system—like a medical practice, an emergency room, hospital, or home health agency—could refuse to be treated at other delivery points within the system. Needless to say *that affects the whole system's bottom line.*[13]

In sum, the provider that survives and thrives will need to have multifaceted approaches and concurrent strategies to meet the needs of a complex customer mix—the government, MCOs, primary care providers, and patients themselves. No one strategy, no one mode of organization or operation will be successful for long. Nor will any strategy be optimal for all customers or all markets.

The life expectancy of decisions that work for a company or health system at any particular time will depend on the rate of change in the markets in which that company or health system competes. In order to succeed, the company must be able to exploit both short- and long-term market opportunities for knowledge-based, customer-configured goods and services. To do so, the company must have the right core competencies with which to create new customer opportunities and to respond to customer opportunities that present themselves.[14] This is a *customer-intimate company.*

The customer-intimate company makes a business of knowing the people it sells to and the products and services they need. It continually tailors its products and services, and does so at reasonable prices. Its position is: "We take care of you and all your needs," or "We get you the best total solution." Customer-intimate companies don't pursue discrete, one-time transactions; they cultivate long-term relationships. They are adept at giving the customer more than he or she expects. By constantly upgrading their offerings, customer-intimate companies stay ahead of their customers' rising expectations—expectations that, by the way, they themselves create. Home Depot is a good example of a customer-intimate company. Cable & Wireless is another organization whose executives knew long ago that their long-distance operation couldn't compete on price with AT&T, MCI, and Sprint. So Cable & Wireless sought to differentiate itself by providing the best ongoing customer support in the industry, along with direct sales consultation that gives the salesforce an intimate knowledge of what makes its customers successful. The result is that Cable & Wireless has turned itself from a mundane commodity business peddling long-distance service into a sophisticated telemanager, a partner with its customers.[15]

Can a customer-intimate strategy pay off for a hospital? You bet! Many provider organizations, such as Bon Secours Health System, are choosing *customer intimacy* as the feature that will create for them some degree of

FIGURE 3–2

Keeping the Patient in the Bullseye

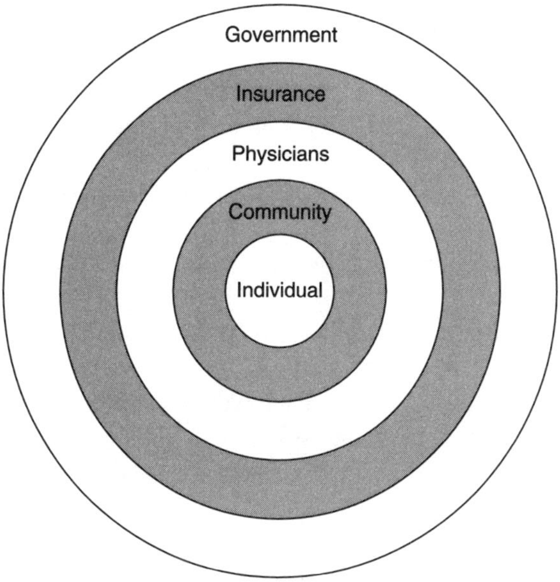

market differentiation. A continuum of care will only be competitive if it is a template response for the needs of the community of individuals it serves. In addition, capitation shifts the incentives toward a wellness model of care. Becoming the patient's partner is what the health promotion movement is all about. For the local hospital that is competing neck to neck with three other metropolitan healthcare centers—or for the community hospital that is trying to build its case as the preferred primary care center—a commitment to customer intimacy may be the most critical strategy for long-term market success.

When mega-health systems begin to compete against each other they will have already demonstrated a mastery of cost efficiency and seamless processes. The new elite will be the providers who never ceased to understand the importance of keeping the patient/consumer in the bullseye (see Figure 3–2).

ENDNOTES

1. Byrd, Kathryn. "Today's Healthcare Confusion Has Quite a Precedent," *Texas Banking,* vol. 83 (8) (August 1994), p. 5.

2. Zarkin, Gary A., et al. "Employment-Based Health Insurance: Implications of the Sampling Unit for Policy Analysis," *Inquiry* vol. 32 (Fall 1995), p. 310.
3. Service, Mary. "Why Health Costs Got Smaller in 1994," *Business & Health* (March 1995), p. 20.
4. "Health Care Costs Rise Again," *The New York Times* (Feb. 4, 1996), p. F–2.
5. Findlay, Steven. "Block Grants for Sale," *Business & Health* (August 1995), p. 55.
6. Findlay, Steven. "California: Edgy at the Cutting Edge," *Business & Health* (July 1995), p. 40.
7. "Agency Plans a Report Card to Rank HMOs' Performance," *The Tennesseean* (Feb. 18, 1996), p. E–3.
8. Addelman, Robert D. "Value-Driven Healthcare," *Healthcare Forum Journal,* (November/December 1995), p. 47.
9. McWhorter, R. Clayton. "America's Health Care System: On the Brink of Change," *Health Care Reform,* p. 3–4.
10. Smith, Tammie. "Technology, Expense Write Prescription for Change," *The Tennesseean* (Feb. 11, 1996), pp. 4–5.
11. "New York Legislation Requires Individual Choice of Doctors," *SHPM Section for Managed Care* (4th Quarter), p. 2.
12. Lumsdon, Kevin. "Inside Track Strategy: Managed Care—More Docs to Pick From," *Hospitals & Health Networks* (December 5, 1995), p. 51.
13. "Patients Rank Interpersonal Issues That Affect Quality of Care," *Society for Healthcare Planning & Marketing* (November 1995), pp. 2–3.
14. Goldman, Steven L., Roger N. Nagel, Kenneth Preiss. *Agile Competitors and Virtual Organizations: Strategies for Enriching the Customer* (New York: Van Nostrand Reinhold, 1995), p. 6
15. Treacy, Michael and Fred Wiersema. *The Discipline of Market Leaders: Choose Your Customers, Narrow Your Focus, Dominate Your Market* (Pennsylvania: Addison Wesley, 1995), pp. 38–39.

4 CHAPTER

Careening Competitive Structures

VERTICAL INTEGRATION FOR SHORT-TERM SURVIVAL

Managed care is serving as a catalyst for delivery system consolidation. Many hospitals have found that survival is their day-to-day challenge. The crunch around reimbursement, combined with new competitive giants entering the marketplace, is fostering a new approach for an old business. Most autonomous providers, that is, physicians and hospitals, have discovered that they can not go it alone. To consolidate, they are choosing one of three strategies:

1. Align with other providers to increase economies of scale, stability, and marketplace leverage;
2. Put themselves on the auction block; or
3. Fold.

To the minds of some analysts, the United States is now witnessing the largest industry reorganization since the 19th century: the corporatization of American healthcare.[1] This first wave of market competition is using the theory that *bigger is better* to define who wins and who loses. Vertically integrated systems have a natural cost advantage over traditional delivery systems (see Figure 4–1). The winners will be facile at applying bottom-line financial analysis and using business principles from other industries.

FIGURE 4–1

Integrated Systems Offer Drastically Lower Prices

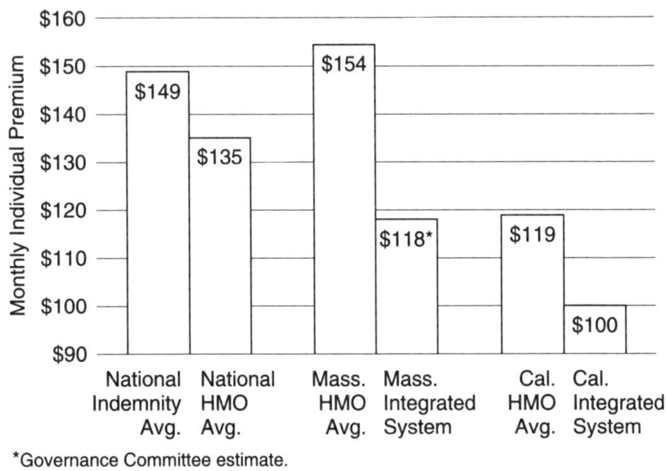

Note: Adapted from *The Advisory Board, "Capitation Strategy"* The Governance Committee, 1994.

The integrated health system is the provider organization at the top of the food chain. Although it is at risk in isolation, the concept of a continuum of care existing across a system actually reinforces the role of the local community hospital as a primary care site. For some hospitals, an interim strategy may be to subcontract with a large system to function as an affiliated service provider. Generally, however, this solution only buys time.

Protecting occupancy rates is another interim strategy that may sustain an individual hospital as long as the market is operating primarily within discounted fee-for-service or per diem rate structures. Although almost irresistible if supported by an even temporary flow of cash, such a strategy will actually cause a hospital to be more vulnerable and at risk as managed care makes greater inroads within a marketplace. According to the American Hospital Association's tracing of nearly 2,000 community facilities through the *National Hospital Panel Survey,* outpatient visits continued to rise in 1995, while surgeries and inpatient revenue slowed, causing profit margins to fall.[2] Hospital administrators who are attempting to "circle the wagons" to protect existing revenue streams must "bite the bullet" and recognize that inpatient care is a non-growth market.

The fundamental goal of all operations is to build a strategic power that will earn a reasonable profit. Market forces are driving reorganization across the industry. Competitive forces are driving integration. In the short run, vertical integration will be a prerequisite for survival. The "lone ranger" will not be able to compete against large forces harboring extensive resources of capital, management skills, and information systems.

NOT-FOR-PROFITS GOING FOR-PROFIT

Breaking even isn't good enough when you have shareholders looking over your shoulder. Hospitals and other healthcare companies are learning this harsh fact of life as a rash of mergers and acquisitions transforms the once primarily not-for-profit system into a for-profit field, according to Irving Levin Associates, a consulting and research firm.[3]

Of the 97 hospital mergers and acquisitions announced during 1994, only four were terminated, which means that the remaining 93 were either consummated or are still pending. Twelve of the announced deals involved multihospital systems, which accounted for 227 hospitals. In total, the transactions actually affected 308 hospitals, 58,928 hospital beds, and close to $14 billion in combined revenues. Of the consummated or pending deals, 22 involved 192 hospitals owned by 11 publicly traded companies (50%); 16 deals involved 49 hospitals owned by private companies (12%); and 55 transactions involved 66 hospitals owned by not-for-profit organizations (38%).

Additionally, the companies doing the acquiring included: 18 publicly traded companies that secured 251 hospitals with 40,731 beds in forty-five transactions; 12 private companies that acquired 16 hospitals with 3,445 beds in fourteen transactions; and 31 not-for-profit companies that acquired 42 hospitals with 14,753 beds in thirty-two transactions. The bottom line? Private companies saw a net loss of 3,524 beds while public companies gained. Similarly, while not-for-profits weathered a net loss of 7,603 beds, the for-profit group gained 11,127 beds.

The three largest deals of 1994 were engineered by three for-profit organizations—Columbia/HCA Healthcare Corp., Tenet Healthcare, and HealthTrust. These three companies alone accounted for 187 hospitals with 29,465 beds, at an average price per bed of $336,000. A second tier of buyers garnered 121 hospitals with 29,463 beds, purchased for an average of $203,000 per bed.[4]

As healthcare becomes more organized and characterized by aggressive business approaches, healthcare providers will be even more accountable for defining their partnerships and alliances in the context of shared vision, mission, and purpose. If the goal is to make money by delivering high-quality healthcare for the lowest possible price, then sign up with a system like Columbia/HCA and move forward in the sick-care business. If, however, the objective is to impact health status, thereby contributing to a societal solution to the problem of controlling healthcare costs in the long run, then it will be critical to come together with other providers with a like commitment.

Vertical integration positions providers into high growth. The developments in patient care which will build a new base for profit making will be beyond the hospital walls. Contemporary strategies for business development will begin with a due-diligence process, investigating opportunities for service development in the areas of prevention, early diagnosis, ambulatory care, and after-care recovery. Defending inpatient beds is a disheartening journey against the wind.[5]

ENDNOTES

1. *Vision of the Future: Briefing for Board Members, Physicians, and Administration,* p. 2. © 1993 The Advisory Board Company, The Governance Committee (1/800–673–1756)
2. "Insights From Playing Patient," *Hospitals & Health Networks,* November 20, 1995, p. 50.
3. "Not-For-Profits Going For-Profit," *Hospitals & Health Networks* (December 20, 1995), p. 24.
4. Id.
5. *Vision of the Future: Briefing for Board Members, Physicians, and Administration* (Washington, D.C.: The Advisory Board, 1993), p. 21.

5

CHAPTER

The For-Profit/Not-For-Profit Showdown*

In a competitive bid to transform the hospital industry into a for-profit, stockholder-owned enterprise, charity care and community benefits have become the device to challenge not-for-profit hospitals in the marketplace. At issue is a rivalry between not-for-profit and for-profit healthcare organizations that may determine who provides hospital care in America in the 21st century. Not-for-profit hospitals are at the center of a growing controversy over whether they behave significantly different from their for-profit counterparts and provide sufficient levels of charity care and other community benefits to merit special tax treatment.

Today's not-for-profit hospitals are mixed institutions, with both commercial and social characteristics that do not resemble the charitable hospitals of the past. The mixed character of these modern hospitals, which produce some services where revenue sources are sufficient to cover costs and other services where revenue sources are insufficient, is at least in part responsible for public and private attempts either to change their behavior to make them more socially directed, community-oriented organizations or to rescind their tax-exempt status.[1]

---

*This chapter was written by Lillian J. Pfaff a marketing consultant doing doctoral research at the University of Southern California in healthcare competition and economics. Because of her area of focus, she has a keen understanding of the non-profit/for-profit competitive rivalry in a changing healthcare arena. In this chapter Ms. Pfaff defines herself as a pragmatic idealist with the potential to serve as a shape-changer for an emerging industry. I am grateful to her for this insightful contribution.

Ironically, the businesslike approach of successful not-for-profits which has made them seem more like for-profit companies than public charities, has invited the current charges that they have abandoned their charitable missions. Competition makes not-for-profits look like any other business.

THE COMPETITIVE ARENA

For-profits are calling for the elimination of not-for-profits' long-standing tax exemptions to "level the playing field" in competitive markets. They argue that the differential tax treatment accorded tax-exempt hospitals provides a competitive advantage, even though operationally there is little that distinguishes the two hospital models. Many not-for-profits, they maintain, provide no more charity care than many investor-owned hospitals do.

As an offensive tactic, accusing not-for-profits of failing to live up to their charitable obligations in a manner commensurate with the value of their tax exemptions has succeeded in raising the temperature on an already sensitive issue. By the 1980s, before the expansion of third-party financing, financially strained state and local governments were already taking a hard look at the revenue value of tax-exemptions granted to not-for-profit hospitals and had begun to question whether the public was getting its money's worth, especially considering the industry's general profitability. They challenged these hospitals to justify their tax-exempt status by validating their charitable community service.

The debate over what constitutes a sufficient level of charity care intensified during the 1980s and 1990s, but it has roots in a 1969 decision made by the Internal Revenue Service (IRS). At that time, the IRS changed the charity standard for tax exemption of not-for-profit hospitals from the narrow concept of charity care to the much broader concept of charitable activity for community benefit. The IRS staff foresaw that the passage of Medicare and Medicaid would eventually lead Congress to deliberations of universal entitlement which, if ever adopted, would undermine the validity of charity care as the basis for tax exemption. If the IRS were to stay in the tax-exemption business in healthcare, the broader concept of a contribution to the entire community was needed, rather than simply to the poor. This larger community benefit standard called for increased accountability—not merely to serve, but to plan and manage the service so that the entire community would consequently be better off.[2]

Following the lead of federal, state, and local governments, and armed with a 1990 General Accounting Office (GAO) study which found that 15 percent of the nation's not-for-profit hospitals provided less uncompensated care than the value of their tax exemptions, Columbia/HCA Healthcare Corporation, the nation's largest for-profit hospital chain, thrust itself into the debate, becoming the hospital industry's most outspoken proponent of tax code revisions. Columbia contends that the taxes paid by investor-owned hospitals are a community benefit commensurate with charity care and bad debt, and that when paid taxes are taken into account, for-profits provide as much charity care and community benefits as their not-for-profit rivals. To prove their point, Columbia devised a formula for measuring community benefits. The formula measures charity care and the sum of federal income, state sales, and local property taxes. It credits investor-owned hospitals for taxes paid plus charity care provided. When applied to not-for-profits, it subtracts charity care from the amount of taxes avoided through exemptions, thus penalizing the hospitals for taxes unpaid.

Beginning in 1993, Columbia commissioned at least five comparative studies in Florida, Georgia and Tennessee. The studies assailed not-for-profit hospitals and the benefits they derived from various tax exemptions. They concluded that nearly half the not-for-profit hospitals in the studies provided community benefits of lesser value than their tax exemptions or "negative community benefits." According to the findings, Columbia's hospitals provided community benefits of significantly greater value than did not-for-profits when paid taxes were added to charity care.

The consulting firm Columbia hired to do the studies contends that the reports fairly represent the documentable amount of community benefits not-for-profits provide. Columbia maintains that the reports are intended to educate the public about the benefits that not-for-profits reap from their tax exemptions. Critics, however, suggest that Columbia's purpose is political. Since losing tax exemptions would raise not-for-profits' business expenses, acquiring them and competing with them on managed care contracts would be easier.[3]

Equating taxes with charity care assumes that governments use these tax revenues to provide services for the poor. In reality, most tax revenues go to other purposes—as, for example, property taxes, which do more for local schools than for indigent healthcare. Not-for-profits argue that it is a fallacy to equate a dollar in taxes to a dollar in charity care when measured by the direct provision of health services.

Many of the industry's other investor-owned hospital organizations reject Columbia's tax argument, acknowledging publicly that tax revenue is a less direct community benefit and not specific to healthcare. Most businesses and individuals consider paying taxes a cost of doing business rather than a charitable act. The argument that paying taxes constitutes charity places businesses of all types, from liquor stores to retail chains, in the same community-benefit category as hospitals. Yet Columbia has used its tax argument to win managed care contracts from competing not-for-profit hospitals and to convince local trustees that selling their hospital to Columbia would increase their institution's level of community benefits.[4]

More persuasive than the tax argument to many trustees willing to consider purchase offers from investor-owned chains is the opportunity to create multimillion-dollar charitable foundations through proceeds from the sale of their hospitals. Columbia has become the industry leader in establishing community foundation spinoffs as part of the acquisition agreement. Communities receive greater benefit, according to investor-owned chains, from having hospitals that pay taxes, provide care, and establish foundations to increase medical research and healthcare services. Critics contend that when hospitals are acquired by a for-profit corporation, their level of charity care drops significantly and other not-for-profits in the area must absorb these patients.[5]

Part of the difficulty in coming to terms with relative contributions of hospitals to their communities is the lack of a generally agreed upon standard for what constitutes charity care and community benefits. Not-for-profit hospitals criticized the Columbia studies as incomplete for not including payroll taxes and the variety of unpaid community services they provide—items not reported on their bottom lines.[6] Experienced professionals caution against too narrow a definition of community benefits that recognizes only charity care. These hospitals have yet to agree on what criteria they should use to calculate the community benefits they provide, however. Thus, the field is open to contradictory definitions, which become the basis for studies that do little more than serve the competing interests of one party over another in the marketplace and fail to provide an accurate picture of services rendered.

The available figures only fuel the debate. The GAO study which Columbia used to support its position included only uncompensated care, defined as charity care and bad debt, in its evaluation of not-for-profits. The report did not include estimates of a dollar value for community services, although it did say not-for-profit hospitals were more likely than for-profits to provide free clinics, subsidized medical education and research, and health screening. Predictably, other reports depict relative contributions differently. The American Hospital Association issued comparative findings for 1988 and 1993, years in which not-for-profit expenditures on uncompensated care increased 53 percent ($6.0 billion to $9.2 billion) compared to a for-profit expenditure increase of 19 percent ($745 million to $886 million).

HOW NOT-FOR-PROFIT HOSPITALS ARE ADDRESSING THE CHALLENGE

The difference between not-for-profits and for-profits is the purpose, not the profit. Tax-exempt hospitals have mission statements that clearly articulate their commitment to treating all individuals regardless of ability to pay, and to serving the healthcare needs of their communities. They are distinguished by the roles and responsibilities that traditionally have justified their tax exemptions. These include: (1) the use of financial surpluses exclusively to advance the institution's charitable purpose; (2) accountability to the public through the board of trustees representing the community's healthcare needs; (3) fulfilling their obligations to contribute to the common good and lessen the burdens of government by providing services that otherwise would have to be provided or financed by state or local governments; (4) charity care to indigent patients; (5) provision of unprofitable services like free clinics, burn and trauma treatment, subsidized medical education and clinical research; (6) educational services designed to enhance individual health, promote primary care, and improve the provision of healthcare; (7) addressing unmet community needs like meals for homebound senior citizens, home health, rural health, child and adult day care, and teen pregnancy programs; and (8) a history of voluntary service to community healthcare.

A recent study distributed by the Voluntary Hospitals of America, Inc. (VHA), shows that not-for-profit hospitals are more likely to provide a wider range of health services, even when these services are not money makers and may lose money for the hospital. For example, of the 4,376 AIDS care units in the nation, the reports shows that 81.6 percent are operated by not-for-profits, compared with 8.2 percent by for-profit hospitals. Of the 881 trauma units nationwide, tax-exempt hospitals operate 91 percent compared to for-profits' 6.7 percent.[7] In short, the not-for-profit hospital is a community enterprise with a strong emphasis on maintaining its not-for-profit, charitable, community ownership structure.[8]

Competition often shapes management behavior and decision making, but survival of the not-for-profit model may rest on accountability for community benefit provision and charity care. In response to the public criticism and competitive challenges, not-for-profits began seeking ways to demonstrate that they live up to their healthcare commitments to the poor and provide charitable services equivalent in value to their tax exemptions.

While there is no general consensus on how to fairly and accurately measure community benefits, there are some generally accepted measurement criteria, and various suggestions as to how hospitals and their communities might measure community benefits to reflect their value. The Catholic Hospital Association (CHA), Voluntary Hospitals of America, Inc. (VHA), and the American Hospital Association (AHA) have developed guidelines and community benefits assessment tools to document the value of charitable services, increase organizational effectiveness, and win back public confidence.

VHA, Inc., for example, issued a list of voluntary standards for self-examination in 1992 similar to those of the IRS. The list includes such specific items as maintaining 24-hour emergency rooms, and general goals involving community representation on governing boards, provision of essential healthcare services, community accountability, demonstrated charitable leadership, and commitment to both community benefit and operating free of private profit.[9]

The Catholic Hospital Association (CHA), headquartered in St. Louis, Missouri, established a model framework for tracking and documenting community benefits. The "Social Accountability Budget for Not-For-Profit Healthcare Organizations," introduced in 1989, set forth definitive guidelines for a broad range of community benefit activities to include not only uncompensated care, but unpaid costs of services to the poor, unpaid costs of medical education and clinical research, and unprofitable services such as trauma, burn, and neonatal units.[10] The framework was developed in association with a number of the nation's tax-exempt hospitals to provide policy direction and a set of tools for hospital executives, professional staffs, and governing bodies. It established measurement criteria and a comprehensive methodology to assist hospitals in documenting and quantifying the value of the broad range of community benefits they provide.

Moreover, many of the leading not-for-profit systems across the country have developed specific community benefit services and reporting tools of their own. The American Hospital Association (AHA) reported that in 1993 approximately 62 percent of the nation's 3,154 not-for-profit hospitals provided health assessment programs and 48 percent issued quality reports, as compared with 46 percent and 40 percent respectively of the 717 investor-owned hospitals.

Critics contend that not enough not-for-profit hospitals have joined the movement to improve community health. In an effort to address that need, the Kellogg Foundation recently awarded $6 million to the National Community Care Network Demonstration Program, collaboratively managed by the AHA, the CHA, and VHA, Inc., to work with evolving networks that demonstrate a community health focus, a seamless continuum of services, community accountability, and a Community Care Network vision of creating strong community partnership.[11]

Social performance would improve if hospitals had a clear perception of their communities' expectations. Often they do not. To make the connection with their constituencies, hospitals need to engage in dialogue with community groups and leaders. Hospitals can be responsive only to the degree that they have accurately assessed community needs.

On the reporting side, almost everyone agrees that as a basic measurement principle the value of a tax-exempt hospital's charitable and community benefit services should equal or exceed the value of the foregone tax revenues. The estimated tax liability of a hospital is a useful performance standard. It is by no means the only standard advanced by people interested in measuring the contributions of not-for-profits, however. Members of Congress have variously proposed that charity care should equal five percent of gross revenue, that other community benefits should be worth 10 percent of gross revenues (both recommended by Representative Donnelly, D-Mass.), and that qualified charity care—the combined values of services to the medically indigent, bad debts, and Medicaid allowances—should equal 50 percent of hospitals' tax liability (Representative Roybal, D-Calif.).

Yet another standard, this one put forth by financial scholars, is the annual return derived from various financial instruments, which represent alternative investment opportunities. Community members may choose to invest funds directly in their local hospital or in financial options such as U.S. Treasury bills or common stocks, the returns of which they can spend on specific charities.[12] Each of these performance standards suggests alternative means of quantifying the level of charity and community services.

In their seven year (1980–87) evaluation of community benefits provided by California's not-for-profit hospitals, researchers Clement, Smith, and Wheeler provided insight into ways in which not-for-profits provide services of measurable social value. Using hospital data, they compared the benefits provided by not-for-profits in each of the seven years to the various performance standards cited above. In using tax exemptions as a performance standard, the researchers found that while the median value of exemption from income and property taxes averaged close to five percent, the total community return paid by not-for-profit hospitals was three to four times the value of the tax exemptions in each year when uncompensated care, education and research, money-losing services, price discounts, and net income (defined as profits used to provide future community benefits) were combined to calculate the value of community benefits. Over 75 percent of hospitals in the study consistently exceeded the estimated tax liability.

With regard to the three Congressional performance standards, results varied significantly, depending upon which of the standards was applied. When the return on charity care alone was compared with five percent of gross revenues, between 20.6 percent and 39.1 percent of the California hospitals exceeded the standard. When "other services" (which the researchers defined as money-losing services plus price discounts from for-profit providers) were compared to 10 percent of gross revenues, approximately 60 percent exceeded the standard. Thirdly, when the researchers applied the standard stipulating that qualified charity care must equal at least 50 percent of the hospital's estimated tax liability, approximately 60 percent of hospitals in the study exceeded the standard each year.

Finally, in comparison to financial scholars' standard of annual returns on financial instruments, the total community return paid by not-for-profit hospitals exceeded rates paid on risk-free U.S. Treasury bills by approximately two-to-one in each year of the study, and in all but one year exceeded returns for common stocks on the Standard and Poor's 500 Index. In a given year, between 63.9 and 75.2 percent of hospitals provided returns exceeding those of Treasury bills, and between 41.1 and 88.6 percent of hospitals exceeded the more variable and higher-yielding common stock returns.

Clearly, hospitals and their communities need to establish agreed upon levels of community benefits and measurement criteria. To the extent that hospitals use the needs assessment process to identify niches for providing services their communities desire, the community benefits planning process has the potential for strengthening the role of not-for-profit hospitals in the healthcare delivery arena. Not-for-profits need to be innovative. They must be committed to restructuring healthcare delivery at the community level, based on what the local residents identify as their needs. The growing "healthy communities" movement extends the hospitals' role to include prevention services like health screening and immunizations; health maintenance services like transportation, food, shelter, and education programs; community-oriented wellness and health promotion services; adult and child day care; and outreach clinics, to name a few.[13]

Community health improvement must be a core business strategy for today's hospital.[14] Not-for-profits need to equate what is best for business with what is right for their missions. Misericordia Hospital in West Philadelphia is a compelling example of an inner-city facility that turned itself around in large part by moving from a medical education model to a community-based model and by renewing ties to its community.

From an outdated institution with declining admissions, decreased medical staff, and insufficient access to capital, Misericordia has become a successful urban-community teaching hospital with an increasing market share, six years of solid financial growth, renovations in progress, and an expanded, board-certified medical staff. As the result of needs assessment findings, community feedback, and an action plan, Misericordia created a family-centered midwifery program which is the foundation for a new Women's Center, provided counseling and parenting classes, and opened a school-based primary care clinic.

Today, Misericordia is the hospital of choice within its locality. By continually reaching out into the community, its administrators and physicians get a realistic perspective on the needs of the people they serve, and are positioned to receive direct referrals and compete successfully for managed care contracts.[15]

NOT-FOR-PROFITS' ALTERNATIVES AND OPTIONS

To Collaborate

The prominent investor-owned hospital chains such as Columbia/HCA, American Medical International, HealthTrust—The Hospital Company, Quorum, Ornda Healthcorp Health Corporation, Community Health System, and Health Management Associates hold common goals of market expansion through hospital acquisition and joint ventures. In choosing whether to collaborate or compete, not-for-profits need to devise institutional strategies for how they will respond to aggressive, often creative initiatives offered by investor-owned companies. Many not-for-profits refuse to collaborate, preferring to compete aggressively in the marketplace instead. For those that decide to take advantage of partnership opportunities, there are four alternative collaborative strategies described by Michael W. Peregrine in the September 1994 issue of *Trustee*. Transactions may follow: (1) the Columbia model, (2) the traditional venture model, (3) the new development model, or (4) the asset sale or disposition model. Because these are relatively new approaches, each strategy raises specific tax issues.

The *Columbia model* raises several such concerns because the partnership is one in which the for-profit serves as the managing general partner and acquires the assets of the not-for-profit. Perhaps the single most difficult issue for not-for-profits entering into these acquisition arrangements is how the transfer of assets will affect the tax-exempt status of their bond issues, since assets financed with tax-exempt bonds cannot be used in operating for-profit businesses.

The Columbia model attempts to blend the operating and management styles of not-for-profit and investor-owned institutions in a way that is appealing to not-for-profits interested in divestiture but wanting to retain strong oversight over their facilities. The participants create a limited partnership in which both parties initially retain equal interest in the venture. The not-for-profit must assure that the investment arrangement does not jeopardize its tax-exempt status. It must assure that partnership income will not be treated as unrelated business taxable income, which can also risk tax-exempt status. Likewise, it must be able to independently maintain its tax-exempt status apart from the partnership, most likely as a charitable foundation, because it will no longer function as a hospital. Part of Columbia's strategy to secure the buy-in of local officials and hospital trustees is to channel proceeds from the purchase of the not-for-profit toward financing community charitable foundations. Any funds remaining after the newly acquired hospital retires its debt goes to the foundation.

For Columbia, the partnership approach not only advances its strategy of building regional networks to dominate managed care contracting, it also enables Columbia to become a general partner without paying 100 percent of the purchase price and to bring people to the table to discuss selling.[16] The creative structure of Columbia's model has attracted the interest of other investor-owned entities considering similar ventures.

The *traditional venture model,* according to Peregrine, involves the new partners combining to jointly own and operate one existing facility. The tax issues involved with a venture model such as this one are not as significant as those presented by the Columbia model, as long as the investor-owned entity contributes the assets. This would be the case if, for example, the for-profit provides the assets of the facility in exchange for a percentage ownership interest, and the not-for-profit contributes cash toward the facility's fair market value plus a percentage of the venture's initial working capital. Since the tax-exempt hospital's assets are not contributed to the venture, the subsequent use of tax-exempt bond-financed facilities is never an issue.

The *new development model* involves the formation of a partnership to jointly develop, own, and operate a new healthcare organization. Examples of successful collaborative arrangements in this category include the formation of general partnerships between for-profit and not-for-profit providers to develop and operate a specialty hospital, clinic, or comprehensive medical facility.

The fourth collaborative alternative Peregrine describes is the *asset sale or disposition model,* which entails the sale of the not-for-profit's assets to the for-profit entity. Here, as in the Columbia model, the sale proceeds fund a charitable foundation or trust to serve the local community. Tax-related concerns regarding this model include the valuation of the not-for-profit hospital's assets to ensure that an equal to or greater than fair market value is obtained in the sale. Otherwise, tax-exempt status is jeopardized and fiduciary and corporate law principles are violated. Moreover, if a not-for-profit hospital receives competing purchase offers from for-profit and not-for-profit entities, and sells to the for-profit, state charitable trust law and not-for-profit corporation law may question whether the sale is in the public interest. At issue is whether an obligation exists to accept the not-for-profit buyer's offer.

To Compete

While the collaborative models offer attractive options to some not-for-profits, others will continue to compete vigorously. For them, there are some legal factors that help. Access to tax-exempt capital, for instance, is not expected to diminish. Increased enforcement of Medicare laws regarding anti-kickback prohibitions may restrict some of the most aggressive marketing strategies.[17]

Hospital associations across the nation view collaborative efforts among not-for-profits as critical to their survival and level of patient care and encourage their members to network. The Hospital Alliance of Tennessee, for example, concedes that the state's tax-exempt hospitals lack the capital to compete directly with Columbia, and encourages its members to form regional not-for-profit hospital networks that link facilities and physicians within broad geographic areas to contract for managed care. Moreover, joint ventures among network members increase effectiveness and community outreach in other ways. Examples include broadening the patient referral base, acquiring physician group practices to form integrated physician networks, and launching outpatient treatment and diagnostic centers.[18]

Hospitals must simultaneously compete for both local patients and groups of patients. Competition in managed care necessitates a series of balancing acts for community hospitals: between geographic patient access and cost control, and between participating in geographically dispersed multihospital systems with centralized decision making and building viable localized community partnerships. Hospitals have a growing need to establish relationships with a diverse array of organizations in their service areas and to develop community-based, integrated networks that will strengthen and reinforce their community ties. In order to continue to win and retain managed care contracts and to receive direct referrals, hospitals must satisfy local consumers. They must become increasingly involved in community health improvement to demonstrate their relevance.[19] Those that do not risk their own extinction.

CONCLUSION

There needs to be a clear public appreciation of exactly what the changes taking place within the hospital community mean. One thing is certain: The pace of competition will accelerate through the 1990s, creating enormous changes in service delivery. As a result, the healthcare environment of today will be vastly different by the year 2000. In many instances citizens stand to lose the community connection with their local hospitals as mergers and acquisitions redefine the healthcare landscape.

Not-for-profit hospitals and their communities need to establish dialogues on standard definitions and appropriate levels of community benefits. A significant potential exists for hospitals in states requiring a "community

CASE STUDY

SAINT THERESE MEDICAL CENTER

When Saint Therese Medical Center, a Catholic not-for-profit hospital in Waukegan, Illinois, decided in 1991 to establish the third free health clinic in the state to serve low-income and uninsured county residents, Sister Christine Bowman, OSF, vice president of administration, took charge of the project. From the start, the clinic was a united community effort in which Sister Christine served as the catalyst for bringing volunteers together to establish HealthReach. Since there was a readily perceived need and desire for the clinic, securing support and participation was easy, and eight months after the first planning committee meeting, HealthReach opened its doors in May, 1992.

Today, the clinic serves 3,000 patients a year, seven days a week on an annual budget of less than $150,000. Medications cost nearly $60,000 per year, by far the largest single expenditure. Funded entirely from private donations, the clinic is supported by individual and corporate contributions and the volunteer services of some 150 medical professionals, including doctors, nurses, dietitians, and nurse practitioners, who provide their services either on-site or from their own offices through clinic referrals. Major financial contributors include Baxter International and Abbott Pharmaceuticals, who in the beginning donated not only start-up funds but office furniture and equipment and building and renovation work, respectively. Saint Therese Medical Center provides executive leadership and many of the direct services such as laundry and food supplies.

benefits plan" to identify and provide solutions to local healthcare problems that will enhance the quality of community life and serve them well in debates over their tax-exempt status. These tax-exempt institutions are community enterprises in which the community invests and expects a return on its investment. Community investments take the form of foregone tax revenues, cash and in-kind donations, volunteer time, and payments in excess of the cost of care that serves to subsidize other patients without means.[20]

Hospital boards of trustees must develop strategies for addressing investor-owned buy-out initiatives and for meeting managed care expectations while retaining a clear vision of their charitable mission. This is a complex challenge. Healthcare professionals and Wall Street analysts agree that the pace of change will accelerate through the 1990s.

In today's environment no one in the healthcare arena, for-profits and not-for-profits alike, has a choice but to be accountable. Success will depend on effective communication with stakeholders and a demonstrated ability to identify and deliver needed services cost effectively.

Concluded

HealthReach serves predominately Hispanic and African-American patients of all ages for conditions ranging from ear infections to asthma, diabetes, hypertension, heart disease, and arthritis. No one is turned away for inability to pay, but $5 donations are the norm.

HealthReach is an example of the community benefits and services that Saint Therese Medical Center provides. Moreover, the clinic exemplifies how a hospital working in concert with the community can bring together local leaders and resources to effectively meet community needs.

Today, HealthReach is one of 16 free clinics in Illinois, making the state the second largest in the nation behind Virginia (with 31) in the number of free clinics serving low-income communities. Illinois' free clinics have established a network to share supplies and maximize financial resources. Together, the volume of patient care the free clinics provide has a significant economic impact on the state's healthcare system in which patients would otherwise go to hospital emergency rooms for treatment at a substantially greater cost. Moreover, the public health system could not handle the patient load alone, and to the degree they tried, the cost would fall on the taxpayer.

Source: Based on interviews conducted at Saint Therese Medical Center, Waukegan, Illinois, by Lillian Pfaff.

ENDNOTES

1. Clement, J. P., D. G. Smith, and J. R. C. Wheeler. "What Do We Want and What Do We Get from Not-for-Profit Hospitals?" *Hospital & Health Services Administration* vol. 39:2 (Summer 1994), pp. 159–178.
2. Sigmond, R. M. "From Charity Care to Community Benefit," *Hospital & Health Services Administration* vol. 39:2 (Summer 1994), pp. 141–142.
3. Greene, J. "Charity Care Falls After Okla. Hospital's Sale," *Modern Healthcare* (March 13, 1995), pp. 36–40.
4. Burda, D. "Critics: Columbia Tax Argument Doesn't Add Up," *Modern Healthcare* (June 19, 1995), pp. 130–134.
5. Greene, J. "Tax-Exempts Feeling the Heat," *Modern Healthcare* (November 20, 1995), pp. 46–52.
6. Greene, J. "Fla. Not-For-Profits Dispute Columbia Report," *Modern Healthcare* (September 4, 1995), p. 36.
7. Cerne, F. "Street Wise." *Hospitals & Health Networks* (March 20, 1995), pp. 38–42.
8. Clement, J. P., D. G. Smith, and J. R. C. Wheeler. "What Do We Want and What Do We Get from Not-for-Profit Hospitals?" *Hospital & Health Services Administration* vol. 39:2 (Summer 1994), pp. 159–178.

9. Lutz, S. "VHA Releases Its Own List of Standards to Help Members," *Modern Healthcare* (April 13, 1992), p. 14.

10. Greene, J. "Fla. Not-For-Profits Dispute Columbia Report," *Modern Healthcare* (September 4, 1995), p. 36.

11. Mower, J. "Community Health Improvement as a Core Business Strategy," Unpublished speech delivered to VHA of New Jersey, Inc. (May 3, 1995), 1–15.

12. Clement, J. P., D. G. Smith, and J. R. C. Wheeler. "What Do We Want and What Do We Get from Not-for-Profit Hospitals?" *Hospital & Health Services Administration* vol. 39:2 (Summer 1994), pp. 159–178.

13. Lee, B. "Connecting With the Community," *California Hospitals* vol. 9, no.3 (Fall 1995), pp. 11–14.

14. Mower, J. "Community Health Improvement as a Core Business Strategy," Unpublished speech delivered to VHA of New Jersey, Inc. (May 3, 1995), pp. 1–15.

15. ibid.

16. Greene, J. "Columbia's Partnership Strategy," *Modern Healthcare* (March 21, 1994), p. 62.

17. Peregrine, M. W. "Facing the Investor-Owned Challenge: Collaboration or Competition?" *Trustee* (September 1994). pp. 24–27.

18. Cerne, F. "Central Tennessee II," *Hospitals & Health Networks* (December 5, 1994), pp. 58–59.

19. Mower, J. "Community Health Improvement as a Core Business Strategy," Unpublished speech delivered to VHA of New Jersey, Inc. (May 3, 1995), pp. 1–15.

20. Clement, J. P., D. G. Smith, and J. R. C. Wheeler. "What Do We Want and What Do We Get from Not-for-Profit Hospitals?" *Hospital & Health Services Administration* vol. 39:2 (Summer 1994), pp. 159–178.

PART THREE

RECONFIGURING RESOURCES TO FIT A NEW STRATEGY

6 CHAPTER

Understanding Your Operating Environment

EXTERNAL MARKET INTELLIGENCE

To remain competitive in a cost-conscious environment a hospital must first understand its operating environment. The successful transition into a managed care marketplace depends on the hospital's ability to build on market strengths, correct inefficiencies of operations, and respond appropriately to external developments and forces. These developments and forces include economic trends and changes in reimbursement, the cost of doing business, the appropriateness or feasibility of its various financial strategies, and the impact of legislative or regulatory activities.

Understanding your market is paramount to developing managed care products that can capitalize on current market dynamics *and* be poised for transition to the next stage. In addition to profiling payor activities, a market intelligence base should include actions by competitors, and demographic trends that affect a base of covered lives as well as physician dynamics. Today's reality is that managed care forces represent threats and opportunities for a hospital's continuing viability. The goal of gathering market intelligence is to evaluate the potential impact of those forces and identify those significant threats and opportunities which will set the stage for the hospital's future performance.

Not paying attention to looming market threats is tantamount to suicide. Particularly in markets where the managed care evolution is occurring more slowly, providers can play out the parable of the boiled frog: If you place a frog in a pot of boiling water, it will immediately try to scramble out. But if you place the frog in room temperature water and don't scare him, he'll stay put. As the temperature rises, the frog will do nothing. In fact, he will show every sign of enjoying himself. As the temperature gradually increases, the frog will become groggier and groggier until he is unable to climb out of the pot and eventually dies. You see, the frog's internal apparatus for sensing threats to survival is geared to sudden changes in his environment, not to slow, gradual changes. Something similar happened to the American automobile industry. In the 1960s, Detroit's Big Three dominated North American car production and sales. Gradually, Japaneses automobile manufacturers began to gain market share. But the change was so gradual—from 4 percent to almost 30 percent over a period of nearly 30 years—that the Big Three didn't feel the heat until it was too late to jump out of the pot.[1]

It is still not clear whether this particular frog, that is, the healthcare industry, will have the strength to pull itself out of the hot water. To start protecting yourself from becoming a boiled frog, make sure you can answer the following questions:

- What are the current measures of managed care penetration in your state and in your local market?
- How rapidly your market is evolving, that is, what was the percentage of penetration a year or even six months ago?
- What new payors are entering the marketplace? What has been their approach to capturing market shares in other states/local markets?
- How are the payors driving your managed care rate negotiations, that is, how rapidly are they shifting the playing ground and moving reimbursement structures from discounted fee-for-service to per diem to global pricing to capitation?
- How are the provider community—hospitals, health systems, and physicians—organizing to respond to managed care?
- What are local employers' level of interest in and readiness for restricting choice and incenting for lifestyle change?
- What is happening at the state and federal levels and how could these actions immediately impact your book of business?
- Can you define the unique features that differentiate your market? With these features in mind, can you identify more mature managed care markets with similar features in order to see who survived and examine their strategies for applicability?

Trend information can be particularly insightful if your market is less mature than other regions within the state. By paying attention, you can become alert to the possible influx of new payors or the rate of change from PPO to HMO enrollment. For example, change in patient days per 1,000 members is evidence of the momentum of the shift away from inpatient care. Similarily, HMO financial performance data will be critical when you begin to entertain the idea of payors as partners. Whatever source you use, the objective is to understand the current environment in which you are operating and to anticipate how rapidly you will be required to transition into a new way of being in business.

RESPONDING TO COST PRESSURES

Scott Moskowitz is a Nashville, Tennessee, based entrepreneur who successfully runs several small businesses and teaches classes on the basics for start-up business success. With his input, the dilemma facing the healthcare industry was stripped of its complexity and encapsulated into the following rather simple postulate:

> Imagine you have business plan that is totally solid if evaluated within the context of current market dynamics. Now imagine the business running according to plan but—all of a sudden—it loses its most significant customer, it has to address a public relations issue that puts the integrity of its whole operation in question, and a new national competitor with the ability to volume purchase enters the market and undercuts your prices by 50 percent. Do you think you'd be in the business long if you were selling shoes or running a local sundry shop? Well, what if you were in the business of healthcare?

As market forces require the provider community to be more competitive, they are also making providers more transparent. Put another way, as costs/charges have gone under the microscope, databases have become big business. Payors are creating and making network decisions from provider performance reports. Financial performance or cost efficiency is the first hurdle of survival.

Do you know how cost competitive you are? See Table 6–1. Can you anticipate your profit and loss ratio in a new managed care equation for reimbursement? Operationally, you can't manage what you can't measure. If your hospital was the first to have an accurate cost accounting system, by all means go to the head of the class. But in the meantime, baseline data is essential for the classic feedback precedent involving hospital efficiency and physician practice patterns. Secondly, on a competitive front, you need to know where you stand when you enter into negotiations. Payors are reviewing data *before* they move into a market, not after. Finally, using actuarial-

TABLE 6–1

Financial Performance Measures

Do you know . . .

- What your *competitive market position* is, globally and by service?
- How *cost competitive* your institution is when compared to other regional providers?
- What *amount of revenue* is generated from each payor?
- How *changing reimbursement structures,* that is, FFS to per diem to per case, will impact your bottom line profitability?
- How managed care will impact *utilization, charges, and service delivery?*

type analysis to predict profit and loss allows you to better understand the threats represented and the opportunities created. You can become armed for proactive planning. (See Exhibit 6–1.)

Most hospitals have reams of data sitting on shelves. The problem is, no one understands what it means to them. Here are some steps you can take to understanding the data that is already available to you:

- Find out what data are already residing in the hospital. (See Table 6–2.)
- Be clear about your objectives; define the question before you start harnessing data.
- Align your data with other data being used in your marketplace.
- Share data with market partners, but be aware that real information sharing is usually contingent on shared assets.
- Begin tying your medical records repository more closely to your ambulatory, rather than your inpatient, business; the best information will come from the fingertips of the physician.
- Translate the data you have into meaningful information that can impact operational cost efficiency, clinical practice patterns, and competitive market strategy.

Financial performance is the first survival test but it isn't the last one. An organizational problem occurs when market revenues stagnate and senior management's reaction is to focus only on cutting costs. These "slash-and-burn" strategies disregard market demands and instead cut costs equally from all hospital activities and departments. While this approach will most likely eliminate some unnecessary costs that have been residing within the system,

EXHIBIT 6–1

Worksheet for Predicting Profit and Loss

	Impact on:							
Type of Development	Financial	Market Share	Service Line Operations	Org. & Mgmt.	Marketing/ Negotiations	R & D	Opportunities Created	Threats Represented
Market Developments:								
A. State/Federal Mandates and Developments								
B. Shifts in Reimbursement								
C. Competitor Actions								
D. Mergers/ Acquisitions								
E. Physician Organization(s)								

TABLE 6-2

Creating a Financial Performance Report Card

Sources of Information:

Internal
- Financial Reports
- Managed Care Contract Modeling Reports
- Marketing/Demographic Reports

External—Public Record
- State Reports
- Regulatory Reports

External—Vendor
- Inforum, HCIA, Medpar Data, Iameter

it can also eliminate many of the more intangible and personal services that patients want, in addition to potentially damaging systems responsible for the efficiency of care so important to the healthcare purchasers. In just cutting costs, organizations can slice away at many of their own competitive strengths and sap the internal leaders of their initiative. Quality and patient satisfaction initiatives must be parallel processes with cost-containment efforts.

REDUCING CLINICAL COSTS*

One of the greatest challenges facing the healthcare delivery system in the 1990s is to lower the cost of providing care while maintaining an acceptable level of quality. To meet this challenge, hospitals work in a close relationship with their physicians to develop a common goal and implement a strategy to reduce cost without reducing quality. Many hospitals have made excellent progress toward meeting this goal. However, others have not established a program to work with their medical staff in controlling cost. Before costs can be reduced, the providers must understand where they are out of line. Usually if the costs and net revenue of providing a service is reviewed in detail with the physicians, they will become active participants in a program to make their service more cost effective.

*This section was contributed by Ed Day, Managed Care Consulting Associates. Mr. Day draws from a background of management engineering, strategic planning, and managed care negotiating to offer practical approaches to operational issues. He emphasizes the importance of fundamental business disciplines, that is, materials management, operational efficiency, and competitive pricing.

The first step in developing a clinical cost-reduction program is to select a procedure that offers the potential for a significant savings—cataract surgery and normal vaginal delivery are two examples. Characteristics of procedures that offer an excellent opportunity to reduce costs are:

- *Volume.* The selected procedure should be a high volume procedure. Often a modest reduction in the costs of performing a high volume procedure can translate into significant cost saving.
- *Physicians.* Several physicians should be performing the selected procedure. Out of the group, if at least one physician has expressed an interest in containing costs, then there is a springboard for additional buy-in.
- *Patient severity.* A procedure should be selected where the patient's severity index rating does not significantly impact the cost of performing the procedure.
- *Financial indicators.* The procedure should not be a complex one such as open heart surgery, neurosurgery, etc. The patient billing should be fairly easy to analyze.

After a procedure is selected, the next step is to determine a sample size. Experience has demonstrated that approximately 125 patients will usually provide an adequate sample size. For the purposes of the project, select a period of time that will yield this number of patients.

Next, patient summary (UB92) bills are obtained for all patients receiving the targeted procedure during this time period. These bills are used to establish a database for the study. Some of the items that can be determined from the billings are:

- Payor mix.
- Length of stay by physician.
- Average total charges by physician.
- Average charge for each charge classification by physician.
- Demographic data such as patient age, patient residence, etc.

Selected patient itemized bills are used to determine practice differences by physicians. These bills can be used to identify differences in ordering patterns for medications, supplies, and laboratory tests. During this process, items that have a significant impact on costs are identified. These items are reviewed by all physicians performing this procedure, either individually or in a group meeting. The most cost-effective physicians are used as the benchmark by the other physicians. During group meetings, the physicians identify accepted changes to reduced costs. All physicians do not have to agree to implement the change; however *each physician* is free to determine which items he or she should implement to make the practice more cost effective. The key is that physicians learn from the quantified data and then teach themselves and each other. With this type of physician-to-physician exchange, the integrity of the physician's role as a patient advocate is never challenged.

This technique for reducing clinical costs has been highly successful. Implemented cost savings have ranged between $60 to $200 per case. While this figure does not appear to be significant in and of itself, because only high-volume procedures have been studied, the saving of each study has been significant. The implemented saving per study has been in the range of $47,000 to $137,000.

Moreover, the literal savings is not the only benefit: It is the cooperation between hospital staff and physicians to control costs that will have an ongoing payoff. The new working relationship should also have a significant impact on developing more cost-effective clinical practices in other areas.

THE SHIFT TOWARD PRIMARY CARE

Financial performance indicators feed directly into strategies for workplace redesign. With this data in hand, you can identify service areas in acute need of attention. Financial performance indicators:

- Allow for evaluation of current services: capacity, cost management, and efficiency.
- Create a framework to assess over- and under-utilization as well as comparative hospital performance.
- Serve as the substance for strategic design of integrated systems.

Remember: Markets drive changes . . . internal efficiency drives profitability. Payors go for the jugular vein when they start cutting costs. About the time the cost of doing business is almost more than the financial pay-off for being in business, payors will look to those who are doing business in a new way in an attempt to save money. With respect to the role of risk in assessing the medical care costs of a population:[2]

- Only 7 percent of all costs are spent on primary, secondary, and tertiary prevention services.
- 45 percent of medical care costs are devoted to acute care services; 10 percent of those costs go toward maternity.
- 33 percent of all medical care services are used for the treatment of individuals suffering from only eight chronic conditions.

- 20 percent of healthcare is devoted to environmental services (mental health, home health, skilled nursing, alternative care, and hospice services).
- With respect to cost structure management: 15 percent of costs associated with delivering care to chronic disease populations could be completely avoided by achieving evidence-based quality of care thresholds (maintaining diabetics at HfA1C levels under 10, maintaining heart disease patients' LDL cholesterol levels under 130, etc.).

The patient–consumer will continue to have needs that require healthcare services and hospitals will continue to exist as facilities that allow physicians to treat very sick people. But most healthcare delivery will occur outside hospital walls. If cost savings can best be achieved through health promotion, wellness, and prevention, then a primary care system will displace the acute care business in the food chain. Across the country, managed care growth has contributed to declining utilization rates, with still more decline in inpatient days predicted. In most urban and suburban markets, utilization declines are already driving the consolidation of acute care business. This is the first signal that the healthcare industry is responding to the basic tenet of supply and demand. The next wave will demonstrate which providers have adeptly anticipated marketplace shifts and, as a consequence, are no longer relying on inpatient business for significant revenue.

For hospitals and health systems today, the objective is to make operations profitable even though the market can't be improved. Once costs have been cut to the bone, the only solution to the predicament about "how to stay in business" is to increase a share of the stagnant overall market. This leads into a strategy for owning a continuum of care.

Where can you augment your existing care continuum to get more business at the local level? Primary care services, demand management activities, and preventive healthcare are part of the answer. These services have, in many ways, been missing—or treated as step-children—from a system vested in acute care. Now they need to be recognized as vital to the future. In the beginning you may operate within a paradox, that is, you may have to spend more money developing these new services without any guarantee that they will bring in more revenue. Still, shifting into the primary care business in a big way could be the only chance for survival because, for most hospitals, the option of reducing costs has already been used up.

An inpatient utilization analysis will generally indicate that there are too many beds in a market area. Utilization declines will continue to pressure area providers to shift business into a primary-care driven system. If you assume California's 1992 utilization rate of 605 inpatient days per 1,000, how many unneeded beds exist in your market today?

ENDNOTES

1. These figures come from the United States Department of Commerce, *U.S. Industrial Outlook,* in 1962 (pp. 58–59), 1970 (p. 355), 1975 (p. 355), 1979 (p. 287), 1981 (p. 320), and 1989 (pp. 34–35); and U.S. Congress Office of Technology Assessment, *Technology and the American Economic Transition: Choices for the Future Washington* (U.S. Government Printing Office, 1988), p. 326.
2. Fetsch, Pamela. "Demonstrating Value to Purchasers of Managed Care Products." *The Academy Bulletin,* (May 1994), pp. 1–2.

7

CHAPTER

Diagnosing Internal Capabilities

ASSESSING CULTURAL READINESS FOR CHANGE

Martha Kathryn Key, Vice President, Quorum Health Resources, Inc., begins her workshop, *Creating The Environment For Continuous Improvement,* by comparing the organizational style of healthcare to stories of the Lone Ranger and the Wizard of Oz. Her point is that in the 1970s and 80s, hospital administrators functioned as Lone Rangers. They were the heroes who could rely on their own instincts and stamina to assuage any medical staff or marketplace crisis. Occasionally a Tonto was also on the scene, but usually not so much in the limelight. Tonto usually took the form of an assistant administrator or director of nursing.

Today, Lone Rangers must radically change their mode of operation or die of their own control. Dr. Key points out that in our current environment of change and uncertainty, healthcare industry leaders are better off using the Wizard of Oz as a parable that can translate to a new organizational order. Like Dorothy, hospital administrators won't be able to get where they want to go alone. Success in the new marketplace will require partnerships, networks, joint ventures, multidisciplinary teams, interconnected processes, and a systems approach to service delivery.

Hospital administrators don't have to go very far to see a working example of a Wizard of Oz team. The emergency room—an example first suggested by Phil Weinzimer, a consultant for Unisys—shows how a team approach to crisis and unpredictable events can optimize performance. Think about it: A trauma case is rushed through the doors. Immediately, the resources at-hand are activated—physician expertise, clinical support services, state-of-the-art equipment, advanced technology, and databanks of information. If the case is too critical to be handled on-site, a helicopter can transfer the patient to a facility with more sophisticated resources. No one component can control the patient's outcome; it is the sharing of responsibility and the linking of people, technologies, and information that influences the outcome.

The authors of *Agile Competitor and Virtual Organizations* build on the emergency room analog with the following observations: The urgency of emergency medical situations creates a climate in which people with complementary expertise work together intensively, joining their expertise to achieve a common goal—restoring the patient's well-being. Now take this image back to the agile competition arena. The analog of the medical situation is to respond to the competitive urgency of a new customer opportunity by synthesizing the expertise required to do so, integrating access to the relevant facilities and knowledge—wherever they may be.[1]

Most hospitals and health systems today are not structured in a way that allows this synthesis and integration to happen. Giving up control is a major hurdle in redefining what business we are in. If you doubt the depth of resistance, just happen into any meeting convened across the country where hospital administrators and physician–decision makers are grappling with questions associated with the organizational structure and governance of new entities. Or check out how many mid-level managers have chronically white knuckles from holding onto their desks after leaving acquisition and merger discussions.

In the past, it was inconceivable for the hospital CEO not to make all the important decisions that directly impacted day-to-day operations. Because important decisions had to be made constantly, most senior administrators got in the habit of working day and night, weekdays and weekends. Saying "I haven't taken a vacation in four years" was a typical comment and one which supposedly evidenced control and indispensability. The CEO truly functioned as a Lone Ranger.

The typical chief executive was also a decision-making machine. Employees supplied the raw data about a problem and presented their alternative solutions. The chief executive then processed this information and spewed forth the answer: "We'll take Alternative 2B." Since he was the only one who saw the overall picture, he was compelled to make important decisions himself. No one else was equipped to do so.[2]

Authoritarian, hierarchical management styles have to go. The Total Quality Management movement has opened the minds of many industry leaders but, on the whole, we all have a long way to go. The silver lining in this managed care cloud is that it is transforming how the healthcare industry must be run. Micromanagement and operating in a vacuum will have to be replaced by the interaction of human and technological resources with customer needs and demands.

New understandings of change and disorder must be communicated throughout the organization. With an aggressive internal education and communications strategy, the continual process of reengineering our system of care can move past the paralyzing forces of chaos, unpredictability, and fear towards the power of innovative thinking, reallocation of resources, and market-based solutions. Change starts at the top.

At Ottumwa Regional Health Center in Southern Iowa, for example, senior management has been motivated for change by proposed budget cuts and market chaos. Lately, they have experienced an accleration in their readiness for change. Their very real commitment to redesign seems to be coming from their communications strategy. In the summer of 1995, three teams of managers holed up in conference rooms several days each week, working out a major redesign of the hospital aimed at lowering costs by 25 percent. "But we're cautious about that figure because we don't want to get too focused on the cost side," says Len Gross, a vice-president overseeing the redesign. "What might be cheapest isn't always best."

One redesign team looked internally, studying ways to reorganize patient care within the hospital; another looked externally, attempting to smooth a patient's path from the hospital to a doctor's office, home health, a nursing home, or the county health department; and the third investigated ways to support the flow of information inside and outside Ottumwa Regional. At a retreat in November attended by managers and executives, the teams unveiled a preview of their ideas, which where then to be merged into a single plan. One team's plan forecasted that the hospital could save more than $1 million a year by shortening hospital stays and improving communication and follow-up care with others in the community. "This may sound strange coming from a finance person," says finance chief Dennis Empey, "But communications is the most important thing we can do."[3] Ottumwa Regional is setting an example for others to follow.

To collapse the hierarchical structure in the healthcare service business does not mean that everyone—every middle manager, physician, clinical professional, clerical employee, or board member—must be involved in making every final decision. Someone will have to have ultimate responsibility; however, *nothing will work* if senior management does not recognize the need for radical transformation and if that need is not communicated throughout the system.

Health system leaders will continue to be accountable to their board of directors and will be charged with pursuing a business strategy. Only after this strategy has been developed in the context of managed care market dynamics and communicated in a way that translates to every listener *what this means to me* can responsibility be delegated effectively.

What's needed in response to the new competition is focus and discipline—unprecedented focus and discipline—to define an unmatched value proposition, build an operating model, and sustain it through constant transformation and improvement.[4] The survival and growth of health systems that range in size from tertiary mega-health centers to rural community hospitals down to clinical departments and outreach services will be made possible by the combination of key principles (or mission objectives) that create the system's overall identity and allow for great levels of autonomy for individual units. This is a major shift and it must begin at the top. Cultural readiness for change will be one of the greatest determinants of who will lead the industry into a new era. Like the frog plunged into boiling water, we've got to move quickly in order to survive. (See Table 7–1.)

DEFINING YOUR BUSINESS

When I trekked off to Emory University in the late 1970s, my mother gave me strict instructions to "*either become a doctor or marry one!*" Believe me, this parental advice was not rooted in a desire to see me shouldering the needs of those less fortunate than myself. No, from my mother's point of view all the doctors in town drove Cadillacs and joined the Yacht Club while the hospitals kept building bigger buildings with marble floored lobbies. In her own way, my mother was trying to steer me toward what she believed would be a lucrative base of business and security. Although few of us could have predicted the current financial upheaval occurring within the healthcare industry, I guess we all would have to agree that *mother does not always know best.*

Anyone who has been in the healthcare business for awhile knows it was hard not to make money if you were in the healthcare business in the 1970s and 80s. In those days, providers gleefully duplicated services, invested in expensive technology, and put up billboards all over town in an effort to capture more market share. Although huge staffs of internal planning and marketing specialists spent incredible sums of time and money developing feasibility studies and strategic plans, it seems that the basics of business development were somehow lost by the time the results were presented at internal meetings.

In the frenzy of becoming bigger and better, it became quite fashionable for competing product/service line managers to have a meeting to schedule another meeting. The plethora of profit centers spawned an abundance of

TABLE 7–1

How Ready (And Willing) Are You?

The following list of questions can help you preview your organizational climate. After responding yes or no, you will have in initial assessment of your cultural readiness for change.

1. ***Marketplace Forces***
   - Are competitive forces at play that are impacting your financial performance?
   - Have you begun to organize to increase marketplace leverage via networks or alliances?
   - Are you a component in a regional delivery system?
   - Are you a target for acquisition or merger?
   - Have you recently downsized?
   - Is reengineering occurring within your own walls?
2. ***Senior Management***
   - Does senior management recognize the need for industry-wide transformation and a new organizational order?
   - Is senior management voicing a commitment to collaborative processes?
   - If so, is this commitment showing up at all, or at least in terms of increased cooperation, in day-to-day operations?
   - Is there a system in place to share internal information, align activities, and interconnect processes?
3. ***Vision, Mission, and Purpose***
   - Do you have a mission statement?
   - Is it widely distributed and understood?
   - Is the mission statement reflected in all planning and operational activities?
4. ***Communications Environment***
   - Is senior management communicating a sense of urgency regarding the need to proactively respond to managed care and marketplace forces?
   - Are there regularly scheduled forums for communication and information sharing?
   - Is there a safe and confidential methodology for airing grievances?
   - Do you have to go through a gatekeeper to get the ear of a senior manager?

TABLE 7–1

How Ready (And Willing) Are You? (*Continued*)

- Are cross-functional teams in place?
- Is customer-based market research widely distributed?
- Is the rationale for prioritizing business development objectives and gauging organizational redesign shared internally?

5. ***Entreprenuerial Spirit***
   - Is R&D an active function occuring within the organization?
   - Are margin requirements, particularly for new programs and services, communicated and understood?
   - In designing a continuum of care, do you ask yourselves whether to make or buy?
   - Are administrative and clinical department managers given the access to information, technical support, and capital?
   - Are there rewards for successful innovation?
   - Are failures tolerated within previously established boundaries of accountability?

Here is one way to interpret your responses. If you answer yes to the majority of the questions in each section, then:

1. Chaos, and possibly fear, are motivational forces for change.
2. Within the organization there is a strategic intent to decentralize control.
3. The mission statement is the driving force for, or at least having an impact on, all operations.
4. The systems are in place for the entwining of multiple objectives and parallel processes.
5. The organization is primed for its role in creating a new delivery system.

middle managers. In fact, I would hazard a guess that only a count of Alabama chiggers in August could have rivaled the number of hospital vice-presidents in place by the end of the 1980s.

While there was a great deal of energy spent writing internal memos and increasing the noise level around individual profit centers, there was little attention given to interconnecting processes or fitting the pieces into a whole, matching strategic goals to new competitive realities. With each specialist group battling to gain a market niche, the healthcare system became increasingly stratified and segmented. Jurisdictional disputes became more important than seamless delivery of healthcare services.

Increasing the supply of healthcare providers and services without limiting utilization or regulating access actually encouraged unnecesssary use and duplication. Competing incentives for healthcare providers have led to an operating environment that is costly and fragmented. Those of us in the industy have had our time of arrogantly surveying the schoolyard to see who can spit the farthest. We can no longer afford the fun of competing among ourselves. Now it is time to grow up and to assume responsibility for the goals we must accomplish. This is serious stuff; our business is at risk.

If we consider ourselves competent business development strategists, our contemporary challenge is to step back and initiate a process of lateral thinking. An adequate understanding of the structure and nature of a hospital's operating environment in the world of managed care is a prerequisite to undertaking the situational diagnosis step of a meaningful planning process. This understanding allows a hospital to zero in on those market variables that truly affect its performance.

Some of the key issues and decisions that must drive business development in a managed care environment include:

- The *values* a hospital or health system holds regarding its mission, vision, and purpose.
- The *basic non-negotiables* in a competitive marketplace, that is, price, quality, patient satisfaction, community service, or market share.
- The significance of more *intrusive regulations* by government and insurers on a hospital's ability to generate revenues and/or control costs.
- The *economic impact* of current and anticipated payor mix as well as possible reimbursement scenarios and projected rate of change.
- The relative *power of managed care payors* on demand issues such as product and/or service characteristics, manpower needs, and information system requirements.

- The fostering of *regional alliances and networks* as a strategy to protect a base of business, attract increased patient volume, access capital, and potentially benefit from selected economies of scale.
- The *demographic, psychographic, and health status profiles* of identified customer segments.
- The *utilization and financial performance trends* associated with existing service lines and product offerings.
- The need for *replacement revenue* creating an urgent need to evaluate the market potential for new or augmentative services and/or products.

These components of business planning set the stage for a set of management decisions that are focused on what a hospital or health system will be doing to be successful in the future. In the most basic sense, addressing these issues sets in motion the process of deciding what a hospital will do to be economically viable and how it will implement the agreed-upon strategy.

For a hospital or health system today, the scope and complexity of the business planning process should mirror the size and complexity of the environment in which it is operating. As the environment continues to become less stable and predictable, leaders within the industry need to recognize the need to commit additional resources to reviewing all aspects of the hospital's or health system's performance. In addition, learning to recognize trends and indicators of market threats can set the stage for anticipatory thinking. Business plan development can then occur along a timeline that extends into the future.

In the past, most autonomous community hospitals could function and plan in much the same manner as the neighborhood grocery did. The planning process was almost a matter of stocking the shelves with staples, watching what customers purchased, and seeing what was left at the end of the day. Hospital administrators usually conducted business with an appropriate inventory of a limited range of services, and relatively simple formulas for service-line pricing and operational cash-flow management. Business development agendas typically floated month-to-month while decision-making authority resided with a few key individuals, that is, the CEO, the hospital board, and a handful of physicians. Success was easy to measure via census, mortality, and morbidity rates.

Today, the few Lone Ranger hospitals that still exist recognize they are target dots for acquisition on the map of some gargantuan health system and know that their days are probably numbered. The current reality for the community hospital is analogous to the story of the neighborhood grocery store that has been usurped by the megamart or the corner drug store that was long ago cannibalized by a large national chain. Acquisitions and mergers are not occurring within the healthcare industry because Columbia/HCA has gone on a crusade and fostered some sort of philosphical conversion. In today's environment, Lone Rangers simply can't compete.

In contrast to the planning approach that was typical of the 1980s, the planning process that is occuring within the industry today involves networks of multiple hospitals and associated healthcare businesses all organized with the purpose of ensuring market dominance by attempting to own a full continuum of care. Strategic decisions must address a much broader range of issues and take into account many market variables—such as increased governmental regulation or new payors entering the market—that are beyond the control of the local decision makers. The challenge is to design adequate and appropriate delivery systems to correspond to market demands at several stages of a complex maturation cycle. A multifaceted strategy is required to interconnect activities associated with integration, reengineering, service mix, cost containment, pricing, and the management and motivation of thousands of employees hysterically guarding turf and position.

Information is essential. Some of the information required for strategic business development can be derived from what is spit out of internal data systems, state reports, and market intellegence purchases from vendors. The problem is that most managers have reams of data in their offices but they don't know how to translate it all into a form that will be helpful. The variable that will have the greatest impact on the restructuring of this industry will be the brains of innovative individuals willing to examine the data, identify systemic issues, intuit, take risks, and innovate a new healthcare business.

Most CEOs, COOs, and directors of managed care that I know are immersed so deeply in the complex issues facing the healthcare industry that they are becoming skilled at putting out the immediate fires but are at risk for evolving into relatively ineffective leaders. As I thought how I might best speak to the challenge we are all facing—that is, too many details with too little time to put them into perspective—I re-read a few chapters of Peter M. Senge's *The Fifth Discipline*. The following passage seemed particularly pertinent:

> The increasing complexity of today's world leads many managers to assume that they lack information they need to act effectively. I would suggest that the fundamental "information problems" faced by managers is not too little information but too much information. What we most need are ways to know what is important and what is not important, what variables to focus on and which to pay less attention to.[5]

Before you read any further I encourage you to stop a moment, turn off your fax machine, put your beeper on vibrate and slide it into a drawer, and let your voice mail answer your calls. In other words, take time and set the stage so that you can really address the question: "What business am I in?"

MANDATING FUNDAMENTAL CHANGES

Defining your business requires that all organizational planning stem from a framework of mission, vision, and purpose. An analysis of the current book of business with environmental threats superimposed onto it can begin to highlight emerging themes associated with the interdependent processes. The following themes emerge as the most salient potential components of an emerging industry.

Leadership

The death of business "as we knew it" has thrust many healthcare leaders into a state of paralysis, denial or reactive postures rooted in fear. Healthcare reform is becoming a critical catalyst for shifting from old patterns of fragmented "who's on first" thinking to a new reality of collective responsibility. Today, the need for organizational redesign has significantly increased the tension for change. Recognizing that moving into a future state is messy and requires a long-term commitment can create a realistic foundation for transitioning through the chaos and confusion.

There is often a great deal of internal confusion regarding the correlation between the hospital's or health system's purpose as a community of care/medical services providers and current activities associated with remaining financially viable in a rapidly transitioning reimbursement environment. If the mission statement is developed so as to ensure an organizational buy-in, then it can become the mirror to evaluate all decisions involving prioritization of activities, resource allocation, budgets, service delivery, and operational policies for consistency.

Information, Education, and Outcomes Monitoring

Moving into the future requires managing multiple processes and relies on harnessing information that profiles baseline performance, measures impact, and describes opportunities for continuously improving upon what is working.

There is an acute need to collect data and create provider performance report cards. Financial and clinical outcomes information must be analyzed and shared in order to provide the framework for developing continuums of patient care and seamless admitting processes. Of immediate concern is the individual hospital's or health system's need to increase operational efficiency. Sharing data internally meets the first requirement for meaningful workplace redesign. Without ongoing dissemination of information, department managers are not equipped to address systems issues and will tend to resort to temporary measures to reduce the cost of care. The most common short-term strategy to increase cost performance is to quickly reduce the number of full-time equivalents (FTE). However, while immediately tangible, this strategy does not directly set the rationale for the long-term objective. Harnessing baseline data is a beginning, but it is critical that managers be educated on how to use it as a springboard for decisions that engineer innovation and then continue to capture data and measure impact.

Physicians must be empowered with information. Hospital administrators cannot use numbers and dollars to develop accountable patient care models. Education and open communication are catalysts for physician-driven clinical-paths and outcomes tracking.

Primary Care Access

Recent legislative changes impacting steerage of Medicaid patients has resulted in an increased sense of urgency around the need to evaluate the primary care delivery systems available to low-income persons. For hospitals, the concern is that emergency rooms and primary care physician clinics could become safety nets for the inappropriate utilization of medical care services to treat chronic concerns. For public health departments, the asymmetry of forces at work makes it difficult to impact this population with broad health promotion activities and thereby significantly impact service demand and utilization.

The opportunity is *now* to create *living laboratories* to investigate approaches for integrating functions across the spectrum of previously autonomous service providers. By working with a defined population in a geographically isolated area, the "partners" have the opportunity to evaluate the impact of merging systems of care while also addressing the operational realities associated with becoming collectively accountable for generating sustaining revenue. The challenge is to aggressively identify divergent perspectives or limiting individual agendas so that stated objectives for the partnership become realistic.

Community Health Status

As hospitals and health systems wrestle with the financial realities associated with changing reimbursement structures, vesting in the health of a defined population shifts from an altruistic philosophy to a pragmatic strategic directive. Baseline data is required in order to first target health education and prevention activities, and then measure impact on service utilization and quality outcomes. Public health departments and community service agencies are grappling with issues associated with changes in reimbursement and funding.

Many services could be endangered if providers do not come together, collapse boundaries, and combine resources. Today there is an awareness of the importance of *working together* to address root causes of illness and injury. Drug and substance abuse, child care, youth and family services, mental health concerns, and domestic violence were among the more frequently mentioned themes.

Industry leaders committed to moving into the future must aggressively invest energies and resources in the following interdependent strategies:

- Equip for managed care and increasing marketplace competition by developing *provider performance report cards.*
- Prepare for the future work of capitation and health status management by committing resources to developing a *continuum of care.*
- Build on existing relationships within the provider community and foster *new partnerships.*
- Arm the management team with pertinent data in order to provide a framework for meaningful *workplace redesign.*

It is the surfacing of these significant underlying elements that has added density to the question "What business are we in?"

CREATING A HOLOGRAPH

When I begin a new consulting engagement, I like to see my new client's current mission statements, strategic business, and/or information systems technology plans before I go on-site. These documents provide insider insight into the current book of business. What is even more telling to me, however, is whether or not I find an obvious common thread running through each document. If the hospital management team is really "up to snuff," as we say in the South, I should be able to read the information systems technology plan, and from its content outline the hospital's business development strategy and/or objectives within a regional delivery network. Similarly, the business plan should be a working document that allows me to immediately derive the health system's mission, vision, and purpose. Finally, the mission statement should act as the original image in a holograph.

While what is on paper is not always a clear reflection of either environmental or organizational culture, confused and fragmented planning documents have, in my experience, been an accurate preface to a confused and fragmented culture. Although I'd like to screen potential clients and choose to work with only lateral thinkers already initiating a multifaceted approach to system redesign, I wouldn't have many clients and my sense of adventure might lose a little edge.

Follow these next steps

1. *Commit to the process.* Recognize that organizational transformation is "messy" and does not occur overnight.
2. *Initiate a collaborative process* to develop and communicate the mission and vision.
3. *Use the mission statement as a holographic image* as you develop managed care business plans, information systems objectives, and community health agendas.
4. Create a framework for *process alignment* and a system to ensure that there is a high level of correlation between all planning, activities, and mission.
5. *Develop a congruent multifaceted approach* incorporating aggressive strategies in each of the following: provider performance report cards/managed care readiness, workplace redesign, continuum of care, and new partnerships.
6. *Harness information, educate, communicate.* Recognize that information sharing is a pivot for fostering collective responsibility. An aggressive and interactive communications strategy can begin with prioritizing educational themes and sharing concentrically in organized forums. (Remember the bulls-eye approach from Chapter 3: Move from hospital board, through medical staff, management team, employees, and into the community.)

Can you find your mission statement mirrored in all of your work plans for change? Is the mission statement a clear enough image for informed workplace activities and job performance? Can your mission realistically create a holograph that integrates current operating redesign objectives and marketplace needs?

Identifying Core Competencies

Hospitals have traditionally been the behemoths at the center of the delivery system. Financial incentives encouraged fragmented delivery of care and micromanagement of utilization and healthcare-related decisions. Hospitals took on *clinical risk* while looking to mortality-morbidity rates to determine how well they were doing. In the 1990s, this created a lot of jobs. The future will require a systemic commitment to expanding continuums of care and creating seamless processes for delivery. This means assuming *financial risk,* which requires that primary care be at the center of the delivery system and that clinical efficacy be driven by prevention and minimally interventionist methods.

Many hospitals are reorganizing—engaging in cost-driven downsizing, down-staffing, labor rollbacks, and elimination of services—but they do not know if it will work. In many instances, hospitals feel compelled to *do something,* but are mostly *shooting in the dark.* A spring 1993 study by E. C. Murphy Ltd. (as reported by Leah Curtin in *Nursing Management*) found a strong relationship between mortality in Medicare patients and cost-driven downsizing. It also found that inefficient systems in the typical hospital "force" employees to waste almost a third of their time. Before hospitals undertake any changes, they need to ask what, in light of their mission, they are doing right as well as wrong. The answers should be organized according to restructuring, reengineering, and job redesign.[6] Business development strategies must begin with an internal audit/operational analysis *before* moving forward.

An internal analysis of operational capabilities provides a complete picture of the hospital's performance. It also identifies areas/departments of inefficiencies. With imminent shifts in reimbursement, this analysis is important to ensure an appropriate meshing between revenue objectives and service capabilities. Economic viability will depend on anticipating the impact of changing reimbursement on revenue and relating that to basic operating costs. Often, proactive business decision makers are faced with the unpleasant task of initiating cost-cutting actions.

A revenue analysis is one of the most important components of an internal audit. It provides the basis for determining if the current mix of products and services is yielding sufficient revenue for the hospital *today.* It also creates a framework for actuarial analysis that can factor in shifts in reimbursement and predict if the current mix of services will or will not provide sufficient revenue for the future. (See Table 7–2.)

Once you have determined potential consolidation of service lines and redeployment of clinical support services, it is important to determine how

TABLE 7–2

Revenue Analysis:
What Will It Cost to Stay in Business?

Must address the critical issues of:

1. The processes and technologies that will be used to deliver services.
2. The requirements for materials, equipment, facilities, and information systems (size, location, staff numbers and skills).
3. The transition schedule required to support business objectives.

the relationship between changes in reimbursement and shifts in operational strategies will feed into an organization and management strategy. An overall labor cost analysis requires a comparative summary of cost and productivity data for each class/type of service worker. For instance, in September 1995 the Connecticut Hospital Association (CHA) looked at the localized impact of the proposed cuts on the region's acute care hospitals. The eight hospitals in the region (most of which are small community institutions) are looking at an estimated loss of $102,735,165 in Medicare funding over the next seven years according to figures compiled by CHA. As hospitals employ over 50,000 people in the state, and two-thirds of hospital costs are labor-related, the reimbursement cuts could have a huge impact upon the employment situation.[7]

There is a great deal of controversy in the healthcare industry regarding who the most appropriate caregiver is. Physicians are concerned about the increasing presence of nurse practitioners and physician assistants. Nurses are concerned about the number of unlicensed assistants on hospital floors. Moreover, consolidation is decreasing the need for hospital administrators, and computerization is wiping out the need for an "Aunt Bea" behind the desk to answer the phone.

Most hospital executives would scan Table 7–3 with equanimity. These familiar figures show total employees by category for a hospital with an average daily census of about 450 patients. A quick mental calculation of FTEs per occupied bed yields a comfortable number (about 5.23, unadjusted for part-time employees and outpatient volume). The numbers and the calculations are so familiar, however, they have nearly lost their meaning. The data point in the table that merits a fresh look is the number of clerks and secre-

TABLE 7–3

Employees by Job Category

Category	# of Employees
Managers and supervisors	147
Administrative professionals	100
Clerical support	455
Nurses and technicians	1,196
Laborers	424
Total:	2,322

Philip Lathrop, *Restructuring Healthcare: The Patient-Focused Paradigm* (Jossey-Bass Publishers, 1993) p. 5.

taries: 455. In and of itself it is just a number, about 20 percent of the total staff. But think again. The clerks and secretaries outnumber the inpatients![8]

Hospital administrators have no shortage of internal and external measures of their operating performance. Full-time equivalent (FTE) positions per occupied bed, housekeeping hours per thousand square feet, relative value units (RVUs) per medical technologist, nursing hours per patient day, and so forth can be tracked internally over time and compared to regional and national databases for hospitals of similar size and mission.[9] The problem with such comparative analysis is not that decision makers are in danger of comparing apples to oranges, the problem is that today most of the apples are rotten. Manpower studies are misleading because no one has yet defined efficiency standards for a healthcare industry whose services are mostly provided outside the hospital.

How do you determine what resource allocation makes sense for the future? A study by the National League of Nursing shows that between 1981 and 1992 administrative jobs grew by 43 percent. (Obviously, all those profit centers needed someone to run them.) In 1994, a survey by the American Nurses Association found that more than two-thirds of 1,800 respondents said their employers had cut registered nurse positions in the previous year. Nosediving hospital admissions and lengths of stay have triggered unprecedented layoffs of nurses and other healthcare workers. And the shakeout wrought by managed care is far from over. One estimate, by the University of California at San Francisco's Center for Health Professions, predicts that 200,000 to 300,000 hospital nurses could lose their jobs by the end of the century, forced to move on by the shifting emphasis to outpatient and community care.[10]

It could be advantageous for nurses to recognize their opportunity to lead the way into a new paradigm. Instead of lamenting the loss of floor nurse positions, nurses should be aggressively scoping out their potential for redefining cost-efficient, mobile, localized, and culturally sensitive primary care services. It is not necessary that a new nursing role be developed for primary health care; most of what *is* primary healthcare has always been within the domain of nursing. In other words, if nurses relinquish the hospital as an anchor of security, they can effectively discover boundless opportunities to define the practice of the primary healthcare provider.

Hospital administrators must be politically savvy as well as financially astute. Those administrators who are still trying to tread softly on the raw nerves of their medical staffs would be wise to leverage the nursing workforce so that it becomes the fulcrum for change. Creatively managing manpower and talents, while at the same time redirecting internal resources, will be fundamental to both short-term and long-term organizational strategies. (See Tables 7–4 and 7–5.)

TABLE 7–4

Challenges of Creating an Organizational Strategy

- Consolidation of clinical service lines.
- Reduction in acute-care beds.
- Redeployment of clinical support services.
- Deployment of case management across the continuum.
- Development of new tools and methodologies for tracking clinical outcomes.
- Reliance on an information system backbone.
- Commitment to health status management for a base of covered lives.

Consequently, an organizational and management strategy addresses five critical issues:

1. The *functions* that must be performed and who will be responsible for performing them.
2. The *organization of the functions* to promote overall cost efficiency, clinical efficacy, and productivity.
3. The *staffing requirements* in terms of numbers, skills, and qualifications.
4. The *procedures* for guiding, motivating, and controlling overall operations.
5. The *extent to which staffing requirements* will be altered, based on shifts in revenue.

As with any business, understanding where the dollars are today and where they may be tomorrow is critical to successful restructuring and reengineering. The question, "What business am I in?" also translates to, "Will I have a job?"

In short, the purpose of an intensive operational analysis is to:

- Give you a snapshot of your current book of business.
- Identify where reimbursement shifts would immediately put you at risk for revenue.
- Provide you with information that will feed directly into your current pricing strategies.
- Assess over- and underutilization, cost performance, and reimbursement trends in order to feed directly into operational/workplace redesign.

TABLE 7–5

Short-term Consequences of Creating an Organizational Strategy

- Lowered operating margins
- Competitive vulnerability
- Internal turf problems

- Create a framework for educating physicians and other clinical caregivers regarding the intersection of clinical outcomes and fiscal realities.
- Enter into negotiations with as much information about your competitive position as the negotiator.
- Move toward per case and global pricing by beginning to integrate delivery systems internally and beyond hospital walls (case manage across functions).
- Develop "shelf products" based on projected shifts in marketplace dynamics and reimbursement trends.
- Protect your autonomy—and market base—by strengthening loose alliances with regional/like-minded providers; or prepare for mergers and acquisitions by understanding your marketplace leverage.
- Get ready to enter risk-sharing arrangements.

ENDNOTES

1. Goldman, Steven L., Roger N. Nagel, Kenneth Preiss. © 1995 by Von Nostrand Reinhold. *Agile Competitors and Virtual Organizations: Strategies for Enriching the Customer,* p. 100.
2. Carlzon, Jan. *Moments of Truth: New Strategies for Today's Customer-Driven Economy* (New York: Ballinger, 1987).
3. Lumsdon, Kevin. "My Town, My Hospital," *Hospitals & Health Networks* (December 20, 1995), p. 54.
4. Treacy, Michael and Fred Wiersema. *The Discipline of Market Leaders: Choose Your Customers, Narrow Your Focus, Dominate Your Market,* p. 13.
5. Senge, Peter M. "The Art of Seeing the Forest *and* the Trees," *The Fifth Discipline: The Art and Practice of the Learning Organization,* (New York: Doubleday, 1990), p. 128.

6. Curtin, Leah L. "Restructuring: What Works—and What Does Not!" *Nursing Management,* vol. 25, no. 10 (Oct. 1994), pp. 7–8.
7. "Connecticut Hospitals Meet with U.S. Rep. Nancy Johnson to Discuss Impact of Proposed Cuts," *CHANGE* (September 22, 1995).
8. Lathrop, J. Philip. *Restructuring Health Care: The Patient-Focused Paradigm,* (Jossey-Bass Publishers, 1993), p. 5.
9. ibid., p. 4
10. Lumsdon, Kevin. "Faded Glory: Will Nursing Ever Be the Same:" *Hospitals & Health Networks* (December 5, 1995), p. 31.

8 CHAPTER

Increasing Market Share Through Partnerships

Once upon a time, hospitals and doctors enjoyed the freedom of parallel play and independent prosperity. In today's managed care markets, solo providers and independent hospitals do not have the depth of resources to provide the scope of services needed to effectively compete. A new vocabulary word is being heralded as the precursor for survival: *integration*. Markets are differentiated by their organizational model for integration, for example, physician–hospital organizations, integrated delivery systems, community-care networks, etc. As new models for consolidation are being devised, it is of ever-increasing importance that hospitals and physicians choose carefully as they come together to form new partnerships.

Merging individual points of access across a continuum creates a delivery system that will meet the demands of the healthcare purchaser. Merging operations creates the opportunity to financially benefit from streamlined systems and economies of scale. Furthermore, merging assets is a contemporary tactic for partners to have access to the capital that will be needed for ongoing expansion. Like marriages, partnerships based on a set of shared values seem to have the most staying power. Those market partners that are able to align goals, objectives, and financial incentives will build competitive strength.

Integration is a complex process. Too often, market forces create a sense of urgency for new partners to come together and develop a defensive strategy. Often, there are simultaneous activities occurring—that is, physician-to-physician, physician-to-hospital, as well as hospital-to-health-system integration.

An integrated system is not a means of preserving territory or building a fortress to keep out managed care. The integration strategy that will most likely ensure survival is one that meets the needs of the managed care healthcare purchaser. If health system executives and physician leaders understand the basic premise that the objective of managed care is to cut costs and, in the process, regionalize and rationalize healthcare delivery, then they will build service networks accordingly. When it works, integration is a strategy that responds to what the market really needs by synthesizing the resources of physicians, hospitals, and other health services providers along a continuum.

MANAGED CARE AND PHYSICIAN MANPOWER*

Before entering into a discussion of organizational models, pause and reflect. The rush of hospitals and health systems to form Physician Hospital Organizations (PHOs) and foundations, while doctors are convening to create Independent Physician Associations (IPAs) and Management Service Organizations (MSOs), is resulting in pseudo-solutions and relatively shallow dimensions of control. Before getting on a bandwagon, organizing providers need to take a look at where the local market is headed. Organizational models for integration are all fine and good—even necessary—but if they are entered into without a template of local *supply and demand* projections, the investment of time, energy, and capital will be premature.

In most markets we know that supply is not the issue. In fact, the proliferation of inpatient facilities and specialists has caused the duplication/fragmentation of care that has driven up costs. Over-abundance and over-utilization are primary healthcare reform targets. The charge today is not to create supply but to manage demand.

Demand projections are defined by local demographic and economic trends. Local healthcare purchasers, that is, employers and the payor community, will generate even more compelling pressures for industry change. For hospitals attempting to match services with need, these factors become important in determining an appropriate physician alignment strategy. Hospitals cannot effectively address the criticisms of high cost, lack of coordination, and poor access without pursuing a strategy of integration.[1]

*This section was contributed by Peggy Garrett, Director of Consulting Services, Harris Kovac Alderman. In this section, Ms. Garrett shares her keen sense of what she contends must be the foundation of any integration strategy: market-specific medical manpower studies. The following text is a synopsis of telephone interviews and written field-based case studies.

Understanding these market forces allows provider groups, that is, physician and administrative health system leaders, to anticipate how rapidly a market can shift from a no-managed care to a high-level managed care ratio. Obviously, the composition of the medical staff will need to change as the market matures. To contribute to overall planning efforts, physician-to-population manpower studies must be dynamic and continuously factor in market pressures.

The first step of this process involves an assessment of physician supply and demand by specialty. To be relevant, current needs must be augmented by at least a 5-year projection. Supply and demand projections should factor in anticipated shifts in demographics and managed care penetration. Before heading off pell-mell recruiting or acquiring the practices of anyone who ever spent Wednesdays on a golf course, organized leaders must use an analytical base of knowledge to determine the composition of the community of providers that will be the most efficient and effective practicing in a new environment.

Once provider organizations know *how many and what type of health professional they need* to adequately meet market demand, the next step is to decide *who they want.* Provider performance and panel selection criteria are the key features in a phased approach; however, they will only be of value if they follow an accurate analysis of market-based supply and demand.

The estimated physician-to-population ratios shown in Table 8–1 and 8–2 utilize data developed in nationwide studies. The Graduate Medical Education National Advisory Committee (GMENAC) ratios are used for fee-for-service and low-level managed care areas. The mid-level and high-level managed care ratios are recommended by the *New England Journal of*

TABLE 8–1

Managed Care Standard Ratios:

Definition:	% Penetration:
No Managed Care	0% HMO
Low-Level Managed Care (categorized as a PPO market with entry level HMOs)	5%–20% HMO
Mid-Level Managed Care (categorized as a PPO/ HMO market with IPA and Staff Model HMOs)	20%–50% HMO
High-Level Managed Care (categorized as a highly capitated HMO market)	50%+ HMO

Source: The Governance Committee, *Future Economic Integration of Hospitals & Physicians*

TABLE 8–2

Low-Level Managed Care:

Physician-to-Population Ratios

Primary Care:	GMENAC 1990 Target Ratios:
Family General Practice	4,000
Internal Medicine	3,500
OB/GYN	10,150
Pediatrics	8,100
Specialty:	**GMENAC 1990 Target Ratios:**
Allergy	118,800
Anesthesiology	12,000
Cardiology	31,420
Dermatology	35,040
Emergency Medicine	18,000
Endocrinology	119,000
ENT	30,440
Gastroenterology	37,460
Hermatology-Oncology	27,000
Infectious Diseases	108,000
Nephrology	89,000
Neurology	44,275
Neurosurgery	92,000
Nuclear Medicine	61,000
Opthalmology	20,990
Orthopedic Surgery	16,130
Pathology	20,000
Plastic Surgery	90,190
Pulmonary Diseases	68,000
Psychiatry	6,325
Radiology	15,000
Rheumatology	143,000
General Surgery	10,350
Urology	31,625

Source: Graduate Medical Education National Advisory Committee, Dept. of Health & Human Services

Medicine, "Special Report: The Marketplace in HealthCare Reform" and the Governance Committee, repectively.

Consolidation is one of the most frequently prescribed remedies for the ills facing hospitals and physicians. Over-capacity, net revenue erosion, poor financial positioning, and high costs are some of the factors driving consoli-

TABLE 8-3

Mid-Level Managed Care:
Physician-to-Population Ratios

Primary Care:	**Target Ratios:**
Family Practice	2,800
General Internal Medicine	2,362
Pediatricians	5,714
OB/GYN	5,714
Specialty:	**Target Ratios:**
Allergy & Immunology	73,000
Anesthesiology	20,000
Cardiology	35,000
Dermatology	40,200
Emergency Medicine	18,000
Endocrinology	161,667
ENT	38,200
Gastroenterology	71,500
Infectious Diseases	183,000
Nephrology	128,000
Neurology	68,000
Neurosurgery	149,750
Oncology	64,750
Opthalmology	28,800
Orthopedic Surgery	20,200
Pathology	58,824
Plastic Surgery	241,500
Psychiatry	23,316
Pulmonary Diseases	83,000
Radiology	16,500
Rheumatology	155,333
General Surgery	19,000
Urology	39,000

Source: "Special Report: The Marketplace in Health Care Reform," *The New England Journal of Medicine*

dation. Physicians are the key to goals of integrating efforts to creating regional continuums of care, aligning physician, hospital, and payor incentives, and providing superior access and quantifiably better patient care at reduced costs. In fact, physicians become the most strategic component of an emerging distribution system.

A pivotal opportunity for achieving equilibrium in a tumultuous marketplace exists when providers come together to define new relationships. Coming together generally begins when a group of physicians approaches the hospital with a request for help in negotiating managed care contracts. It may also begin when a fire is lit under local hospital senior management because of a rumor that PhyCor, Inc., MedPartners, or other for-profit physician management company, is coming to town. Occasionally, integration begins with a hospital or health system that has a deliberate, proactive strategy for creating a system of care that serves all functions across the continuum and, essentially, corners the market. Regardless of its point of inception, physicians and hospitals can view integrated systems development as either a defensive strategy or as an opportunity to work together to undertake a fundamental positive restructuring of the healthcare delivery system.

In their rush to lock down doctors, most provider organizations are not creating organizational structures derived from an in-depth understanding of the market. Haphazardly creating new organizational structures for physician participation is not enough. Both hospital and physician leaders must first step back, look at the market, and ask: "What do we need? Who do we want? and What will it take to make this thing work?" Without a manpower study and conscious recruitment plan, the provider organization can fall into a political trap and be loaded down with specialists who will be dead weight as managed care accelerates. If this happens, the new "partners" will soon encounter a labyrinth of operational and functional issues that can ultimately trigger collapse and business failures.

To prepare for managing a more capitated population base, certain tools will be needed to successfully make this transition. Proactive administrators and physician leaders realize they need ammunition to secure the resources that will allow them to move strategically forward. A manpower study lets health system leaders look into the future (see Table 8–4). Future provider organization needs are based on an equation that factors in both the projected rate of managed care maturation and population-based algorithms for determining supply and demand.

Again, physician manpower needs will change with the market. What meets market needs today will be significantly different when the incentives encourage less—not more—treatment. Primary care, with its potential for cost savings through preventive medicine, is fast becoming the most important component of an aggressive strategy for business development. The driving forces that will alter recommendations as to a "best mix" of physician specialties include:

TABLE 8-4

A Manpower Study Should Accomplish the Following:

1. Document projected five-year changes in service area demographics, socioeconomic characteristics, market share, and managed care levels.
2. Define and document the total number of physicians and other healthcare providers needed, by specialty, in order to meet community needs and obtain optimal hospital utilization levels at each stage of managed care market evolution.
3. Become a working document and an essential component of an overall strategy for integration, especially as it relates to the increasing impact of managed care and the preferred position of physician partners.
4. Serve as a justifying document for current and future physician recruitment, acquisition plans, and panel selection.
5. Serve as a catalyst to solicit better understanding and improve working relationships between hospital management and medical staff.
6. Follow suggested government regulations and guidelines, including both objective data and subjective documentation.

Source: Peggy Garrett and Genie James

- It is becoming increasingly evident that primary care physicians are in the best position to thrive in the new healthcare world order. Managed care and other market reforms have put a renewed emphasis on primary care. The industry is demanding more generalist physicians. This marketplace reform is sweeping the country. For example, the American Academy of Family Physicians' 1995 annual practice profile survey indicates that 87 percent of the respondents see some managed care patients. Seventy-five percent of the responding family practitioners reported an increase in such patients in the last year. Of those physicians, 21 percent saw increases larger than 50 percent.
- Evidence also indicates that solo practice is becoming obsolete. The American Academy of Family Physician's reports that 21 percent of members have either considered or accomplished a move from unaffiliated, independent practices to a full-time contractual or salaried position with an integrated delivery system or other managed care organization.
- Medicare risk will be a critical component of generalists' future. Health systems will need a strong base of primary care providers to get Medicare risk business.
- More graduating U.S. medical students are choosing primary care for their first-year residencies. According to the National Residency

Matching Program, in 1995 more than 50 percent of U.S. medical school seniors secured residency positions in one of the generalist disciplines.

- 70 percent of 1995 medical residents surveyed indicated a preference for an employer setting (group, HMO, hospital) over a more independent, entrepreneurial setting (solo, association, partnership). Many residents are looking for career opportunities in a managed care environment.
- Primary care physicians' compensation is rising rapidly due to increased demand. Most first-year practice primary care physicians expect to earn $100,000–$125,000.
- Surveys show that mid-level practitioners are rapidly moving to the top of most healthcare providers' needs lists. The demand, especially for physician assistants (PAs) and registered nurse practitioners (NPs) has skyrocketed. Statistics indicate that mid-level practitioners justify their presence by *increasing productivity, thus increasing the bottom line.*

A manpower study should be an integral part of any total planning process. If the objective of business planning activities is to anticipate what services, personnel, and facilities will be needed to maintain and increase market share, *then a manpower study should naturally correspond to any actuarial analysis.* Healthcare facilities and physician groups need to be certain a manpower study is a working document. A manpower study can provide a detailed situation analysis and identify market opportunities. It also represents another step toward the future system of integrated organizations. This analytical base of information can help convince boards of directors, physician members, and senior management that the favored specialists who filled their beds in the 1980s is no longer king. Manpower studies are the analytical framework for expanding a base of primary care revenue and creating the foundation for future business. The benefits of and steps involved in manpower study are summarized in Tables 8–5 and 8–6, and Exhibit 8–1.

What will separate the winners and losers in the new healthcare environment? It won't be the specific legal structure for integration; it will be what you do with that structure once it's formed. What you do with the foundation, Management Service Organization, Independent Physician Association, or Physician Hospital Organization will have a lot to do with the leaders' beliefs about what it will take to survive in the future. Under any scenario, the prerequisite for winning will be *the ability to begin with the understanding of local market need in order to build a model that corresponds to supply and demand.*[2]

TABLE 8–5

Why Execute a Manpower Study?

A manpower study:

- Is a positive, proactive step toward strategic planning and medical staff development.
- Determines market share.
- Determines physician supply and demand by specialty within both the community and the organization.
- Provides a comprehensive medical staff profile.
- Provides an overall physician age analysis and succession planning.
- Documents/justifies recruitment; it keeps the organization in compliance with IRS and OIG guidelines.

In short, a medical staff manpower study provides direction for the future in a competitive healthcare environment.

Source: Peggy Garrett and Genie James

GETTING ORGANIZED*

There are many alternative models for integration. Understanding what each can do for you and how it fits with your strategy for managed care business development is the first step. New alliances are being formed every day. In the sharing of capital, management, and business resources, provider groups are getting organized to successfully lead the transition of health systems in their markets. Only the local players have the hands-on knowledge to address the intricacies of personalities and personal agendas; however, most physicians and hospital administrators are looking to outside consultants for the business and legal expertise required to get them going.

It is commonly believed that managed care market pressures will require that area providers come together to develop a fully integrated delivery system. With vision in mind, entrepreneurial providers are experimenting with a multitude of models including physician–hospital organizations (PHOs), independent physician associations (IPAs), group practices without walls (GPWWs), and management services organizations (MSOs). Trying to

*This section was written by Sally Sjobeck, Principal, SIDUS, LLC. While working at Travelers and HealthTrust, Inc., Ms. Sjobeck built a reputation as a problem-solver—never simply a vendor of popular 'band-aid' tactics. Ms. Sjobeck has founded SIDUS, LLC, a consulting firm that builds its reputation on customizing integration strategies according to local market needs. She shares her philosophy and technique in the following section.

TABLE 8–6

Manpower Studies: What Information Should Be Provided?

- *Market Definition*
- *Situation Analysis:* Description of current scenarios, immediate competitive threats, and pending financial tensions
- *Internal Cultural Audit:* Overview of organization's strengths and weaknesses, opportunities and threats
- *Managed Care Market Dynamics:*
  Including: Percent of penetration
  Payor profiles
  Trends
  Governmental reform variables
- *Physician Need in a Managed Care Setting:*
  Including: Current covered lives/MD
  Comparitor covered lives/MDs; Stages I–IV in a managed care evolutionary cycle
  Shortfalls
  Surplus
- *Patient Origin:* Number of patients per zip code, trended for five years
- *Existing and Projected Community Population,* trended for five years
  Including: Total service area
  Primary service area
  Secondary service area
  Zip code
- *Existing and projected Utilization by Major Diagnostic Category*
  Including: Total service area
  Primary service area
  Secondary service area
  Zip code
- *Overview of Competitive Position*
- *Medical Staff Profile*
  Including: Composition
  Practice descriptions, i.e., solo vs. group
  Profile by specialty/board certification
  Primary care/specialty ratios
  Hospital inpatient utilization report
  Physician inpatient utilization analysis
  Physician utilization report
  Age analysis by specialty
  Age analysis compared to national distribution
  Succession planning
- *Physician Recruiting Priorities*
- *Acquisition Targets/Objectives*
- *Time line for Integration Strategies*

Source: Peggy Garrett and Genie James

EXHIBIT 8–1

Physician Manpower Development Model

1. **Integrated Strategic Business Plan**
   - "A hospital without a strategic plan is like a large ship without a rudder in a changing current."
2. **Medical Staff Manpower Study**
   - "Positions hospital for practice management of its medical staff asset."
   - Highlights physician shortfalls and surplus. Becomes the *justifying statement* for the preferred medical staff composition of an integration strategy.
3. **Physician Recruitment**
   - "The lifeblood of any hospital's future."
   - Winning hospitals of the 1990s are more active than ever in primary care physician recruitment.
4. **Targeted Physician Practice Assessments**
   - "How does the hospital strengthen its referral base?"
5. **Physician Practice Valuations/Acquisitions**
   - "It's all about gaining and protecting market share."
   - "A *physician* practice acquisition strategy is a *patient* acquisition strategy."
6. **Physician Retention Programs**
   - "Physician *recruitment, practice acquisition, and retention* determine the hospital's product distribution of the future."

Source: Peggy Garrett and Genie James

figure out the defining attributes of each can be as daunting as trying to spell out the Gettysburg Address using alphabet soup! This can be where potential partners get frustrated and the objectives for integration get aborted.

In very simple language, provider independence decreases with increasing economic integration. The strategy for developing a model that works at the local level should occur at the intersection of the providers' motivators for coming together and the financial tensions threatening profitability. (See Table 8–7.)

Consulting firms are often brought in by local organizing provider groups to help sort through the alternatives and to operationalize a model for integration. It is a good thing to "know what you don't know" and to seek outside expertise when needed. Problems occur, however, when consultants or lawyers come in with a ready-made solution without attending to the unique concerns of the partners or the features of the market. This situation can be likened to a man who knows he needs shelter for the winter but does

TABLE 8–7

Model Descriptions: Collabcration Alternatives

Model	Defining Attributes
Equity	Physicians are owners of the for-profit health system and all subsidiaries
Employment	Physicians become employees of the (typically not-for-profit) health system
Foundation	Not-for-profit subsidiary of health system purchases the tangible and intangible assets of physicians' practices, although physician group maintains separate legal identity and legal structures; 100% of groups' revenue from foundation
Full Management Services (MSO)	Health system or jointly owned company acquires the tangible assets of physicians' practices and provides *comprehensive* management services (to include contracting) for which physicians pay a market price
Physician–Hospital Organization (PHO)	Joint physician–hospital organization negotiates payor contracts on behalf of the hospital and member physicians
Open	Open: all medical staff members free to join, physicians retain 100% ownership of practices
Closed	Closed: only a select group of physicians are offered membership based on high-quality, cost-effective profiling
Service Bureau	Health system subsidiary provides practice management services to interested physicians. Physicians select from a menu and pay a market price
Group Practice Without Walls (GPWW)	Physicians create a vehicle for contract negotiations and also contract for management services; looking for benefits of shared systems and economies of scale
Independent Physician Association (IPA)	Physicians band together to increase marketplace leverage and negotiate managed care contracts
Totally Independent	Physicians and health system operate as independent providers within a marketplace.

Complexity & Capital

Competitive Forces/Economic Tensions

not have a home. He has the option of sharing space with relatives or friends; renting an apartment; buying a pup tent, trailer, tract home, or luxury condominium; building a custom-made home; or renting a room at the Ritz Carlton for the season. All of the above options meet his immediate need for shelter but, needless to say, there is significant variance in terms of his level of personal and financial investment.

Similarly, a fully integrated provider services model is sort of like building a custom-made home. It requires a significant infusion of capital and, usually, a long-term commitment. Instead, when local players first come together they may be better off initially contracting for practice management services or creating a structure that can jointly negotiate payor contracts before they commit to shared equity arrangements. In other words, providers can "rent an apartment" before they sink their capital reserves into "the home of their dreams."

What any provider group needs is a "broker" not a "Realtor," intent on selling one particular (and potentially wrong) model. No outside source can come in with a ready-made solution that will work in every market, nor can the design of an organizational structure occur in a vacuum without the critical input of all key players. A consulting firm that effectively brokers alternatives will focus first on educating the providers as to what each model might mean to them. Next, a consulting firm can assist in identifying shared motivators for change, common objectives for growth, and an appropriate starting point for unity.

Again, the initial juncture of any effort to integrate must be a function of the marketplace. The scenario will become more complex as managed care market forces and financial tensions increase. Providers must first invest time and energy in a learning environment before they can adeptly determine how to best organize for survival.

Examining strategies organizing and for choosing a long-term partner can ensure success in a future, more sophisticated managed care environment. As physicians come together, their objectives will include the need to:

- Protect against income erosion.
- Reduce overhead via cost sharing and economies of scale.
- Access proactive management expertise.
- Associate with professional medical colleagues whom they respect and trust.
- Retain a measure of control.
- Gain access to market share via managed care contracts.

For physicians, focusing on the development of a physician organization can create a firm foothold. Physicians can work through this organizational structure to enhance operating performance, contract with managed care organizations, and refine relationships. It is not an "end-game" but rather a powerful kickoff. As physicians and hospitals join forces, their partnerships will need to be based on:

- Capital/financial strength.
- Local presence, existing market share, and reputation.
- Commitment to integration; willingness to give up control and to align financial incentives.
- Experience in managing operations within a capitated reimbursement environment.
- Ability/willingness to assume risk.

As managed care reduces hospital census and length of stay, everyone—physicians and hospitals—will increasingly be in the outpatient business. Consequently, partnerships will have new requirements that cut across functions. (See Table 8–8.) The most competitive systems within the healthcare industry will be the ones that are able to synthesize provider functions at a low cost and market them to healthcare purchasers.

If the market allows, a phased approach to getting organized—which does not immediately require the merging of tangible assets—can be advantageous. Contracting with outside consultants will only make sense if they work *with* you to clarify objectives and analyze options. Getting organized is the first step toward market dominance (see Table 8–9); it is important for providers to start by getting the analytical base of information and the additional professional expertise that will be needed to manage a complex and dynamic process.

TABLE 8–8

New Requirements Cut Across Functions

Traditional Hospital Functions	Traditional Medical Staff Functions	Individual Physician or Physician Group Decision	New Requirements
Recruiting	Credentialing	Partner addition	Physician manpower planning
Unit pricing		Unit pricing	Payor contracts
JCHAO standards Productivity	Quality assurance	Individual practice patterns	Clinical protocols/ standards
Technology acquisition Marketing		Some marketing	Volume targets/ strategies across the full spectrum

MOVING ONTO COMMON GROUND

Physicians are the hub on which the healthcare industry turns. Physician practice patterns determine the dollars spent on healthcare—either directly through the cost of patient encounters, or indirectly through ordering habits for both inpatient and outpatient services. The new organizational order recognizes that physicians must be partners, both financially as well as philosophically. More and more doctors are recognizing their market power. Although they may understand that their own organization's success may be restricted by lack of sufficient capital, they are upping the ante when they come to the table to negotiate with health system partners. This creates an immediate legal barrier for some tax-exempt systems, but a distinct differential advantage for investor-owned systems in many markets. Today, doctors demand partnerships that offer them both control and equity.

Health system executives have to accede their old ways of thinking when it comes to looking at survival. Filling inpatient beds and creating specialty service profit centers is the old paradigm. The new paradigm requires that business executives get in the minds of the local physicians.

At the local level, the need to integrate physician–hospital services results in several functional dilemmas, among which are:

- Trust: Who will need to come together to "own" the marketplace?
- Control: Who is on first?
- Growth: What will the strategy be for differentiating within a marketplace and capturing greater market share?

These concerns can be addressed on the provider side of the market by integrating provider functions with appropriate incentives. Neither hospitals nor physicians can develop such a continuum of care alone. Physician–hospital integration offers the potential scale and scope to develop a continuum of care.[3]

Hospital administrators must be attentive to how they communicate and relate to physicians. The old, condescending attitude that portrayed physicians as inept at business must go. Successful organizations share several qualities, but the most important is the awareness that a strong base of clinically respected physician–leaders is their most important core competency. Often, it is a group of like-minded physicians—not a team of hospital executives—that drives an organization to become proactive and market-focused.

The notion that hospital executives might actually play a *nurturing role*—as opposed to just an accommodating one—is even taking root. However, in the words of Robert Frost, there are "miles to go before I sleep." Just ask Steve McDermott, CEO of Hill Physicians Medical Group in San Ramon, California. This independent practice association of 2,500 doctors

TABLE 8–9

Physician–Hospital Integration

I. Hospital

- Competitive Cost Position—overall and for high-volume tertiary services (based on adjusted costs/case, length of stay by diagnostic-related grouping, FTE/occupied beds, etc.)
- Financial Position—overall and by major products and payors
- Utilization/Case Management Systems (approaches, protocols, and information systems)
- Contracting experience by plan and plan type
- Customer service ratings and other competitive position measures versus competition
- Degree of collaboration/system (or group) development among providers
  - Horizontally between hospitals or physicians
  - Vertically between hospitals and/or managed care organizations and physicians
- Source of referrals to major inpatient and ambulatory programs (e.g., self referral, volume by specific community physician)
- Geographic coverage in terms of patient origin
- Competitor assessments, including community providers and tertiary providers by key product line
- Physician profile (concentration of admissions and location, specialty, other hospital alliances, and managed care participation for highest volume admitters)
- Nature of affiliation(s) (if any) with community physicians and/or hospitals

II. Physician Profiles (segmented by the nature of their practice)

- Practice configuration—current and planned
- Indicators of pressure on practice profitability
- Overhead cost trends, volume and declines, and/or experienced
- Extent of use of information systems to track referral sources and utilization by patient by plan
- Volume of referrals by source (e.g., self referral volume by insurance plan by specific community physician)
- Plan membership

TABLE 8–9

Physician–Hospital Integration (*Continued*)

- Profile of referring physicians (e.g., locations, age distribution, plan membership, alternative specialist alignments) (hospital as proxy as appropriate)
- Use of physician extenders to triage patients
- Level of experience with capitated plans
- Utilization rates/practice patterns compared to major competition
- Credentials

III. Future Success Criteria and Timing

- Case studies of successful hospitals and physicians from markets in the same stage (and one stage more advanced)

  Cost/utilization position

  Core managed care capabilities (e.g., systems, use of triage)

  Degree of horizontal and vertical integration

  Managed care strategy (e.g., subcontract as a tertiary services niche provider, act as an agent for the full spectrum of health services)

  Competitive threats/need for urgent action

  Capital requirements

  Comfort with collaborative models that involve sharing various responsibilities and authority with (or sometimes shifting it to) physicians

  Readiness for significant change (could include conducting survey of “readiness for change” on a larger number of managers)

manages 10 HMO contracts covering 250,000 people. Says McDermott: "When the idea for developing formal partnerships between doctors and hospitals first materialized in this market, I thought hospitals could mimic some of the companies like 3M or IBM in their early days and fund start-up integrated systems as [research and development] projects—not control them but help get them started." Well he's been disappointed: "In the process of starting PHOs and MSOs, hospitals tend to smother them and kill them."[4]

Now is the time for hospital executives to stop trying to preserve their territory because, without the physicians, they won't have any turf at all. It is possible to be creative when designing very palatable alternatives for cooperation. This does not necessarily mean employing doctors or buying up their practices. It means treating physicians as equals and entering into partnership discussions with respect.

How attractive a partnership opportunity is to a physician depends on several features of the arrangement. Retaining the role of patient advocate, developing the parameters for quality assurance, and having the independence to adjust their own service mix are high on the physician's list and begin to meet his or her needs for control. Physicians also differentiate potential market partners based on their willingness to enter into shared-risk arrangements and pay physicians relative to the money they save the hospitals.

Most hospitals have in operation some form of physician–hospital partnership. As steering committees decide key issues and move toward implementation, certain things are becoming clear about the optimal way for them to work together. First and foremost, everyone must *focus on common ground.* The motivators drawing physicians and administrators together as business partners include loss of revenue and market share, an increase in operational costs, and decreased profitability. While both parties have other factors affecting them as well, by building on this common ground they can gain greater control over their future position than physicians and hospital administrators making decisions independently.

Here are some additional tips for moving hospital–physician partnership talks along:

1. *Vent first.* Plan the first session to include venting on both sides regarding past grievances and doubts about a partnership; allow the bloodletting to occur. It'll turn into that anyway so you may as well put it out there first.
2. *Make sure that senior hospital executives talk personally with physicians.* Never talk down to doctors; be willing to eat "humble pie." It is best if the CEO and the CFO meet with as many physicians as possible on an individual level as well as a group level.

It is important to recognize that physicians are not naïve about the business pressures they are facing. Propelled by dramatic changes in a healthcare system and reforms that have shrunk their income and authority, modern physicians have taken it upon themselves to obtain education and business training. As a result, they are often as sophisticated as health system administrators in their understanding of organizational structures or governance options for new entities.

Also, executives should ask physicians individually what *qualitatively* makes a difference to them. And it's important for executives to begin their discussions with physicians by acknowledging past sins. For example, when trying to build a base of primary care physicians, administrators may point out that they've often shown favoritism to specialists, which was the business of the 1980s. But the 1990s are different and somewhat unique.

3. *Recognize that the two groups may have different problem-solving styles.* Hospital executives traditionally problem-solve with long-term goals in mind. Physicians tend to be oriented toward quick decisions, and receive immediate gratification from their jobs. Therefore, while both sides want evidence and are disciplined thinkers, physicians see hospital executive as "talkers" who come out of their meetings with strategic and marketing plans in hand. Conversely, executives see physicians as prone to making snap judgments.
4. *Communicate about managed care in terms of "what this means to you."* Few physicians may be willing to get involved if they do not understand the power of market forces and the potential impact on their practices.
5. *Share case studies from various markets nationwide.* Find case studies from markets like yours and from other, more mature. Discuss how these markets are similar to yours, so that physicians can relate. The tricky part is that none of these case studies will be "finished." They are still evolving. Therefore, present market case studies as "options" and "probabilities," each with certain advantages and benefits.
6. *Share the integration strategy.* If the plan is to enter into a shared-risk arrangement or have a managed care product, hospital executives must demonstrate to physicians how they will bring resources to the table to secure a base of business.
7. *More broadly, create common visions of what the new partnership will entail.* Develop a specific vision so that physicians will see long-term possibilities of partnership. With the market changing so

rapidly, the knowledge that three to five years out they will still be in business can be a reassuring thought.

8. *Give physicians control over decision making in the new integrated system.* While trust is a key issue in any type of integration partnership, hospitals won't get far with physicians without tangible evidence of partnership. This equates to turning responsibility over to physicians. Credentialing, panel selection, and systems for quality assurance should belong to the physician–partners. Give physicians control of areas such as critical path development and outcomes tracking. Physicians have traditionally been involved in the clinical component of care without taking financial responsibilities.
9. *Assure physicians that they will still be the patient's advocate.* In the physician's experience, managed care companies, employers, insurers, and others have all gotten in the way of solid physician–patient relationships. This has caused physicians to feel that they no longer have control over patient care.
10. *Recognize how managed care shifts the power between primary care physicians and specialists.* Managed care is creating new leaders in the physician community. This is a difficult gap for hospital executives to bridge. It is helpful to recognize that there are style differences between the two physician groups.

    Accustomed to being revenue producers, specialists tend to be driven, analytical, and bottom-line oriented. Primary care (PC) physicians, on the other hand, tend to be more expressive or amiable. They want a track record with the people they work with, and they want to know that potential partners are trustworthy and will deliver. This may give the impression that it takes them longer to make decisions. Therefore, negotiations with PC physicians are best pursued quickly and quietly, through one-on-one interactions with physicians. Find out what most PC physicians want in order to be enticed into working for a physician group. For example, they may be interested in keeping their own office staff. If so, offer some type of management services organization to allow them to have their staff in place while handling the billing and managed care contracting centrally.
11. *Lay out the tangible details of the proposed partnership.* For example, spell out how equity arrangements, shared governance, office management services, and information systems may work. Physicians may believe that they can do it themselves because—after all, the hospital is only a facility—they have the patients.

Underscore the importance of the deep pockets, that is, the capital, that the health system brings to the table.

12. *Use economic modeling to examine hospital–physician relationships.* If you can explain and predict, you can motivate and move towards consensus. As has been mentioned previously, information systems are crucial in an era emphasizing ambulatory care. Patient information has to be at the physician's fingertips, especially physicians under capitation. However, development of information systems is very expensive and physicians in groups generally do not have that kind of money to invest up front. Physicians must evaluate if potential health system partners can meet their needs by bringing that type of capital to the table.
13. *Delay bringing lawyers and accountants in as long as possible.* You may need a facilitator, but don't jump into discussions of organizational structure prematurely. Iron out everything before bringing outsiders into the room. You will undoubtedly want lawyers and accountants to assist you, but the more trust you can build up with physicians before these parties enter the picture, the stronger the partnership. Bringing in outside parties too quickly can make the atmosphere antagonistic.

DEVELOPING NETWORKS: A SMALL WORLD?

The first stage of market consolidation among providers is usually characterized by loose alliances, managed care consortiums, and some kind of shared-services arrangements. These create less-formal structures that allow for some enhanced competitive clout but have a limited lifespan when measured by the market power of merged entities.

Although not the end goal, loose networks do have a purpose. In essence, they provide an opportunity for partners who are considering equity models to "date before they get married." Forming a network is also a way to experiment with less-threatening components of an integrated system—that is, seamless admitting/patient transfer protocols, patient tracking and utilization reports, standardization of critical path guidelines and even shared forums for continuing education.

As the market evolves, so too will the resource requirements for providers wanting to remain competitive. Some original network affiliates will be weeded out because their functions do not add enough value to be profitably used in a continuum of care. Similarly, other alliances may dissolve in the face of new competitors entering the market.

Proprietary chains have become increasingly aggressive in creating comprehensive local networks of care. These companies are investing billions of dollars acquiring hospitals and buying physician practices, as well as other types of medical providers, so they can be positioned to meet all the healthcare needs of managed care payors. Obviously, the scope and intensity of market partnerships is increasing.

The goal, then, is to assemble loosely organized providers with an array of skills and outfit them with the technology and facilities they need to manage the health as well as the acute care needs of a given population. From the perspective of a healthcare purchaser, a continuum of care is actually a one-stop-shop. According to Robin Walsh, vice president of the Partner Group, the increased level of network development activity in the market is in direct response to the growth in managed care, competitive positioning of providers, and the stronger role of insurers. "In markets nationwide, we see providers jockeying for position, racing to secure primary care relationships, and looking for ways to ensure their inclusion in managed care contracts," says Walsh.

Scores of provider networks and affiliations have formed over the last three to five years. Some have created the opportunity for horizontal integration and others have set the stage for vertical integration. This means we are now witnessing the coming together of a variety of provider groups such as physicians, community hospitals and tertiary care centers, home health departments, primary care outreach and pharmacy services. The most powerful networks are those that have merged assets, identified core competencies, synthesized functions into a continuum of care, and then marketed the package successfully within a managed care environment.

What is particularly striking about all these new deals is that, in the world of healthcare, your enemy can often become your friend. Former direct competitors are coming together in order to survive. This is not a unique business strategy. In Atlanta, for instance, Columbia's drive for market dominance has initiated a dialogue between two provider systems that have competed for years for market share: Saint Joseph's Hospital and Emory University Medical Center.

The need to price competitively is usually the first incentive for coming together to diffuse operational costs as well as financial risks. Pricing is now the number one determinant of health provider choice in many markets. Consequently, the one with the lowest costs eventually becomes the one with the most covered lives.[5] While exploiting cost competitiveness is important, it will be what happens next that determines the winners and the losers. Centralized resources must support decentralized operations. In the healthcare new industrial order, the winners will demonstrate that healthcare is a local issue—best managed at the local level.

An increasingly intense competition with for-profit hospital chains to secure managed care contracts has prompted the nation's largest association of not-for-profit hospitals to cross the rubicon. In concert with a unit of Chemical Bank and four Texas healthcare executives, Dallas-based VHA has invested an undisclosed sum for a 10 percent stake in InteCare, a newly organized for-profit Dallas company planning to buy 50 percent stakes in some of the nation's largest tax-exempt hospital systems. The initial four to six acquisitions expected to form the core of InteCare will generate about $2 billion in annual revenue, making it the third-largest proprietary chain in the United States.[6]

Not-for-profit hospitals are uniting in an attempt to withstand the shake-out that is happening in markets across the country. One school of thought is that by coming together the not-for-profits will not only strengthen their competitiveness by becoming more cost-competitive, they also have the opportunity to gain access to new markets and to exploit their perceived strength of enhanced customer intimacy. Market access and customer choice can be very valuable once the price window narrows. Some call this phenomenon the "halo effect."

Like many not-for-profits, academic medical centers face a number of critical challenges. The key question is whether or not teaching medical schools can compete in an environment that is increasingly cost-competitive. With the erosion of state-funded safety nets and federal medical school training funds, academic medical centers are at risk. Many are working hard to position themselves as tertiary centers of excellence but—except for a few carve-out diagnoses like burns, sick babies, and transplants—the payors aren't necessarily buying. Managed care organizations are not prepared to incur the higher cost of teaching.

According to David Fine, president of the New Orleans Division of Columbia/HCA, Tulane University was one of those academic institutions that recognized that "life as we knew it was over." In 1993, the Board of Tulane University's Medical Center created a self-study group to evaluate a variety of financial scenarios. The debate vacillated between two identifiable options for developing sustainable revenue: merge or sell.

"At first it looked like Oschner [a competing facility] might be the market partner that made sense. Although it was quite similar to Tulane in many ways, the respective power brokers for each institution were unsuccessful in negotiating terms for a merger. Medical politics nulled this marriage," says Fine.

The idea that did come to closure in April of 1995 was the sale of Tulane's Medical Center to Columbia/HCA. Many critics looked at this venture as a "sell out" but, according to Mr. Fine, "Tulane got to eat its cake and got to keep it too." The attraction for Tulane was that it was able to realize a one-time infusion of capital that could be applied to its teaching facility. It still has the Medical Center; it just doesn't own it. For Columbia/HCA, this approach is congruent with a strategy that is being enacted across the country: target major metropolitan areas where Columbia has limited market share and increase market presence by purchasing an academic medical center or public hospital. Tulane's objective to ensure long-term solvency for its teaching facility converged with Columbia/HCA's strategy for new growth. From the perspective of each, the acquisitions strategy was a "win–win."

HealthTrust, Inc., has served as an example of a lean, mean competitive machine in previous chapters and here again it serves as a valuable model. As a national company, Healthtrust, Inc., used its national presence to build clout and negotiate contracts. Still, its structure and strategy were defined and executed at the local market level through a synthesized system offering geographic access and a continuum of care. The rationalization of the system, the design of a continuum of care, and the development of strategic market partnerships reflected local needs. Now that HealthTrust, Inc., has been acquired by Columbia/HCA, the provider community is watching this market power in order to either develop a defensive strategy or to learn enough to replicate what works.

In just seven years, Columbia/HCA has grown from two for-profit hospitals in El Paso, Texas, to an international healthcare delivery system of over 330 hospitals in 37 states and two European countries, nearly 150 ambulatory surgery centers, and a variety of other, tightly integrated delivery services. This explosive growth has been driven by the aggressive acquisition of proprietary hospital chains—like HealthTrust, Inc.—and, more recently, by purchasing or partnering with tax-exempt, not-for-profit systems. Columbia/HCA's dramatic growth has been achieved with a well-prepared, very experienced acquisition team; an aggressive, flexible, and persistent approach; amazing speed in deal-making; ready access to large sums of money; and a reputation for not over-valuing acquisitions. Most of Columbia/HCA's future growth in new market areas is expected to be through acquiring or partnering with not-for-profit hospitals. In areas where the company already has a strong presence, future growth is expected to be through consolidation of its local-area delivery system into a complete and tightly integrated operation. In nearly all markets where Columbia/HCA has a presence, the response of competitor hospitals has been to seek rapid consolidation, with heightened anxiety.[7]

What can be learned from examples like Tulane Medical Center, HealthTrust, Inc., and Columbia/HCA? Here are a few salient points:

- Develop an aggressive communications strategy to apprise all stakeholders of the importance of decisions at hand.
- Make sure your own business is cost efficient.
- Analyze local market utilization patterns, purchasing trends, health status indicators, and current market share indicators.

- Use the statistical market area analysis to define the makeup of a continuum of care.
- Determine your fit within that continuum and your strategy for securing your place.
- Identify opportunities for vertical integration, that is, physician partnerships, local hospitals and ancillary providers offering a complement of medical services.
- Organize into a network that recognizes competitive forces as the catalyst for eliminating excess capacity, the duplication of services, and the need to streamline operations.
- Align goals for growth with financial analysis.
- Recognize the market advantage inherent in merging assets.
- Be willing to trade off some control and autonomy for access to capital and increased contracting leverage.
- Time is of the essence—first move forward to organize to meet local community need. If you don't, your competition will.

PROFILING PROVIDER PERFORMANCE

What is recommended here will be short, sweet, and to the point. Market requirements necessitate that healthcare providers' track outcomes and indicators of providers' performance, and hospitals should track and report appropriateness indicators related to utilization. The development of sophisticated clinical indicators for outcomes tracking, however, must remain in the hands of the physicians.

Current market requirements mandate the collection of some very basic data, usually financial data that serves as an indicator of utilization. The most frequently requested quality indicators today are those that also measure the hospital's ability to provide cost-effective care. The initial goal of capturing this information is to ensure that only necessary care is being delivered. The rationale is that—by closely monitoring indicators of length of stay, incidence rates for common procedures, and physician ordering patterns—there is the opportunity to eliminate unnecessary utilization and simultaneously improve quality.

Outcomes need to be tracked for those areas which are important to the performance of an integrated system. These will obviously include high-risk, high-volume cases. For hospitals, this decision is sometimes easy, because they can look at diagnostic-related grouping (DRG) volume and DRG costs. However, as they start connecting up with other parts of the healthcare system, such as managed care, they need to start thinking about conditions for which hospital care is not a critical component. For example, in the evaluation of chest pain, hospitals must have critical pathways on CABGs and angioplasties. If hospitals are linking with managed care to look at populations of patients, they need to have guidelines for screening and evaluating patients who do not go on in the hospital setting and perhaps even guidelines that address prevention, such as stop smoking methods, patient education, and cholesterol screening.[8]

According to the Healthcare Advisory Board's report on outcomes strategy, "The cost of tracking these indicators is virtually nil; most hospitals already have the information systems and personnel in place to monitor appropriateness and length of stay (LOS) for major conditions, procedures." Once the hospital has the information, the question then becomes *what to do with it.* The answer: *Give it to the doctors.* Also, the hospital must work closely with the physicians—and be humble in their sharing of information—because the bulk of the information needed in the future resides beyond their domain. It is in the hands of the doctors.

While purchasers will require that health systems track financial and appropriateness indicators in the short term, data on procedure volume and utilization will become less significant in the future. Why? Because the focus on costs is already standardizing measures of appropriateness, that is, the level of resource utilization that corresponds to a particular diagnosis. As capitation becomes a market reality, economic forces should eliminate concerns regarding the overuse of resources. With new incentives in place, the concern becomes the *underuse* of needed services. Healthcare reform demands the flipping of financial incentives that once encouraged too much medical care. The problem is that, once inverted, the reimbursement system is set up to reward for too little care. If capitation is the operative reimbursement system, then one important function of clinical indicators of quality will be to send a red alert when there is evidence of underutilization.

The case for keeping outcomes tracking within the domain of the physicians will be made by returning to the original intent of each of the players participating in this healthcare game. The healthcare purchaser's role is to get the best buy for the money. They track outcomes primarily to see how much was paid out. The hospital administrator is in business to make a profit from health services delivery. From an administrative perspective, the primary function of outcomes indicators is to be alert to opportunities to change utilization patterns in a way that will favorably impact the bottom line. The physician, however, is in place to serve as the patient advocate. Of course, altruism does not generally displace the need to earn a living, but even in the face of perverse fee-for-service incentives, most physicians remain true to their original intent to practice good medicine.

Physician peer review is one vehicle that can move the provider community into an era that will demand more sophisticated measures of quality. According to Richard M. Cooper, M.D., former HMO medical director/executive director and founder and chairman of a medical risk management company, peer review is an essential element in any meaningful quality assurance program. The purpose of peer review is to *modify,* not simply monitor, provider behavior, and to *enlighten,* not control. Peer review leads to continual self-improvement through a process of critical and constructive introspection. To be optimally effective, peer review must:

- Not be punitive.
- Be educational in orientation.
- Include active involvement and participation by *all* providers.
- Not be based on the objective of ensuring only that minimum quality standards are met; it must earnestly strive for the unattainable goal of perfection.
- Not rely exclusively on analysis of computer data.
- Include a thorough evaluation of the documents contained in the medical record.

This last piece, the chart audit, means nothing more than a group of physicians together reviewing each others' work. It also means nothing less. Chart audit, done well, is the most highly educational activity in which physicians can be involved. But chart audit requires a fair amount of finesse.

Another powerful medical management device, though more passive than chart audit, is the "practice profile." If you plot an aspect of physician behavior, say laboratory-test ordering, you typically find the data create a classical bell curve: some order lots of tests, some order few, and most order a medium number of tests. If you then distribute the profiles to the physicians (the "feedback loop"), depicting each physician's behavior relative to the others (without any judgments or editorial comments), and later re-plot the same behavior, you will most likely find that the curve has become taller and narrower: the extremes at either end have disappeared and a clustering has occurred around an implied group norm. Practice profiles work because of heightened awareness and passive peer pressure. Most physicians don't know what their own profiles look like, let alone how they compare to anyone else's. Most physicians are also bright, highly motivated individuals who want to practice good medicine.[9]

Hospitals will have to continue to use financial indicators to demonstrate cost effectiveness in order to stay ahead of the market. The prevailing focus on cost containment means that in the near future, the importance of appropriateness and efficiency indicators will not be diluted. Still, if one predicts that more mature markets will hold providers accountable to objective standards of clinical quality and functional outcomes, then a system for enhancing provider performance across several different dimensions needs to be put in place now. Tracking outcomes is a way of informing clinicians' decisions, changing behaviors, and improving healthcare.

Hospitals should provide physicians with data, then empower them to drive the processes for clinical outcomes tracking and critical path design. In other words, clinical care is the domain of the physician. Physicians must be the ones setting any parameters impacting practice. They are the ones who know what is the standard of the community and what is not. According to Joseph C. Hutts, chairman, president, and CEO of PhyCor, Inc., "It is certain that the performance of physicians will drive healthcare reform. Physicians' organizations must demonstrate that clinical results and patient satisfaction are not only protected but enhanced as we restructure our system."

As the market threshold for acceptable quality rises over time, those hospitals, health systems, and provider organizations unable to relinquish control to the health professional touching the patient may risk losing marketplace leverage and, ultimately, being locked out.

VENTURING INTO THE BERMUDA TRIANGLE (OR, INVESTING IN INFORMATION SYSTEMS)

Efforts to integrate healthcare systems are on the rise. While getting organized into groups and networks is the first thrust of this trend, the long term test of these new entities will be how well they operate. Initially, barriers to operational efficiency include structural legal issues, medical staff politics, income distribution models and the redeployment of staff. A concentration of time and analytical thought can usually allay these issues. What really challenges emerging integrated systems is the need to create seamless, coordinated systems to store and process information.

As the role and mission of integrated delivery systems evolves, timely and accurate information becomes increasingly vital to every key player. Capturing inpatient data is not hard, but as patient volumes move outside the hospital walls to a lower-cost environment, technology must be most closely linked to ambulatory care. For this to be effective, we need information systems that allow the physician to navigate all environments of care—outpatient, inpatient, long-term care, home care—from a single work station through the use of standardized protocols.

Most people say that the computer is the piece of technology that has most dramatically changed how we operate. There is undoubtedly some truth to that statement, but someone recently countered that it was the refrigerator—

not the computer—that ushered in a new age across domestic and industrial fronts. Think about it. All of a sudden, by storing food until time for use, the refrigerator increased the flexibility and mobility of an entire culture. Every healthcare executive signs off on the investment of large sums of money to buy sophisticated information systems technology, a lot of which is still in the R&D stage. What we really need is a repository for information that can store pertinent data and allow it to be accessed as needed. The electronic medical record will become the "refrigerator" of information systems.

The idea of seamless, coordinated systems that eliminate wasteful fragmentation makes sense, but making it happen is not so easy. One problem is that hospital departments have been assaulted by vendors hawking their solutions which usually only address a narrow focus of information needs. All of a sudden the lab, the pharmacy, and the patient accounting office are automated. The cumulative effect is that the multiple platforms that are put into place actually aggravate, rather than reduce, the fragmentation that has been so characteristic of the industry. Instead of a *relational* system that could move patient data across access points, most health systems have invested a great deal of money in a la carte proprietary databases with narrow-purpose applications.

In his article, "The Infoswamp," Owen Edwards makes the following pertinent observations:

> In his book, *The Road Ahead,* Microsoft co-founder Bill Gates defines information as the "reduction of uncertainty." Of course, as a captain of non-industry in the business of selling information systems, Gates might be expected to come up with such a simple, sunny definition. But, hesitant as I am to contradict a man who, as of yesterday, was worth about $15 billion more than I, it simply has to be pointed out that Bill is dead wrong. In truth, information is anything that can shout, wheedle or wiggle itself into the path of our attention. It is nothing more or less than data, decibels, bits, bytes, pixels, pheromones and vibrations (both good and bad). Though sometimes it may be a reduction of uncertainty, more often than not it is a contributor to confusion.[10]

Paul Ellwood, CEO of Minneapolis-based InterStudy, says:

> The current proliferation of medical databases demonstrates how large in size and broad in scope they can become and how fragile they are to maintain. Each database represents an advance in its own field, but perhaps because of the fragmentary and proprietary nature of the data and the difficulty of converting medical records across systems, clinical database developments are now held hostage by our tendency to create information repositories independently of each other. This incompatibility in data systems, rooted in history, function, pride, and money, creates added urgency to adopt a uniform subset of health outcomes data.[11]

Despite the obstacles, interest in the automated medical record is burgeoning, according to research by Charles J. Singer. In fact, a 1994 survey of 137 health systems showed that 86 percent of them were either implementing or at least developing automated medical record strategies. Singer's study found that large organizations such as the Mayo Clinics, Allina Health Systems, Kaiser Permanente, CIGNA, and PruCare were piloting various systems at clinics throughout the United States, while hundreds of small- to medium-sized practices were already operating electronic medical records acquired in the previous one to three years. Furthermore, some health systems had decided to set aside \$50 million to \$150 million per year for systems development because they'd realized that the investment was essential to maintain their competitive advantage.[12]

Sentara Health System, a Norfolk, Virginia, based integrated delivery system, is one of those organizations that has been willing to make substantial investments in enabling technologies which have the potential of enhancing inter-system information processing and clinical communications. In 1994, Sentara initiated a comprehensive evaluation process to select a computerized member/patient record system with a companion ambulatory care system. Sentara Health System consists of 4 hospitals, 8 urgent care centers, 11 staff model healthcare centers, 1000 nursing home beds, 170 employed physicians, and an independent physician association (IPA). Needless to say, the need to link information across sites was a strategic imperative.

Sentara realized at the beginning of the process that these systems would be the most expensive computer systems it acquired. A consulting initiative with Ernst & Young was engaged to perform a benefits study to identify enterprise-wide cost savings, as well as key strategic qualitative and operational benefits for the integrated delivery network. The early projections for capital funding missed the mark. The systems would cost approximately double the anticipated projection (over \$30 million) to automate these environments. OUCH!

According to Bert Reese, corporate director of Information Systems, and Donnie Belangia, director of Enterprise-Wide Initiatives, the big issues that made this project seem almost like a journey into the Bermuda Triangle included:

- The lack of standardization of medical nomenclature.
- The fact that, unlike an automated order entry process that tracks a patient across an inpatient visit, there is typically no navigational tool that guides outpatient practice patterns.
- The lack of functionality of a master member/patient index that initially had been assumed to be an operational component of certain vendor systems.

- The fact that the usage of clinical workstations by physicians was less than expected.

To date, Sentara remains committed to the process but has modified its approach to occur across several phases. Phase 1 will produce the "seamless member/patient recognition" for hassle-free access into the Sentara Integrated Delivery Network. The "feared process" of system integration will be tackled with assistance from outside system integrators to interface the master member index to subscriber membership databases and legacy registration systems. This approach will allow Sentara to "go to school" as an organization on enterprise-wide integration prior to associating clinical information member/patient population. Also, this provides the option to furnish the master member index as a "plug-and-play" database as it relates to the computerized record.

Phase 2 will begin with funding for a free-standing pilot of clinical workstation capabilities within one of the physician practice groups. This will provide an opportunity to understand the impact of automating physician workflow before the large investment of the computerized record is made. The reality is that there are no vendors that have fully implemented integrated delivery systems. Signing up to be a beta test site does not guarantee that the investment of time and dollars will pay off in critical functionality. This R & D effort can be costly.

IS director Bert Reese recommends that smaller market players considering a strategy for technological investments should remember that "less can be more," particularly if discussions regarding acquisitions, mergers, and network developments are in the wind. "Local-level strategies should mirror that of large system partners. You can spend a lot for systems which have a relatively short life-cycle and can be in danger of becoming obsolete as data and communications architectures evolve rapidly." A guiding principle is that your systems should not be a barrier that hinders other entities from doing business with you.

"When you do invest," he adds, "be sure to 'look under the hood' of the vendors' products. Conduct a detailed analysis of technical/integration alternatives with an emphasis on performance and depth of service. Devise scripted demos of key processes based on your most immediate needs and then ask for product demonstration. Extensively probe to determine vendor issues, specifically determine what the vendor has truly operationalized versus what may be in developmental stages." Negotiate from a "try it–buy it" position. That is, if the installed system meets your clearly defined expectations, you'll buy it. If it does not, you will uninstall it and owe nothing.

Although no provider system can ignore the importance of developing strategic integrated information systems, this is one growth area where it behooves providers not to overshoot the marketplace. Like the personal computer market, there is great possibility that the cutting-edge-technology of today will be commonplace tomorrow—or at the least more affordable.

In addition, it has yet to be determined how the Internet might undercut its competitive vendors. Both personal computers and the Internet distributed network provide the essential character for decentralizing information within centralized organizational structures. Clinical protocols could be accessed via a home page; protocols are not proprietary. Clinical experts from around the world could conduct peer review meetings in a chat room and benefit from the low cost format and real-time information exchange. Indeed, databases may be the cost-effective solution for complex and expensive medical record technology, if the issue of confidentiality can be addressed.

Organizations like Columbia/HCA, Oxford Health Plan, and HealthWorld are developing online services hawking health promotion, wellness, and preventive services. Their goal is to use the Internet to replace health professionals' hands-on role in working with patients and enrollees to enhance individual responsibility for health and lifestyle choices.

One recent electronic link-up will connect 500 hospitals around the world via cyberspace. Organizers of the new "global hospital" have set up a site on the World Wide Web—Health on the Net (http://www.hon.ch)—which offers contacts, information, and advice for individuals, and healthcare providers and professionals. "Hospitals and doctors will have instant access to health and medical facilities around the world," says Marc Selby, president of the Health on the Internet Foundation, a non-profit group that pioneered the hookup. The link will:

- Allow hospitals around the world to look at each other's services, learn from each other's experiences, and share information.
- Help experts share advice and research data. If a hospital suddenly must deal with earthquake victims, doctors can turn to the topic listing on the site to find out how doctors in an area like Kobe, Japan (hit by a huge earthquake in 1994), handled injuries and dispensed care. The site is also designed to serve as a resource, allowing users to contact experts.
- Put patients into virtual support groups, through a directory of health support groups.

With support from AT&T and the Aga Khan Foundation, the "global hospital" has raised $1 million to start up. The plan is to have all 500 hospitals linked by December 1997. The group also is asking IBM and the World Bank for $1.2 million to fund post-medical school studies in tele-medicine. "In return, the students (would) provide assistance in helping the hospital get on the Net," says Selby, a former Digital Computer Corporation executive.[13]

It will pay to watch if and how the Internet displaces all those expensive IS vendors on the market today. Cyberspace may be a useful tool, but it will never be the nirvana for the healthcare industry. Fancy information systems and the Internet are missing the most essential ingredient: human aspects. Health systems need only look to their customers to understand that the important aspects of human interactions must never be de-valued.

Instead of depleting precious reserves, this may be the one area of healthcare where it makes sense to wait and see what a potential large system partner accomplishes through its investments. If it works, then a deal to merge interests might have some real attraction.

The bottom line for developing integrated information systems for the future is:

- An organization must strategically align its technology plans with its business objectives.
- The best designs for integrated systems should be natural extensions of what is already working well to streamline processes and encourage real-time communication.
- Information systems will need companion education and training programs if they are ever to be used.
- The most important information will occur outside of the hospital and will come from the fingertips of the hands-on caregiver.
- Don't venture into the Bermuda Triangle, that is, don't overshoot the market and deplete capital resources *particularly if there is the potential to pursue a tighter relationship with a systems partner who has deeper pockets.*

AVOIDING PITFALLS

Businesses fail because they are undercapitalized, they have no leadership, they lack expertise, they suffer from poor management, the timing of new product and/or services launch is out of sync with the market, and/or the business venture is not founded on a sound base of local market knowledge. The new business of healthcare will have to avoid the same types of planning pitfalls if it is to be successful. Healthcare must act as a business and be accountable to both the bottom line and the local market if it is to earn the right to enact its social mission. In general, planning pitfalls can be grouped accordingly: dollars, data, delusions.

Dollars

Having access to a tremendous amount of capital will be the strategic tool that ensures long-term, viable provider organizations. Underestimating the power of the dollar can be a fatal mistake. Large health systems, not individual provider entities, are the ones with the capital resources that will be needed to build the infrastructure for a strong bottom-line business.

Data

You can't change what you can't measure. Information equips healthcare decision makers with the power to be aggressive, opportunistic, and pragmatic. Tactical mistakes will be unavoidable when moving into new service lines and forming new partnerships. Providers must have systems in place to quickly ascertain what is working and what is not, in order to not diffuse capital resources or make the same mistake twice.

The failure to invest time and money to obtain local data is a very treacherous planning pitfall.

Delusions

Get used to it: *There is no status quo and you can't survive alone.* To profit, industry leaders will need to be strategic in identifying partners with like intentions and objectives. The best returns will come from those organizations that focus on a fundamental tenet of business development: Local market demand must drive supply, that is, systems integration and new product/service development.

Do not delude yourself that you are keeping market forces at bay. If a provider system is not simultaneously getting organized, streamlining operations, and piloting new ways of being in business, then it is at risk. Denial is the most dangerous planning pitfall.

ENDNOTES

1. "Making Strategic Choices," *Integrated Healthcare Report* (January 1993), p. 4.
2. "Organizing to Manage Risk," *Integrated Healthcare Report* (May 1993), p. 1.
3. Gregory, Douglas. "Strategic Alliances Between Physicians and Hospitals in Multi-Hospital Systems," *Hospitals & Health Services Administration,* vol. 37, no. 2. (Summer 1992), p. 257.
4. Sandrick, Karen. "How to Succeed With Doctors by *Really* Trying," *Hospitals & Health Networks.* (February 5, 1996), p. 28.
5. "Investor-Owned Systems: Déjà Vu or New and Improved," *Planning & Marketing* (December 1995), p. 1.
6. Fox, David A. "Not-for-Profit Hospitals to Unite: InteCare to help them compete," *The Tennessean,* Nov. 12, 1995.

7. Heineccius, Lance. *Columbia/HCA: A National Profile,* A Report for the Washington State Hospital Association. December 1, 1995.

8. "Out in Front: Managed Care Helps Push Clinical Guidelines Forward," *Hospitals* (May 5, 1993), p. 31.

9. Cooper, Richard M. *Buyer Beware: A No-Nonsense Guide to Health Care Cost Containment* (Brentwood, TN: Richard M. Cooper, M.D., 1988).

10. Edwards, Owen. "The Infoswamp," *Sky* (March 1996), p. 14.

11. *Integrated Healthcare Report,* (December 1992), p. 9.

12. Appleby, Chuck. "The Mouse That Roared," *Hospitals & Health Networks,* February 20, 1996.

13. Olsen, Elizabeth. "Web Site Lets Hospitals Link Up," *USA Today* (March 20, 1996), p. D–1.

9 CHAPTER

Physician/Hospital Risk-Sharing*

In most major metropolitan areas across the country, the local healthcare delivery system is undergoing a major reform process. The "revolution" caused by managed care and the pressure from healthcare purchasers, has had a tremendous impact on most hospital and physician providers. Some providers have embraced this forced change to decrease the cost of care as an opportunity to improve the system in a positive way. However, most have gone into a form of denial and have responded by either refusing to change or by moving very slowly to fix a system that is in bad need of repair.

The current healthcare system has had one major flaw dating back to the earliest days of health insurance and entitlement programs: the fee-for-service method of reimbursement. Although this payment mechanism seemed logical when it was designed, it failed to recognize the need to promote "value" in the healthcare services that were being delivered. If the value purchasing equation is value = cost + quality + patient satisfaction, healthcare providers—mainly

*This chapter was written by Joane H. Goodroe, RN, MBA, and Tom Andrews.

Joane H. Goodroe was formerly the vice president of Cardiac Services at Saint Joseph's Hospital of Atlanta and was responsible for the implementation of the Medicare Cardiac Bypass Demonstration Project. She is now president of the consulting firm, Goodroe & Company, which works with hospitals and physicians to create partnerships to enhance quality and cost effectiveness.

Tom Andrews is currently the Director of Managed Care at DeKalb Medical Center in Atlanta, Georgia. He has over 20 years of health care experience and has spent the past 10 years in managed care, working with both payors and providers.

hospitals and physicians—were given the open opportunity to disregard the cost component of value. As technology improved and services became more readily available, the natural evolution of the fee-for-service system sent the cost of care out of control. Contrary to some recent accusations, it was not provider greed that caused the system to implode. The entire revolution can be attributed to the pure and simple lack of market incentives inherent in the fee-for-service system under which the system operated.

One area that obviously lacks incentives is the way hospitals and physicians currently do not have the natural financial need to work together in delivering healthcare services. Historically, physicians and hospitals have been paid independently and neither payment was based on how the other performed. Many times, hospital payments have been denied based on the lack of clear evidence that the service was necessary, while the physician who is responsible for making most of the decisions regarding the services was paid in full. Again we return to the basic tenet that was true of hospital operations in the 1980s: Physician practice patterns were a primary determinant of cost.

Managed care has introduced a number of new and different reimbursement methodologies that are assisting the purchasers of healthcare in decreasing cost. Most of the more popular reimbursement terms are focused on discounts off billed charges and per diem payments to hospitals and discounted fee-for-service or capitation for physicians services. Unfortunately, these new forms of reimbursement do not get at the kernel of the issue: appropriate utilization. With discounted fee-for-service, providers may couple decreased rules with increased volume. In capitation, providers can potentially make more money by doing nothing at all. Neither discounted-fee-for-service, per diem payments, nor capitation necessarily addresses the fundamental component of risk sharing: the financial incentives of the hospital and the physicians.

Managed care payors in some of the more evolved managed care markets are recognizing that merely reducing the amount of reimbursement is only a temporary fix to the cost problem. A more permanent solution lies in a reimbursement methodology that involves a true alignment of the incentives between the providers. These new mechanisms are designed around a shift in the risk to the provider under some type of capitation or global payment basis. Early results have indicated that when the providers assume the risk they are more apt to aggressively reengineer the patient care process, which improves not only the financial outcome, but the quality of care as well.

MEDICARE PARTICIPATING HEART BYPASS DEMONSTRATION

One of the first opportunities to explore the effects of physician and hospital risk-sharing occurred with a special demonstration project designed by the Research and Demonstration department of the Health Care Financing Administration (HCFA). In 1988, HCFA gave every hospital in the country performing a minimum of 250 open heart surgeries the opportunity to be selected to participate in a demonstration project that would pay one combined fee for all hospital and physician services associated with Medicare coronary bypass surgery.

Although the concept is simple, there are several complicated aspects to this type of payment plan. Traditionally, Medicare has paid hospitals a fixed fee for services based on an assigned diagnostic-related grouping (DRG) and physicians have been paid a discount fee for service (RBRVS). Again, there had been no shared risk or alignment of incentives for hospitals and physicians.

Applications were solicited from hospitals who were willing to accept a fixed physician/hospital fee for DRGs 106 and 107, coronary bypass surgery with or without catheterization. Medicare had asked the hospitals to discount the current hospital and physician reimbursement in order to be part of the project. The areas of evaluation for selection of project participants in 1990 included the price of the service, breadth of covered services, quality of patient services offered, and information systems available. Hospitals and physicians were reluctant to accept less money with no guarantee for additional volume. Therefore, only 24 hospitals in the country submitted applications with meaningful financial discounts. Four hospitals were chosen to participate in the project that began May, 1991. They were:

- Boston University Hospital–Boston, Massachusetts
- The Ohio State University Hospital–Columbus, Ohio
- St. Joseph's Hospital–Ann Arbor, Michigan
- Saint Joseph's Hospital–Atlanta, Georgia

The authors of this chapter were in charge of the implementation of this project at Saint Joseph's Hospital of Atlanta (SJHA). As part of the contract, the hospital was to be paid one fee and then pay the physicians. The hospital had agreed to an aggregate five percent (5%) discount for the hospital services and a three percent (3%) discount for the physician services. However, the amount that was paid to the physicians was negotiable. HCFA did not dictate the split between the physicians and the hospital, and in fact encouraged the hospitals to be "creative" with respect to physician reimbursement.

SJHA had an open medical staff structure and there were over 300 physicians who would be required to participate in the project. The physician specialties included the cardiac surgeons, cardiologists, anesthesiologists, radiologists, pulmonologists, neurologists, hematologists, pathologists, and infectious disease specialists. The majority of the physicians were reluctant to participate in the project because of the loss of economic autonomy. However, the cardiac surgery group that performed the majority of open heart surgery cases at the hospital was supportive of the project. Since the cardiac surgeons represented the largest component of the physician fees, the decision was made to go forward.

The first step to set the initial fees for each specialty was to review past claims history associated with each DRG. Since the relative base resource value system (RBRVS) had not yet been initiated, there were many diverse physician charges for the same service. There were also significant variations in the physicians' practice patterns. For example, there were over 100 cardiologists who could participate in the project. Some of these physicians followed a post-operative coronary bypass patient on a daily basis while others relinquished total patient control to the surgeon. In order to set the appropriate physician fees, the overall average patient situation had to be determined. Since the surgeons, anesthesiologists, and radiologists were involved in every case, their average fees were more predictable. The other physician services were more difficult to determine since there was not common involvement in every case.

Negotiations with the physicians on fees was based on the review of data with a "gentlemen's" agreement that the actual claims history would be monitored to determine the actual discount that physicians were taking under this project. The fees would be recalculated each year based on a retrospective analysis to ensure that the physicians were not taking additional risk.

One of the key cardiac surgeons immediately identified the opportunity for the surgeons to take an aggressive posture in reducing cost if there was true alignment of the hospital and physician incentives. It was determined that the physicians controlled 85 percent of the variable costs associated with an admission. Further analysis of the data confirmed that the surgeons controlled the majority of cost from the date of surgery until discharge. It was determined that anesthesia controlled between 12 and 15 percent of the cost. In contrast, radiology had no control over cost. The radiology services utilized were based on the ordering patterns of the surgeon. The consulting physician usage was also controlled by the surgeon. Routinely, when a consulting physician was utilized, the overall cost of the case increased due to the ordering of new laboratory tests and other services. Therefore, it was determined that costs were controlled by the cardiologists before the surgery and by the surgeons and anesthesiologists following the surgery.

Once there was agreement on who controlled the cost, it was important for the physicians to have detailed data and information on the actual cost of all services. The initial review of data was surprising. Length of stay is so often referred to as an area to reduce cost. However, the review of data demonstrated that the largest cost areas from open heart surgery until discharge were in the operating room followed by the intensive care unit. This accounted for 75% of the total variable cost.

The Medicare Bypass Demonstration project accounted for 52 percent of the total coronary bypass cases performed at Saint Joseph's. For the surgeons, this was a significant part of their total practice. Since the hospital had agreed to structure a payment system that would align the financial incentives for the surgeon and the hospital, the variable cost began to decrease.

A "RISK/INCENTIVE" PAYMENT MODEL

By the end of the first full year under the demonstration project, it became obvious to the hospital that the cost of care on certain cases was decreasing based on the efforts of key surgeons. The hospital recognized that under the fixed reimbursement methodology the reduction in cost across all cases would result in a tremendous impact on the net income associated with these bypass surgeries. Therefore, it was in the hospital's best interest to examine how it could share with the physicians the cost savings and/or the increase in net income.

The hospital began to work with the surgeons on modifying the original payment methodology to include an incentive-based system. First, it was determined that the most essential criteria under a new incentive-based reimbursement system was to ensure that the quality of care was not impacted by cost reduction activities. Therefore, the physicians developed a list of quality indicators that were monitored by the case manager for all bypass cases. In order for surgeons to participate in the new incentive-based program they were required to be within a certain standard deviation from the hospital norm on each of the quality indicators. If the physicians met the quality criteria and performed a minimum number of cases annually, they would qualify to participate in the incentive-based program. The new payment program was designed around an analysis of the physicians' individual (or aggregate for the group if desired) average variable cost per case prior to the demonstration. This average variable cost was compared to the average at the completion of one year under the demonstration. The surgeon(s) was then "credited" for 25 percent of the cost reduction.

The incentive program made its first payment to the surgeons in a lump sum payment based on the first year's activity. Only a few physicians realized any sizable incentive payment because the majority had not begun to aggressively manage the care. During the following year, however, the cost reduction activity increased tremendously and the hospital decided to modify the methodology once again. This time in lieu of a lump sum distribution of the cost savings percentage, the hospital modified the physicians' reimbursement to include the "credit" for the reduction in cost. Therefore, the historical cost reduction was used to determine the physicians' reimbursement prospectively.

Over time, most of the surgeons began to modify practice patterns significantly. The surgeons were also responsible for working directly with the anesthesiologists in gaining their cooperation to reduce cost. A similar cost savings/incentive program was then developed for the anesthesiologists.

RESULTS AND IMPACT

Of the four original hospitals in the Medicare Heart Bypass Demonstration project, Saint Joseph's Hospital of Atlanta (SJHA) was the only program that developed a formal risk-sharing relationship with the physicians. The results of the program at (SJHA) were astounding. The variable cost of services for coronary bypass surgery (DRG 107) decreased over 40 percent. The other hospitals involved in the project showed average decreases of 10 percent.

In order to assess the impact on the patients in this type of integrated hospital and physician billing system, The Gallup Poll Organization was hired by SJHA to determine overall patient satisfaction. The results demonstrated higher than national average satisfaction levels and somewhat higher than SJHA's overall satisfaction levels. In review of these findings, it was noted that the patients had not been treated differently from other patients. However, their perception of better service was related to the simplified approach to billing. All of the services received were bundled in the one billing and payment system. The result for the patient was a tremendous decrease in paperwork and out-of-pocket expense that exists in the normal Medicare system.

In the first 18 months of the project, Medicare saved $15.3 million. SJHA alone generated $5.5 million of that savings. These numbers can be doubled within the official three-year completion of the project.

The Medicare Heart Bypass Demonstration project had four major results in a program that had aligned its physician and hospital incentives:

1. Medicare saved a significant amount of money.
2. These cases were more profitable for the hospital.
3. The physicians were sheltered and in some cases increased their reimbursement.
4. By the patients' perception, quality had increased.

FUTURE APPLICATIONS AND PRACTICAL SUGGESTIONS

The principles and lessons learned from the Medicare Heart Bypass Demonstration can be applied to all aspects of healthcare as it relates to physician and hospital financial relationships; however, the current antitrust laws make it legally very difficult for hospitals to adopt these strategies. As mentioned earlier, several managed care companies have adopted the idea of global pricing, especially for cardiac services. These contracts are excellent vehicles to begin risk-sharing relationships. Health Care Financing Administration has plans to continue its efforts to expand the current global payment demonstration plans. The expansion will provide hospitals and some physicians with these opportunities.

A broader issue is also raised by this example. A global pricing strategy addresses the need to merge the fiduciary interests of interdependent provider components: the physician and the hospital. What it leaves unaltered is the incentive to use the system and, with a per case discount, there is the danger that such a reimbursement system could incent cardiologist and cardiovascular surgeons to access the system even more. As an example, the Rand Corporation has embarked on studies of carotid endarterectomies and coronary artery bypass procedures. The need for these procedures was assessed, given the outcome, and in only 36 percent and 56 percent, respectively, of the cases studied was the need unequivocally appropriate.[1]

If discounted arrangements can set the stage for over-utilization, then capitation creates the potential for under-utilization. What is needed is a reimbursement scheme that puts the hospital and physicians at joint risk for cost and quality, but remains incentive-neutral. Perhaps then cardiologists and cardiovascular surgeons would be conditioned to consider a behavioral modification program for lifestyle change as an alternative to surgery. In order for meaningful and lasting efforts to be made possible, financial incentives and overall objectives for service utilization must be aligned for hospitals and physicians.

Hospitals and physicians who want to remain competitive in the future must recognize that it is essential they find avenues to accept risk-sharing relationships. What we have described here is only one model. There are many other creative mechanisms being developed as the healthcare industry evolves toward a value-oriented delivery system.

ENDNOTES

1. McCune, Walker S. "Watching Practice Patterns Change," *Southern Hospitals* (January/February 1992), p. 14.

10 CHAPTER

Outcomes Tracking and Monitoring*

We need to bridge the gap between knowledge of what produces desirable outcomes within a particular healthcare practice and the information needed to generalize about that knowledge to and from similar practice systems. Often when examining outcomes, information related to the system of a healthcare practice context may be incomplete or missing. This chapter is not a call for an extensive retrospective organizational review to develop a system for tracking and monitoring outcomes, but a call for developing a healthcare system that offers an *ongoing* critique of itself and continuously assesses its progress toward desired outcomes.

Of critical importance is the realization that *the processes used to achieve outcomes may not be obvious* and may not have been examined by the organization in the past. As important as outcome measurement is, real effort is needed to develop systems that not only focus on outcomes of importance, but also on the realities of the processes at play behind those outcomes. The purpose of this chapter is to provide an overview of one approach to outcomes tracking and monitoring that looks at both.

---

*This chapter is contributed by Tom Cook, PhD. Tom Cook is a nurse who has worked extensively within healthcare organizations including clinics, for 30 years. In 1994 he received his PhD in policy development and program evaluation from Vanderbilt University, where he currently teaches and does research within community systems.

The operational strategies of outcome management itself are multifaceted. The strategies include:

- Identifying the resources directed toward outcomes and the tools used to gather the data on those outcomes.
- Focusing primary on patients/clients.
- Developing and applying guidelines to groups of patients/clients whose care, while similar, is managed by multiple provider groups.

The strategies also include managing providers who have not always seen themselves as members of a team but rather as independent professionals. These tasks of outcome measurement itself are daunting and complex.

"The secret of medical management lies in the control of the patient care process."[1] Control of the patient care process is necessary if the organization is to be effective and efficient. The medical care organization that is able to work directly with managing patient care will have more control over its production process. Market intelligence means understanding the need to focus on outcomes and at the same time being aware of the processes needed to achieve them. While these processes can be reduced to a conceptual formula, or model, that formula is not the same for each outcome. It is important for the reader to individualize the framework offered here into a plan that matches his or her unique environment, set of players, and program outcomes.

WHAT IS "THE MODEL "?

The model is a framework, a graphic which depicts the elements associated with the healthcare program(s) for which you are responsible. The model helps us visualize the components that lead to outcomes. It also helps us see how the outputs from one phase of the process become the inputs in another phase. The model varies from one organization to another. Some of the questions upon which the model varies include: Is the institution a hospital or an HMO/PPO? Is the environment urban or rural? Who are the populations served by your program? Who are the providers? These issues will have a direct effect on the components and processes of the system model you are developing. Furthermore, how do the model's elements lead to outcomes? What outcomes are of interest to the organization: satisfaction, quality of life, costs, and so on? Will one outcome serve as a proxy for other outcomes? What effect does one outcome have on another outcome? Within the model, what are the key elements in patient and provider processes and how are they linked?

Include inputs or outcomes that impact the organization's outcomes but are not part of the organizational structure.

THE THEORY BEHIND THE MODEL

The program's theory is a map of how expected events, elements, or components are linked within the system or organization. It describes the usual way in which often disparate elements link together in the expected order that lead to specific desired outcomes. It is important to identify the theory of how components are related before measuring outcomes. The theory can be conceptualized in rough blocks as you start, and in more formal frameworks as you proceed. The theory describes how the pieces of the program model work or should work together to achieve desired outcomes. Is the theory shared by the program or organization's stakeholders?

BEFORE YOU BEGIN

Determine why you want to monitor or track outcomes and how you will use the information. Identify what you will assess and, in some detail, which program outcomes you are interested in knowing. Will you use a forward or backward strategy to develop a flowsheet on the outcomes of interest? Based on the assessment, present a practical tool set, or plan, for proceeding with the process of outcomes tracking and monitoring. What does the model look like? How large is the overall system to be managed? What are its components? What is the program's "theory"? How well-integrated is the system (how well does your system relate to the larger organization)? Do you provide primary care management and disease state management systems (with and without practice guidelines), as well as a demand management system? Do case managers integrate treatment decisions? Are any of the providers cross-trained? Who are the customers? Are they both internal business people and providers, representatives of the payor segment, and the community at large, as well as governmental (regulatory), legal (antitrust), and individual patients/clients (both adult and pediatric)? What minority groups are being served? What are the demographics of the organization and of the consumers? Are any of these groups already joined as PHOs, physician–hospital organizations or the like? How much of the system is capitated? What sort of information systems and databases already exist? Databases provide data upfront so that you can evaluate and validate outcomes. Are there information systems that support collaboration between sites, providers, clients, and programs? To what extent do the system's components have a shared constancy of purpose?

DESIGNING SYSTEMS

The mode of monitoring you choose depends on the purpose, the people, and the organization. Planning for outcome monitoring includes an understanding of the inputs and processes at work within each input, as well as the processes at work when one input is linked to another input (collaborative work). It is the people and the product and the components of the overall system that must be understood.

Outcomes Tracking

A focus on outcomes measurement is a relatively new phenomenon in healthcare. Conceptually, outcomes management is healthcare research development. It is recognized that outcomes for similar health problems are achieved using a variety of resources.[2] The medical literature reflects diverse patterns of medical practice for the same illness.[3] Such variation in practice may negatively affect the quality of care as well as its costs. Outcome measurement is both an activity of outside accrediting agencies and a concern of a healthcare organization's internal management. Specifically, the outcomes of interest include clinical outcomes for a specific illness, a client's functional activities in terms of activities of daily living, including mental and emotional well-being, the client's satisfaction with the care received, and, importantly, its cost.

Healthcare organizations whose outcomes are measured externally are increasingly interested in knowing and improving their own outcomes before accrediting agencies challenge the healthcare organization's ability to provide care and be reimbursed for same.

Organizations interested in measuring targeted outcomes typically engage in the following activities:

- Identify which outcomes you are interested in.
- Locate tools to measure those outcomes (well constructed measures are out there).
- Measure outcomes in both the aggregate and in subgroup levels.
- Identify outliers and system weaknesses.
- Take corrective actions.

Today's healthcare outcome manager not only wants to know if an outcome is present in a population or not, but to what extent is it present or absent. What is the outcome most frequently "in line" and which is most inconsistent with the organization's mission and survival: clinical outcome in a diagnostic category, functional status, client or provider satisfaction, or costs? While costs are often the pressing concern, they frequently follow standardization of elements in clinical practice, optional functional status, and moderately good levels of client satisfaction. Effective outcome tracking is also interested in the processes associated with those outcomes.

Ultimately, the effective healthcare organization will link the systems tracking interests as well as monitoring the processes associated with those outcomes. What the organization needs to understand about its outcomes is both the actual measurement of those outcomes and the knowledge of the factors/processes influencing those outcomes, that is, organizational support and use of resources.

System Thinking

Information on outcomes leads you back into the processes used to achieve those clinical results. Monitoring outcomes is the biggest challenge in healthcare management today. The best outcome tracking system plans arrived at in any healthcare environment become useless if no one does anything with them. We want to be sure we are gathering information on the outcomes themselves and not on some artifact associated with how, when, and where the outcome is actually measured. Even if input on desired outcomes was gathered inclusively using a consensus-building process or using a focus group approach, the early task in monitoring is to be sure everyone is aware and knows the decisions made on what outcomes would be tracked, when they would be measured, and what tools would be used to measure those outcomes.

An essential first step in monitoring or measuring processes is the identification of those processes. Identification includes all of the various components of the system that produces the outcomes the organization is interested in. Put a label on each component. Once you have named it, describe the purpose of that component or element. Identify the linkages between components (how input from one element is used to become an output for the element you are working on). The model and theory work suggested earlier is a useful place to begin identifying these elements and processes. You may rename the elements later on, but for now you are trying to illuminate the structure and processes you will measure which, until now, were rather vague. These are the elements and processes that produce the outcomes you already know and are interested in. Let's remember that the reason you are engaged in this activity is to more completely understand the ways outcomes are achieved in your healthcare endeavor.

Once you've identified the components, pull them apart. One approach to exploring the processes is to develop a flowchart. A flowchart is a roadmap, picture, or schematic representation of the steps used to produce a product. The concept of flowcharting is borrowed from the field of engineering. Creating a flowchart requires working with the various people who work in and are responsible for each of the components of the organization. Further, the flowchart depicts methods and materials used (what, when, where, how) to produce a product. You may be able to do this at a larger meeting or working with two to three individuals at a time.

While constructing this chart or roadmap, it is critical that you chart the way the system *should* work. Blame, negative evaluations, and so forth, will not be useful at this point. To do this you must have the right players—those who actually know—not just those who should know. You need only enough information to understand the component itself and the processes used to achieve their "product." List out the steps in a process and number them. Numbering the steps amplifies the processes at work. Once you have done this, you have a document which should reflect the way the program or organization should work. (Decide later how best to address each of the problem areas.) Develop a flowchart for each of the elements. Each element or component has a start and stop point—many elements are dependent on previous elements while others work simultaneously. Once you've constructed these flowcharts, draw them out and put them up on a wall. Invite everyone connected with the outcomes and processes you depicted to review them. You want them to be as accurate as possible.

Your flowchart will look something like the example in Figure 10-1.

FIGURE 10-1

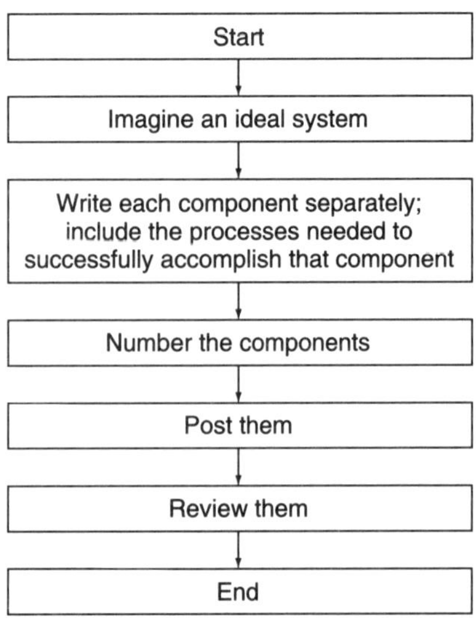

The flowchart may be as brief as one-to-two pages, or as many as 20 in length. The length of the chart depends on the number of components and details of the processes associated with your program and organization.

CONCLUSION

The information derived from systematically approaching outcomes and their processes will be invaluable to your organization. The specifics detailing what your program looks like (the model) and how it works (the theory) will make your tracking and monitoring work more concrete. Not only will you derive data on what works and what doesn't work (outcomes). You will also have ample information on processes associated with outcomes you want to reinforce, as well as on processes that need correction. The strength of this approach needs further refinement in practice. This chapter has attempted to encourage managers who work on broad programs associated with outcome measurement and those who work on more isolated elements of a healthcare program to link their outcomes with the processes that create them.[4]

ENDNOTES

1. Rohrer, J. E. (1989). "The Secret of Medical Management." *Health Care Management Review,* vol. 14, p. 7–13.
2. Wennberg, J. E., Freeman, J. L., Culp, W. J. "Are Hospital Services Rationed in New Haven or Overutilized in Boston?" *Lancet,* 1, 1185–90.
3. Roper, W. L., Windenwerder, W., Hackbarth, G. M., Krakauer, J. (1988). "Effectiveness in Health Care: An Initiative to Evaluate and Improve Medical Practice," *The New England Journal of Medicine,* vol. 319, no. 18 (1988), pp. 1197–1702.
4. Batalden, P. B., and Ucton, T. W. "Knowledge for the Leadership of Continual Improvement in Healthcare," in Robert J. Taylor (ed.), *Manual of Health Services Management.*

REFERENCES

Batalden, P. B., Nelson, E. T., Roberts, J. S. (1994). "Linking Outcomes Measurement to Continual Improvement: The Serial 'V' Way of Thinking About Improving Clinical Care," *Journal of Quality Improvement,* vol. 20 no. 4 (1994).

Bolmon, L. G., and Deal, T. E. *Reframing Organizations.* San Fransico: Jossey-Bass, (1991).

Cordray, D. S. "Prospective Evaluation Syntheses." In Wulker, M. and Derks, J. (eds.), *Rekenschap: evaluatie-ouderzoek in Nederland, de stand van zaken.* Utrecht, Netherlands.

Lipsey, M. W., and Pollard, J. A. (1989). "Driving Toward Theory in Program Evaluation: More Models to Choose From," *Evaluation and Program Planning,* vol. 12 (1989), pp. 317–328.

Spitzer-Lehmann, R. (1994). *Nursing Management Desk Reference*. W. B. Saunders Company (1994).

PART FOUR

CREATING A NEW DELIVERY SYSTEM

11 CHAPTER

Owning a Continuum of Care

CUSTOMIZING THE DELIVERY SYSTEM

As providers complete the transition to managed care, they are functioning in a much more competitive environment. Health systems that emerge as the center point of evolving competitive networks will be differentiated by their ability to coherently link together health professionals, services, products, technology, and information. In other words, they will operationalize the concept of a continuum of care.

Developing a continuum of care is a complex process. Building the infrastructure takes people, systems, and resources. To pay off, the design process must be intensely market sensitive. Continuums of care that succeed and create value in this new managed competition environment will bring to the market a spectrum of care that mirrors local market needs.

Once again, local market data is the rubric for success. The crux of the process is understanding demand scenarios. In order to be competitive, health systems will need to have a deep understanding of market features. (See Table 11–1.)

This is not a case of "if you build it, they will come." Both the intermediary customer, that is, the payor, and the end-user, that is, the patient consumer, should set the standards for the array of customer-centered services to be included. As described in Chapter 6, quantitative health status analysis combined with qualitative profiles of perceived needs can provide

TABLE 11–1

Market Features

- Target Geography/community
- Population size & growth forecast
- Population % over 65
- Health status and perceived needs
- Current and projected manpower ratios
- Payor market share (in covered lives)
  - Traditional
  - Managed care
  - Medicare and other
- Growth rate for managed care
- Hospital use rates
- Number of admissions by payor category
  - Forecasted number and size of new payor contracts
  - Forecasted number and size of direct contracts with employers
- Number of admissions per physician
- Outpatient volume per physician
- Outpatient visits per department/clinic
- Emergency room visits
- Number of admissions from ER
- Volume % of Self-Pay "Retail" Activity in Wellness, Health Promotion, and complementary therapy arenas

an overview of the end-user's needs and wants. With this base of data in hand, a process of obtaining deep market intelligence from the payor should ensue. (See Tables 11–2 and 11–3.)

The goal of customizing a delivery system is to make sure that all customers get exactly what they want. Please note that identified areas of need may be broader than a profile of wants. For instance, a high percentage of risk factors may indicate a need for health promotions and education, but if the payor is not willing to pay for it or the individual consumer is not concerned, then those in the business of health services delivery will probably not give a lot of attention to the health promotion component of a continuum of care.

As long as reimbursement is contingent on service utilization, providers will have a hard time justifying the development of such socially responsible services. As reimbursement shifts more and more towards capitation, however, providers will be incented to have a continuum of care that addresses needs as forcefully as it does wants. When a health system

TABLE 11–2

Market Intelligence:
Managed Care Company Payors

- Current managed care products
- Premiums charged
- Percent of contracts in various payment plans
- Number of covered lives in each type of plan
- Providers approved for various panels
- Premium dollar distribution
- Primary employers under contract
- Plans for expanding market share
- Method of utilization management
- Receptivity to relinquishing UM/QA functions to a new, integrated entity
- Purchase criteria: customer satisfaction and importance
- Major competitors
- Critical success factors
- Perception of local provider's cost quality positions
- Level of interest in contracting with integrated entity
- Level of interest in health promotion and wellness products

becomes responsible for the health status of a base of covered lives, the continuum of care considers the value of a full spectrum of well and sick care, not just the profit and loss incurred as a result of an episode of illness or injury.

FROM BIRTH TO BURIAL

The health status of a community depends on the makeup of the population. Age, sex, and genetics combine with lifestyle and behavioral choices to create a portfolio of risk factors. When attempting to impact the health status and corresponding utilization behaviors of a base of covered lives, health services providers are advised to first concentrate on clinical interventions that have the potential to alter the path of chronic diseases. Consequently, when designing a continuum of care, a provider organization can consider expanding the thrust of certain acute care services to include an emphasis of health promotion and immediately preview a return on investment. Cardiac rehabilitation programs, heart attack risk and breast health screening services, and telemedicine consults for complicated cases are examples of ways a continuum of care can be expanded.

TABLE 11–3

Market Intelligence:
Self-Insured Employers

- Local areas of operation and number of employees
- Present healthcare plan alternatives
- Recent changes in healthcare plans
- Importance of managed care today, and in five years
- Current average annual healthcare cost per covered employee
- Rate of healthcare cost increase during past five years
- Level of interest in health promotion and wellness products
- Willingness to incent for lifestyle changes
- Total healthcare cost as a percentage of profits
- Satisfaction with value provided by healthcare dollars
- Purchase criteria for health plans, satisfaction, and importance
- Definition of healthcare quality
- Current measures of outcomes/quality or utilization
- Interest in direct contracting
- Perception of provider organization

It *almost* makes logical sense for providers to focus only on expanding their existing service mix. However, when one factors in the negative financial impact of cost shifting, then suddenly pre-natal care and elder-care services move back onto the priority list. The result is that the delivery of healthcare service from early intervention to assisted living to long-term care all fall back under the business umbrella of health services delivery.

An integrated delivery system must develop a continuum of care that will respond to health needs occurring across the incumbent dimensions of life. These are:

1. *Preventive Medicine, Health Promotion, and Wellness*
   a. Community health status management
   b. Worksite health promotion
2. *Community-oriented Primary Care*
   a. Family practice
   b. Pediatrics
   c. Women's health
   d. Sports medicine
3. *Acute and Sub-acute Care*
4. *Chronic Disease Management*

5. *Elder Care*
   a. Healthy aging
   b. Alzheimer's disease and senile dementia
   c. Assisted living
   d. Long-term care
6. *Dying*

A continuum of care should entwine the following components of a delivery matrix:

- Outreach education, health promotion, and screening programs.
- Clinical health professionals; emphasis on primary care providers.
- Accessible ambulatory care settings.
- Ancillary service, that is, laboratory, X ray, and so forth.
- Mental healthcare/psychosocial services.
- Behavioral medicine.
- Worker's compensation care.
- Pharmacy services, including infusion care.
- Acute care facilities.
- Advanced technology and state-of-the-art equipment.
- Home healthcare.
- Rehabilitation services.
- Assisted living programs.
- Long-term care facilities.
- Hospice.
- Communications and marketing programs.

A health system will not want to give each component equal weight. Where resources are concentrated will correspond to where the dollars are, that is, who is paying and what are the margins for profitability? Anticipated shifts in reimbursement may move a low revenue service up the list if it has the potential to impact utilization in a way that will correspond to incentives.

As in the collaborative model for community health, the health system's role may be to analyze the data and create an architectural plan for the continuum (see Chapter 13). It may be cost efficient—and better business—for the health system to concentrate on its provider capabilities and outsource certain functions. Still, the opportunity to secure a competitive advantage pivots around a shared infrastructure, particularly information systems capabilities.

The keys to designing a continuum of care that will meet the needs of a population across its lifespan while also working to lock in a competitive presence will be:

- Using local market data to create the blueprint for design.
- A spectrum of care that links clinicians, programs, and services.
- An understanding of the potential for replacement revenue that will color business decisions associated with the choice between R&D investments, loss leaders, and outsourcing.
- A centralized medical record or patient information repository that resides within the health system.
- A commitment to use outcomes tracking to add density to those programs and services that are having an impact while weeding out the ones that are not.

A NEW DELIVERY SYSTEM

Access is a pivotal issue in healthcare reform. In an era of capitation, access to appropriate care and the need for behavioral medicine become priorities. The need to impact utilization is fostering innovative approaches to getting to the end-user. Within the industry, we are already seeing some unique methods for provider organizations to meet the consumers where they are, instead of waiting for the consumers to come to them.

No one will deny that the new business of healthcare revolves around outpatient care. Satellite primary care clinics are very real evidence of this phenomenon. Here are a few more examples of moving beyond hospital walls to deliver care. Healthcare has gotten mobile. We now have sophisticated diagnostic equipment—mobile cardiac catheterization units, mammography service, and fully equipped primary care "doc-in-the-boxes"—moving around from parking lot to parking lot. Most healthy people will not take time to come in for screening but many will use the services that come to them. Convenience and quality are the keys.

Worksite wellness has also become a new area of growth. Frustrated employers no longer want to wait and see what it will cost them to treat their employees. Instead, they want to avoid the bill altogether by avoiding the episode of illness or injury in the first place. Consequently, large employers are developing on-site clinics staffed by a primary care health professional. This person is usually an RN, NP, or MD—skilled in prevention, education, and triage.

Have you been to the mall lately? Large health systems are setting up booths for breast health screening and women's services. This is a new competitive front. Still, this may not be a long-lasting strategy. Recent changes in the retail industry may be applicable in healthcare. For example, French Silks, a retail clothing manufacturer that makes high-end silk fabric ready-to-wear for women, used to distribute its products through department stores like Macy's and I. Magnin. After years of success with this strategy, French Silks discovered its profit margins were shrinking. The problem? Women are too busy to go in the malls and spend days shopping. The new strategy? Home trunk shows. By targeting the high-end customer, understanding her needs, and going to where she already is, the company has realized exponential sales growth.

Dell Computer is another example of a company that focused on delivery and achieved radical success. Michael Dell was a college student in Austin, Texas, when he saw a chance to undercut IBM and Compaq in the personal computer business. His strategy? Direct contracting. Dell built to order and sold to customers directly. He aggressively cut the middleman out of the process, effectively listened to the end-user, and provided high-quality, user-friendly products.

What is the application for healthcare? How can providers cut out the third-party administrators and managed care organizations and work directly with the end-user? How do providers get face-to-face with the patient consumer? Go to where they work, live, eat, play, and worship.

Some HMOs are sending out case workers to go into new enrollees' homes. Their purpose is to access lifestyle conditions that impact health choices. Case workers conduct a personal interview, look in the refrigerator, scan the medicine chest, and check the stairs and walkways for ease of access. They look at the bathtub and railing. They immediately begin to work with the individual to develop a plan to address any health risk behaviors or environmental hazards. The theory: It is less costly to fix a stairwell than to mend a broken hip.

In most communities, churches have always been a center point for personal growth or improvement. Some health systems are finding churches to be excellent distribution centers for health education materials. In addition, parish nurse programs reach beyond the hospital walls, touch the patients, but do not drive up the cost of care.

School-based clinics are also increasing in number. Many communities are working with their local hospitals to impact the incidence of such concerns as teen pregnancy and substance abuse. Providers chip in with staff and resources as much out of concern as out of an awareness of the bottom line result of cost shifting.

Finally, the Cancer Consortium is trying an innovative approach. Targeting a high-risk African American population, the outreach coordinators surveyed to determine where they might best "capture" this group. Their findings indicated two prime opportunities: the church and beauty/barber shops. With creative energy, the beauticians and barbers were mobilized into a prevention program, health education materials were distributed through their shops, and one-on-one encouragement supported the content of written materials.

A new delivery system is emerging now. Protecting inpatient beds is like spitting into the wind. We need to go beyond the hospital walls. The opportunity for growth exists in healthcare that is local, mobile, and flexible.

PATIENT-CENTERED CARE

According to Michael Johns, executive vice president and director of the Woodruff Health Sciences Center and CEO of the Emory System of Healthcare, "The future of healthcare is going to be centered around teamwork and teams of professionals working together, delivering the best quality of healthcare for the best price by allowing the professional best able to deliver the services to do so." At Johns Hopkins, Johns encouraged joint appointments among medical, public health, and nursing faculty, and was involved in bringing nursing into the clinical practice plan.[1]

If the patient is the hub, then all caregivers are the spokes of the wheel. For the wheel to turn, patient education, individual responsibility, and multidisciplinary approaches must be integrated. The new vehicle will move a delivery system into an emerging paradigm of health.

Cross-training and multidisciplinary health team approaches are, in themselves, the subject for a book. Here are some of the core concepts:

- *Access is Key.* Healthcare must be decentralized; ancillary services must go to the patient, not the other way around.
- *Continuous Care is Cheaper.* When multidisciplinary teams of health professionals work together, share information, and jointly manage patient care, the benefits include less duplication, more efficient coordination of services, and improved outcomes information. Healthcare services can be assessed in relation to the impact on a patient's overall health rather than only the treatment of symptoms.
- *Health professionals enjoy serving the patient.* In their book, *Patient-Focused Healing,* Nancy Moore and Henrietta Komras report:

> Patient-focused restructuring results in measurable improvement in satisfaction for physicians and other staff. . . . Typically, nursing turnover in a hospital's patient-focused care unit is the lowest of any of the units. Lower turnover has a significant cost benefit because it costs $1,000 on average, to orient a new nurse. . . . Physicians report increased satisfaction based on significant improvement in nursing care and in the quality of test results, reduced turnaround time, reduced paperwork, and increased efficiency.[2]

Just as importantly, physicians report that they resent managed care and its punitive approach to utilization review. Many cry loudly that "I am responsible to my patient and my ethics, not to a voice at the end of a 1–800 pre-certification phone number." Physicians feel their primary role is to serve as the patient's advocate. Putting the patient at the center of the delivery system brings the physician's role back into focus.

- *Patients like being the center of attention.* Intense market competition means that all providers must be accountable not only for patient outcomes but also for patient experiences. At Bishop Clarkson Memorial Hospital in Omaha, Nebraska, hospital administrators found that in the patient-focused units patient perception of nursing care, hospital environment, and concern for the patient rose from the 13th to the 92nd percentile in Gallup-SRI patient satisfaction surveys. This is certainly a significant difference. At the same time, length of stay decreased by 10 percent. Satisfaction levels were 13 percent to 17 percent higher on these units than on conventional units.[3]

Patient-centered care is a multifaceted phenomenon. The Fetzer Institute and the Pew Health Professions Commission convened a task force to explore the many dimensions of relationship-centered care. The following interrelated relationships are essential within a reformed system of healthcare. Each involves a unique set of tasks and responsibilities.

- *The patient–practitioner relationship:* The work of the practitioner within this relationship includes organizing information about the patient and his or her care; providing comprehensive biomedical care; critically reflecting on practice to increase self-awareness; practicing from a caring, healing ethic and perspective that seeks to preserve the dignity and integrity of the patient and the patient's family; listening and communicating openly and effectively; seeking to eliminate abuses arising from power inequalities with regard to race, sex, education, occupation, and socioeconomic status; encouraging the active collaboration of the patient and family in decision-making, care and treatment; and promoting health and preventing illness in the individual and family.
- *The community–practitioner relationship:* The community is a central context for health and human development which has the potential for producing injury or healing. Individuals simultaneously belong to multiple communities formed by neighborhoods, cultures, work groups, or circumstances. As an example of the latter situation, a person hospitalized for an extended period of time becomes part of

the hospital community. Through their relationships with—and memberships in—various communities, practitioners are advocates and workers for health policy. They need to understand the broad social, political, cultural, economic, and political determinants of health; recognize and act in accordance with the values, norms, social, and health concerns of the community; develop a sense of community responsibility; be able to recognize harmful elements within the community; and work to improve the health of the community and change harmful aspects of the community.

- *The practitioner–practitioner relationship*: Effective, empathic care requires a community of practitioners who commit themselves to working together to serve the complex matrix of individuals' needs in health and illness. Relationships among practitioners include those within or across disciplines, and those between practitioners and practitioners-in-training. These relationships require teamwork, shared values, learning from and making use of the expertise of others, helping others learn and develop, integrating services at individual and systems levels, and setting aside issues of specialism, hierarchy, and privilege. Such relationships serve the needs of practitioners as well as patients: Building communities enables healthcare providers to care for one another and to give and receive the support and encouragement that produces personal and professional maturation and more effective patient care.[4]

THE MAKE-OR-BUY DECISION

Health systems that want to dominate a market will need to find a way to "own" the continuum of care. This does not mean that the health system has to add all the above-listed components of a continuum into its mix of services and products. What is does mean is, if the market demand exists, then the health system will need to know where to go to get what it lacks in order to present itself as a one-stop shop. The option is to make or buy.

The decision of whether to make or buy is really one of inventory management. The costs associated with lost business is a tradeoff with the costs associated with developing customer-centered services that are not identifiable profit centers. The challenge is to simultaneously add new service lines, achieve operational efficiencies, meet purchasing objectives, and generate enough revenue to support the integration process. The good news is that there are alternatives. Fostering cooperative arrangements with other providers or contracting with a vendor are two options for responding to market demand in a costly and timely manner.

Integration sets the stage for the design of a delivery system that will have the scope and capacity to respond to local market needs. Integration allows for operating models that deliver a much broader and deeper level of services and functional support. An integrated system's continuum of care is created by tailoring a mix of services and customizing products. If this means acting as a broker to obtain these services and products from network partners and outside vendors, then individual assets can remain intact for as long as it is economically justifiable to do so.

Some examples where *buying* (or *renting*) makes sense include:

- Management services organizations (MSOs).
- Utilization management (UM).
- Home healthcare and home infusion services.
- Mail-order pharmacy businesses.
- Wellness programs.
- Complementary medicine.
- Hospice care.
- Marketing and communications functions.

The formula for success for health systems and provider organizations is changing dramatically. Hospitals and physicians must concentrate on the part of the continuum of care that is critical for their own success. To do this effectively requires a lot of energy as well as deep resources of capital and information technologies. Making the transition into a new operating environment will not leave a lot of anything—time or money—left over.

Deciding whether to make or buy comes down to economics. If the health system sees the opportunity for replacement revenue, or if it determines that the integration of a specific component will enhance its efficiency and performance under a capitated system of reimbursement, then opting to "make" is sensible. If, however, the return investment is not easily projected, then the health system should factor developmental cost estimates into the computation of overhead budgets. This kind of financial evaluation helps determine the desirability of choosing the option to buy (or rent).

Savvy administrators are already putting this st[illegible] to work and are joint-venturing with home health agencies, practi[illegible]ent service organizations, mail-order pharmacy companies, an[illegible] of critical importance that is n[illegible]ommonly outsource[illegible]tention, is *marketing*.

As the playing [illegible]r choice will impact competitive [illegible] efforts funnel into the need for br[illegible] They are indirect revenue producers; success is most often measured in terms of increased market share. Because consumer education will become increasingly important as managed care markets mature, marketing and communications strategy is an elemental part of a continuum. The question is: Does this function need to reside within the hospital?

According to Bressler and Yauger, an Atlanta-based healthcare company, the answer is NO! To support their response they provide a financial analysis comparing the cost of departmental operations versus the cost of contracting with a vendor to get what is needed.

The example begins with a 276-bed med-surg community hospital located in suburban Virginia. Hospital leaders believed in the power of consistent, well-directed marketing efforts and had made the commitment to the resources necessary for intensive image enhancement and subsequent product-specific marketing and advertising efforts.

As time passed, hospital budget problems arose and intense scrutiny had to be applied to every expense category. Marketing efforts had been very successful in that positive market share trends were in play. There was a committed desire not to back away from the gains that had been made. Executives wanted to keep their plans in force but internal resources were scarce. The hospital considered its options and made the strategic decision to outsource this critical function. The contract contained the following highlights:

- The Director of Marketing at the hospital was placed on the management company's payroll. This resulted in the immediate decrease of one FTE with the added benefit of keeping a valuable and talented employee.
- There were other employees in the marketing department including a secretary, a physician referral coordinator, a corporate services sales representative, a patient advocate, and a public relations assistant. The hospital had the option of transferring the salaries of these employees to the management company but elected to keep them on the hospital payroll.
- The budget was broken into five main categories: salaries, production, media, public relations, and other. The "other" category contained such items as printing and office supplies.
- The hospital maintained a centralized approach to budgeting marketing dollars in which all dollars spent throughout the institution were allocated and expensed through the marketing budget. Each year the budget process involved extensive planning sessions with other department heads to estimate their marketing dollars and resource requirements for the year.

The marketing function was effectively interconnected within the hospital infrastructure. The hospital retained control of the dollars spent by approving an annual budget and requiring approval for any amounts not accounted for in the budget. Monthly meetings and quarterly planning sessions between the hospital CEO and management company principals kept all informed of appropriate issues and allowed for alteration of spending patterns and the like.

The management fee was based on the production, public relations, and other budget categories. The amount charged was based upon a percentage of each budget and invoiced at a flat rate on a monthly basis. The management company billed the hospital at net for travel, printing, original or stock photography/illustration, broadcast production, and market research. Negotiated rates were charged for media time and space. As a result of this subcontract, or "buy" agreement, the hospital's total dollars for marketing services that had previously been produced in-house *decreased immediately by nearly 30 percent.* Even without supporting the full scope of interval marketing functions, the hospital was able to provide full-service marketing that could impact consumer choice.

Health systems need to look to the local market to find partners to be responsible for secondary processes. The output should be a continuum of care that has market value and is flexible in its delivery. The result can be a win–win. When providers enter into joint ventures or partnerships to create continuums of care, they must share a sense of accountability for performance and outcomes even when they do not have the same bottom line. (See Table 11–4.)

TABLE 11–4

Criteria for Choosing Partners

A potential partner:

- Has a shared vision.
- Has a congruent philosophy and approach.
- Is available at local market level.
- Demonstrates operational efficiency.
- Has the potential—and the willingness—to participate in data capture and contribute to relational databases.
- Understands the need to interconnect across functions in order to provide seamless care.
- Recognizes that there is shared accountability for provider performance and outcomes tracking.

RECOGNIZING THE R&D PAYOFF

According to a *Business Week* survey, American major industry spent about $70 billion for research and development (R&D) in 1990.[5] The amount of money spent on R&D by U.S. businesses seems like an enormous amount, yet when it is expressed as a percentage of gross national product (GNP), the United States is actually lagging behind other countries. While U.S. R&D expenditures equaled 1.8 percent of its GNP in the same year Japan's R&D expenditures equaled 2.8 percent and West Germany's amounted to 2.6 percent of their respective GNPs.[6]

Investments in R&D appear to pay off. The Japanese have more than doubled the number of patents they have received for electronics technology since the mid–1970s and they license their patents more often than do companies in the United States. In 1990, the top three recipients of U.S. patents were in Japanese companies: Canon, Hitachi, and Toshiba. Only three U.S. companies were in the top 10: General Electric, U.S. Philips, and IBM.[7]

As we work to redefine the healthcare industry, we need research and development to prepare for the sweeping changes that will accompany its implementation. I am convinced that R&D is the key to forging competitive success in a tumultuous environment. Instead of investing time and dollars to maintain the status quo, emerging industry leaders are commanding greater market share by listening to the customer, understanding the local marketplace, and being the first to respond with what the customer expects in a continuum of care.

More and more hospital and health system administrators are waking up to the fact that the survival of their organization—and their own professional tenure—will be determined by how well they interpret market forces and how quickly they cross the threshold between economic competition and a new industrial order. Of course if you ask most hospital administrators today, they will say they are so stressed trying to operate under the increasing crunch of managed care reimbursement that they would have a hard time finding the funds for innovative trial and error exercises. As pressure on earnings intensifies, there are fewer dollars available for what we call R&D. The challenge becomes how to strategically target all activities so as to minimize risk and maximize the "bang for the buck." Again, the answer is first to grasp the importance of *identifying local marketplace needs* and then *to consider the cost of lost opportunities.*

In the 1980s, the healthcare industry greedily created demand, so it was easy—even incredibly comfortable—to sit back and watch competitors bring new products and services to the market. You could observe their process for market entry, learn from their successes and, more importantly, from their glitches. If it worked, your strategy was to duplicate like crazy because when demand is created, there is always enough business to go around. If it didn't work, on the other hand, they took the hit, not you.

Today, competition for market share has become so intense that no one can relax or "wait and see." If a competitor is the first to expand a continuum of care that more effectively meets a marketplace need, they will be the first to capture new market share and, with increased volume, expand a base for profit. In competitive contracting situations, the "best" continuum wins. Competing providers will be sorted by the success of their R&D efforts.

Research and development can be supported by simulation exercises and actuarial analysis. The goal is to ask the question "What if we did *x?*" and then simulate the environment in which the action would occur. These forms of strategic modeling can predict economic success or failure; however, they cannot accurately portend the powerful undercurrents of organizational politics. R&D creates a dilemma: You can commit to an intensive process of due diligence for any new idea, you can systematically plan for the launch of new programs and services, but because many of the variables impacting success cannot be quantified, *you can't know until you act—and you have to act to know.*

R&D activities can get messy and laborious if they are not rooted in a cross-functional team approach. Take, for instance, the idea of seamless admitting processes. Sounds good, right? Everyone likes the idea of reducing paperwork, decreasing costs, and eliminating the duplication of services. The suggestion is made to pilot a seamless admitting program with an identified target population, such as AFDC recipients. But no one asked the information systems people if their admitting screens were set up to sort patients in this way. They cannot, and the process goes back to the drawing board for revisions. In this example, it is easy to imagine how much more efficient the development process could have been if, from inception, representatives from all functional components had been represented, that is, admitting, IS, billing, physician offices, finance, patient care services, clinical quality assurance, network development, and anyone else who might be impacted or contribute.

The important point is that investment in research and development represents a cost to a hospital and should therefore be tied to the achievement of some objectives—whether in the short or long term. Thus the primary bases for evaluating the R&D strategy are:

1. Can you afford to invest now to reap a benefit in the distant future?
2. Have the identified objectives been accomplished?
3. Have the results of R&D activities justified the level of investment made?
4. Are current R&D activities still appropriate in light of marketplace developments?

These questions, in effect, define the efficiency, the efficacy, and effectiveness of R&D activities and should be a litmus test for determining how well the vision, marketing, and production objectives mesh.

ENDNOTES

1. "Michael Johns Named Executive Vice President for Health Affairs," *Campus News* Emory University.
2. Moore, Nancy and Henrietta Komras. *Patient-Focused Healing: Integrating Caring and Curing in Health Care,* San Francisco: Jossey-Bass (1993), p. 45.
3. ibid., p. 47.
4. Tresolini, Carol and the Pew Fetzer Task Force. "Health Professions Education and Relationship-Centered Care: Report of the Pew-Fetzer Task Force on Advancing Psychosocial Health Education," p. 11.
5. "The Brakes Go on in R&D," *Business Week* (July 1, 1991), pp. 24–26.
6. "Report Warns of Decline in U.S. Electronics Industry," *The New York Times* (June 9, 1990).
7. "Foreign Investors Get 48% of U.S. Patents," *Research-Technology Management* (July/August 1991), p. 6; Himmelfarb, Philip A. *Survival of the Fittest: New Product Development During the 90s* Englewood Cliffs, NJ: Prentice Hall Professional Publishing (1992), pp. 2–3.

12 CHAPTER

Expanding Your Primary Care Base of Business

If the objectives of healthcare reform are realized, providers will operate in a demand scenario that requires fewer hospital days, ancillary procedures, and requests for technological support. Even with the emerging awareness that yesterday's profit centers are likely to become tomorrow's cost centers, most hospital CEOs are not happy to see empty beds in their facilities. While healthcare decision makers recognize that today's and tomorrow's financial incentives are perversely related, they are struggling to survive the current economic pressures in order to have the resources to invest in new business strategies portending future viability. Expanding a base of primary care business is an immediately doable strategy that can demonstrate a positive bottom-line benefit today, increase market share and contracting leverage tomorrow, and provide a strategic business foothold for the future.

Real-life scenarios provide healthcare decision makers with equations for factoring the revenue impact of shifts in reimbursement and supply and demand. Innovative models now exist within the framework of primary care business for operating structures that can enhance cost and service performance.

THE PHYSICIAN SEAT OF CONTROL

Physicians hold the seat of power in a "reformed" environment. While physicians only receive around 20 percent of healthcare expenditures, their decisions determine approximately 80 percent of healthcare expenditures as they manage the diagnosis, treatment, and care of their patients. It is accepted that the performance of physicians will determine the value in competitive networks as we move from treating illness to managing care and ultimately to managing the health of a population.[1]

As changing incentives associated with inpatient utilization erode the existing delivery system, the physician who most often touches the patient outside the hospital walls becomes the central change agent. This reality has put the primary care physician in the spotlight and served to "up the ante" in terms of his or her market worth.

With physicians as the key component of the distribution system, primary-care anchored multi-specialty groups become the most important component of an aggressive business development strategy. Consequently, competition for physician practice acquisition increases. Networks that have not shored up their stable of local primary care providers will be at risk.

All primary care physicians are aware of their position of power and most are leveraging it for all it is worth. According to the American Medical Association's report entitled *Socioeconomic Characteristics of Medical Practice 1994,* "Although doctors have the best interests of their patients at heart, these undesirable aspects of the profession would not be undertaken without at least some expectation of appropriate economic remuneration." Does it make a difference if the primary care physician practices in a multi-specialty or single specialty healthcare organization? Yes, according to the Medical Group Management Association (MGMA). Its study, *Physician Compensation and Production Survey: 1994 Report,* compiled data on 52 physician and 14 mid-level provider specialties with responses from nearly 23,000 providers in over 1,300 medical practices. Findings include:

- Primary care physicians in multi-specialty practices earn more per year than those in single specialty practices.
- The gap between the compensation levels of primary care physicians in single and multi-specialty practices has narrowed. Family practitioners in multi-specialty groups had a median compensation about $4,500 higher than single specialty groups in 1993, compared to $9,000 the previous year. For pediatricians, the gap narrowed from $13,000 to $1,300.
- Primary care physicians in practices that have high levels of managed care earn more than those in practices with low levels.

There is money to be made from acquiring and managing physician practices. Practice management groups can reap from 10 to 50 percent of pre-tax earnings. Press reports suggest that Caremark International's revenue from managing physician practices soared from $190 million in 1994 to $400 million in 1995.[2] Similarly, PhyCor's 1994 annual report indicated that, for the year, net revenue was $242.5 million, up 45 percent over 1993. This kind of revenue is incredibly seductive, but it does not mean that every hospital and health system needs to take on full responsibility for this function.

If health systems do not have practice management expertise and information systems, they could lose their proverbial shirts. This is a perfect example of a make-or-buy decision scenario. A joint venture with a practice management company can perhaps meet a health system's needs by securing a local primary care base of business, broadening a thrust into new markets, creating a source of replacement revenue, and reducing the financial risk of entering into a whole new business. Of course, health systems will have to give up control and honor that the physician is in the power seat. But which is better: *control or profit?*

WHO'S WHO IN NURSING

Advanced-practice nurses and physician's assistants constitute an evolving middle ground between highly trained physicians and registered nurses:

Nurse practitioners: Can handle about 80% of a primary-care doctor's chores but often specialize. Widely used as front-line providers in managed-care plans. Practicing: 20,700.

Nurse-midwives: Provide full maternity care. Practicing: 2,600.

Clinical nurse specialists: Provide specialized care and case management—cardiology, oncology, etc.—usually in hospitals. Practicing: 11,500.

Nurse-anesthetists: Provide anesthetic services. Being replaced by anesthesiologists, but still sole provider in 49% of hospitals. Practicing: 18,100.

Physician assistants: Provide expanded primary and specialty care—diagnosis, treatment, referral, some prescriptions—under supervision. Practicing: 25,700.

Sources: Alliance for Health Reform; American Academy of Physician Assistants.

NURSE PRACTITIONERS PULL AHEAD*

Nurse practitioner clinics are receiving a lot of attention within the primary care business. Nurse practitioner clinics can withstand economic pressures, choose to face daunting market competitor dynamics, and still remain financially viable. Two key facts differentiate them in the marketplace:

*Contributions to this section were made by Frances K. L. Bushnell, RNC, EDD, MPH.

1. **The nursing model is very competitive**: Nurse practitioners are not as expensive a commodity as are physicians. Anecdotal evidence also indicates they have a customer-intimate advantage. Patients generally choose to access a provider whom they feel will listen. TLC, or patient-focused care as we call it in the 90s, can provide a marketplace advantage and result in *significant market share increases.*
2. **Caring, community outreach, cost efficiency, and contracting strategies** are congruent terms with organizational objectives for business development.

The bottom line is that nurse practitioners can provide primary care at a reduced cost to consumers.[3] Just as importantly, a nurse practitioner clinic may be a new "hook" for enhancing customer intimacy and creating a unique brand identity. Review the following facts and decide for yourself:

- An internal medicine study found that nurse practitioners could be judged to be adequate in dealing with 98 percent of old problems and 85 percent of new problems. Multiple studies have found that the quality of care provided by nurse practitioners was similar to that provided by physicians in a primary care practice.[4]
- Studies demonstrated that the morbidity and mortality of nurse practitioner patients with chronic illness was the same as for those treated by physicians, and patient satisfaction and reduction of disability was better in the nurse practitioner group.[5]
- The components of practice that are related to good outcomes seem to be the following: time spent with each patient, less use of drugs, patient satisfaction, fewer days of hospitalization with chronic conditions, and cost efficiency.
- 57 percent of nurse practitioner employers find that the *extension of health services* is their most significant contribution; another 40 percent considered *improvement in the quality of care* as the most significant effect.[6]
- Physicians who supervise nurse practitioners rate them as good or excellent in the performance of 85–90 percent of tasks in primary care. Nurse practitioners are considered to require less supervision than physician assistants.[7]
- Employers report that they hire nurse practitioners to improve the quality of patient care and to assist or substitute for busy physicians. More than 93 percent of the employers felt the benefits outweigh the costs.[8]

- On average, nursing centers reported that 1,952 individuals were cared for in 1990. Those individuals visited an average of five times. Clients are recruited largely without advertising, but with significant help from professional referrals and word-of-mouth referrals. In fact, word-of-mouth referrals generate over half of all nursing center business, and professional referrals one-third.

The long-term success of the nursing center model will center on the ability to strategically position it in the marketplace and to create around it a type of brand image. Examples of nursing centers that are successfully competing in a managed care arena include Vanderbilt's Vine Street Clinic in Nashville, Tennessee, and Arizona State University College of Nursing's Community Health Services Clinic in Scottsdale, Arizona. It is important to note that in both cases these centers assumed new prominence within a competitive environment as a result of changes in Medicaid regulations.

THE FEMINIZATION OF HEALTHCARE

Captivating a niche market of female healthcare purchasers is another means of adding strength to the nurse practitioner model. Females make about 70 percent more office visits per year to primary care physicians than males. (See Figure 12–1.)

Women drive provider selection decisions for themselves and their families. However you come out on the issue, one thing is certain: The medical establishment is finally becoming more aware of women—as patients

FIGURE 12–1

Doctor Visits by Gender

Visits by Specialty (in millions)

	Females	Males
Family Doctors	133	86
OB/GYN	68	.06*
Internists	56	42
Pediatricians	47	49

*For conditions men/women share, of general prescription.

Source: Dept. of Health and Human Services, National Center for Health Statistics, American Academy of Family Physicians for 1992 (latest available).

and as consumers of family medical care. According to a report by the Boston-based consultancy Marketing to Women, women make 75 percent (some put it at 80–90%) of consumer healthcare decisions.[9] When it comes to influencing market share, women are customers worth cultivating.

More women are turning to nurse-midwives to shepherd them through the birthing process, a trend that must dismay the OB/GYNs who are losing baby business. The number of babies delivered in hospitals by certified nurse-midwives climbed 12 to 15 percent annually between 1990 and 1992, according to the first-ever study of nurse-midwifery practices, released by the New York advocacy group Public Citizen. That added up to nearly 180,000 newborns delivered in hospitals by nurse-midwives in 1992.

Certified nurse-midwives provide a viable alternative to doctors when it comes to childbirth, Public Citizen's report indicates. The study suggests that pregnant women receive more pre- and postnatal care from midwives, more education, and greater emotional support. In addition, going with a nurse-midwife lessens the chance that a cesarean-section will be performed. Women who choose to deliver with a nurse-midwife instead of a physician cite their preference for a high-touch, personalized delivery experience. When TLC (tender loving care) coincides with reduced resource demand, then payors also become new cheerleaders.[10]

Because the nurse practitioner field is still primarily populated by females, the trend of women choosing women is a plus for the NP clinic model. The primary focus of women's health centers has shifted from abortion to mainstream women's healthcare. Even though these centers do *not* focus exclusively on the concerns of menopausal women, they are poised to embrace that priority as the population ages. Their approach is already holistic—from premenstrual syndrome, to cholesterol screening, to breast cancer, to psychological counseling. Adult women's medicine is a growth industry, an area of specialization with a guaranteed clientele—perhaps a specialty all those obstetricians who have left the baby business due to astronomical malpractice insurance might want to consider.[11]

If a health system has not fully considered the nurse practitioner primary care center as a viable alternative to the physician-staffed clinic, then it should. The evidence suggests that this model can offer a cost advantage as well as a leg up on capturing market share.

PREVENTIVE MEDICINE, HEALTH PROMOTION, AND WELLNESS

In July 1993, the *New England Journal of Medicine* reported that the 10 leading causes of death, such as heart disease, cancer and diabetes, are actually secondary to the nine *actual* causes of disease, which include nutrition, lifestyle choices, tobacco use, and alcohol and drug use. The article suggests that all nine "actual" causes are preventable. Similarly, the "Healthy People 2000 Report" of the Department of Health and Human Services states that at least 70 percent of all disease is preventable. This common sense information must be recognized for its importance; it is the market intelligence that is directing the reengineering of the healthcare industry as it is known today.

In the next few years, the focus of healthcare delivery must transit from the treatment of the "leading" causes of death to addressing the "actual" causes of disease. This move from a system based upon the remediation associated with episodic care to one vested in the payoff associated with health status management will largely be addressed outside the acute care institution. The first goal will be to develop and evaluate innovative health and medical programs. The second goal is to evaluate the efficacy of these programs according to their health and cost outcomes. Research must be transferred into what works for the community at the local level.

A model that integrates health promotion and acute care services should be designed to increase individual responsibility for health and well-being while simultaneously reducing demand and cost. Information, education, and access to more natural (and less costly) approaches to self-care will be essential elements for a system committed to facilitating individual and community health improvement. Ultimately, a new and rapidly emerging system of care will *foster demand reduction and individual self-determination.*

Many hospitals have already invested in some form of wellness programs, whether by way of a significant outlay of dollars for bricks and mortar to house a fitness center, or an investment of manpower to staff outreach community education and health screening programs. Until recently, these programs typically have been viewed as goodwill services or limited means of obtaining upstream referrals, *not* as components of an aggressive business development strategy. Today, shifting financial incentives are causing a change in focus and consequently, health promotion/disease prevention programs are receiving new attention and some real impetus for growth.

While emphasizing prevention and health promotion is almost always congruent with a health system's mission, these objectives can get lost in the development of strategy when not enough attention is paid to their potential for contribution to the hospital's profit margin. Too often, hospital administrators have pacified resident health enthusiasts by housing a couple of classes, offering some screening programs, creating a space for some exercise bikes or Stair Masters, and sprinkling some health promotion activities throughout the community. That's nice, but that's not business. When taken seriously, preventive medicine, health promotion, and wellness services can be a source of *real* revenue.

If making money on health promotion seems like a far-fetched idea, learn from those who have been doing it for more than a decade. In 1978, Riverside Health System in Newport News, Virginia, asserted that its wellness initiative was going to be a revenue producer. Riverside's management team was convinced they had to support prevention with dollars, not just rhetoric. The health system invested a substantial amount of money into creating a model that would make the concept tangible. Riverside's commitment to mission *and* margin paid off. In a little more than 10 years, Riverside has recouped its entire $14 million investment. In 1992 alone, the health promotion operation generated $1 million in excess revenues. Riverside has now ventured beyond developing its own programs and has created a licensed product that teaches other hospitals how to develop such centers as the core business of their future healthcare delivery system.[12]

WINNING EMPLOYER CONTRACTS

Most healthcare leaders would agree that healthcare reform has been driven more by large employers than by the federal government. The January 11, 1993, issue of *Business Week*, predicted that medical costs would exceed $900 billion in 1993, with 51.7 percent paid by employers, 33.7 percent by the federal government, and 14.4 percent by the states in Medicare and Medicaid. No wonder employers—large and small alike—are being forced to face the task of appropriate managed care within a global budget plus an emphasis on patient demand reduction through health promotion and disease prevention programs. Within managed care, with a renewed emphasis on demand reduction through health promotion, is the opportunity to create a true healthcare system rather than the current disease management industry.[13]

Financial tensions and a renewed commitment to employee satisfaction are creating fertile ground for innovative approaches to preventive medicine and health promotions. Employers are generally not altruistic when determining where and how to spend their healthcare dollars. They want healthcare plans that reduce the days lost from work, get people back to work in better shape, and lower disability costs. If they consider a package that integrates complementary therapies, employers are demanding increasingly sophisticated means of tracking health and cost outcomes. The emphasis on wellness, health promotion, and improved health outcomes at lower costs can be an advantage.

The link between costs of care and access to services seem so obvious that healthcare reform has become preoccupied with containing costs. The cost-containment imperative has led to massive restructuring in the delivery of physician and hospital services. This response, however, has not been viewed as adequate, as national spending for health has exceeded the rate of growth of the GNP. Anticipated savings have not been squeezed from system changes to give relief to employers, customers, or taxpayers.[14]

Several factors are motivating the large, self-insured employer to demand that primary prevention become an integral component of primary care services, among which are:

- Continuing concern about ongoing increases in healthcare costs and the need for effective interventions before disease or acute episodes occur.
- A growing awareness of the potential cost savings associated with accident prevention, injury control, and stress reduction.
- Increased employee interest in information about improving personal health behaviors.

Offering health promotion and wellness services at the worksite should be a core component in an aggressive strategy for growing primary care business. Making health promotion an integral part of a delivery system requires establishing strong linkages with physicians, inpatient facilities, ancillary services, outpatient care providers, payor representatives, local employers, and individuals.

Instituting preventive services can also create links to potential users of other hospital services. To help hospitals to develop their own programs, the AHA Division of Ambulatory Care, in cooperation with the Preventive Services Committee of the Society for Ambulatory Care Professionals, has developed the new resource, "Prevention Strategies in Ambulatory Care: A Manager's Guide." The guide, published in 1992, provides a concrete, step-by-step process for involving all areas of the hospital in identifying community prevention needs and designing preventive service interventions.[15] The AHA is approaching prevention as if it were a viable new service line.

The good news is that if you've got the product, the customer is ready to buy. More and more employers are analyzing insurance data on treatment costs, placing dollar figures on the loss of productivity due to absenteeism, and determining the average short- and long-term disability payment costs for employees suffering from specific chronic conditions. When confronted with the total cost outlay associated with acute care, employers are more willing to make an equivalent commitment to wellness and prevention.

Suddenly the hospital has an enthusiastic new customer base that is ready and able to contract for health promotion services. The employer's motivation to buy is not soft; it is the potential for significant financial savings that drives them to encourage healthy lifestyles for their workers.[16]

A great example is the Stanford Corporate Health Program of the Stanford University School of Medicine.[17] Since 1984, the goal of this program has been to develop and evaluate innovative medical and health promotion programs in the workplace as an integral part of managed care for both purchasers and providers. Under the direction of Dr. Kenneth R. Pelletier, the research program involves a unique collaboration between the Stanford Center and 21 corporations.

Participating corporations include:

Aetna	
Amdahl	Johnson & Johnson
American Airlines	Kaiser Permanente
ARCO	Levi-Strauss
AT&T	Motorola
Bank of America	Pacific Bell
Blue Shield	San Mateo County
Bristol Meyers Squibb	Shaklee/Yamanouchi
HealthNet	State of California
Hewlett-Packard	Sybase
IBM	Xerox

Among the research and development areas in progress in the Stanford program are:

- Behavioral management of hypertension and coronary heart disease.
- Computer and/or telephone health delivery systems.
- Early cancer screening, especially mammography for women.
- Smoking cessation.
- Health promotion programs to reach minorities, dependents, and retirees.
- Alcohol and substance abuse programs.
- Dietary and nutritional counseling.
- Physical fitness and back saver programs.
- AIDS prevention and policy formation.
- Applications of meditation and relaxation for stress management.
- Reaching small and/or remote worksites.
- Comprehensive program evaluation.

The strength of the program and its increasing customer base is attributed to its emphasis on tracking outcomes. The framework for tracking health measures and cost-effective outcomes is as follows:

1. Assess corporation needs, goals, resources, and objectives to develop program specifications.
2. Build evaluation into beginning of program.
3. Assure appropriate control groups.
4. Obtain baseline data.
5. Determine appropriate data points and formal risk analysis.
6. Include dependents, retirees, and small remote sites.
7. Develop profile of high-risk areas (coronary heart disease, stress, cancer).
8. Develop research designs and statistical methods.
9. Generate appropriate reports.
10. Create mechanisms for feedback to evaluate and refine program.

Core funding for the project from the participating companies is used to maintain the ongoing meetings, pilot projects, data exchanges, and consultations between these major corporations and the Stanford Corporate Health Program. When projects of mutual interest are identified, grants are written conjointly between the corporations and the program to private foundations and government agencies for major research and development support.

Results of the Stanford Corporate Health Program are utilized to determine which health promotion programs can work most effectively in the managed care business environment and how such programs can be developed and evaluated in a practical, cost-effective manner. The results of this program are also disseminated to businesses and other national and international organizations.

Once initiated, promotion programs can be self-sustaining as well as a source of financial support for an ongoing program of research and evaluation to improve the delivery and efficacy of medical and health promotion programs. Dr. Pelletier has reviewed 77 studies of work-site promotion programs published since 1980. Of those that have been analyzed for cost-effectiveness, all but one have shown positive effects on workers' health, as measured by risk factors and by rates of actual illness.

In 1989, I had the chance to test out Dr. Pelletier's contemporary approach to health promotion while I was working with Saint Joseph's Hospital of Atlanta. As health marketing coordinator, my responsibilities included packaging the hospital's mobile mammography service and securing direct contracts from local employers. Having studied Dr. Pelletier's work, I devised some very simple equations that allowed benefits directors to see for themselves what their financial implications for health promotion activities might be (see Figures 12–2 and 12–3). It worked! Within nine months, Saint Joseph's had 62 new relationships with corporations including Delta, Coca-Cola, and Southern Bell.

MOVING THE "CARROT" AND INCENTIVE FOR CHANGE[18]

Gordian Health Solutions, Inc., is profiled here as one of the most innovative companies looking to make prevention and wellness a profitable venture.

FIGURE 12–2

Mammography Screening Program Costs

Estimated cost to provide screening mammography to the female employees 35 years of age and older:

Number of employees screened:

Employer paid full fee:

_________mammograms × ________________=________________

Employer paid partial fee:

_________mammograms × ________________=________________

Employee paid full fee:

_________mammograms × ________________=________________

Benefits administration

_________mammograms × $2.00 =________________

Employee away from job:

_________hourly rate × 0.5 × ________________ =________________

Treatment Costs

Number of malignancies detected: *(Between 2–5 breast cancers diagnosed per 1,000 women screened)*

*_________× $24,000 = ________________ early

*_________× $84,000 = ________________ late

Number of biopsies: *(2% of women screened require biopsies)*

_________ × $2,700 = ________________________________

Number of ultrasounds completed: *(5% of women screened require ultrasound)*

_________ × $100 = ________________________________

Number of magnifications: ________________× $46 =________________

TOTAL COSTS: ________________________________

(Cost to company for screening and ultrasound and magnifications)

*Will want to monitor consequent health insurance claims to determine total cost of follow-up treatment.

Source: Saint Joseph's Hospital of Atlanta, 1989

FIGURE 12–3

Total Company Cost of Late Detected Breast Cancers
(Without Mammography Screening)

Projected # of Late Breast Cancers:

A. Direct Medical Cost:
$96,000 × 1 = $96,000

B. Short-term Disability Cost:
(Based on six months of full salary—average annual salary of $48,000)
$24,000 × 1 = $24,000

C. Long-term Disability Cost:
(Based on 60 percent average salary—1/2 of the women live beyond 4 years)
$28,000 × 1 = $28,000

D. Employee Replacement and Training Cost:
$24,000 × 1 = $24,000

Total Cost: $172,000

The American Cancer Society statistics indicate that *one out of ten* American women will develop breast cancer during her lifetime. Statistically, out of the ____women screened for your organization, ____could develop breast cancer. Without mammography screening, the risk is much greater that such a cancer, once found, will have progressed to a later stage. Consequently, the total cost to your organization could be as great as________________× $172,000 = $ ________________.

Source: Saint Joseph's Hospital of Atlanta, 1989

This model warrants intensive review as it is the opinion of this author that this is the wave of the future.

Company Background

Gordian Health Solutions, Inc. (GHS), began operations in 1995 under the direction of its three founders: Yonnie Chesley, President and CEO; Keith Rye, COO; and Clayton McWhorter, advisor, board member and former CEO of HealthTrust, Inc. (HTI). HTI, a $4 billion, publicly traded company on the NYSE, owned and operated approximately 116 hospitals across the United States. Mr. McWhorter recognized that he could improve his company's bottom line and increase its attractiveness to investors by decreasing healthcare costs for his own employees. Ms. Chesley and Mr. Rye were instrumental in designing a health benefits program that aligned lifestyle choices and financial incentives. The program was offered to its employee group of approximately

40,000 people and was administered by an independent company, ETHIX Risk Management (ERM), located in Portland, Oregon. As a "flagship" client, HTI helped shape programmatic design, service methodologies, and health promotional policies and procedures of ETHIX Risk Management. To accelerate the development of the company's mission and objective, GHS acquired ERM in July 1996. The experience levels gained through the development and administration of the HTI program from "both sides of the table" offer a unique combination of experience to GHS clients.

The Gordian management team is comprised of the only management team known in the United States who has pulled together and accomplished the implementation of a comprehensive (total employee and spouse population) health promotion initiative in a large employer environment with multiple sites. In addition, the management team has extensive experience in the medical benefits development, management and administration, and in human resources administration. Therefore, GHS understands the complexities (need for cost justification, employee relations and legal issues, benefit program management, logistical and administrative issues) associated with the development and implementation of this kind of program for a large population. This experience, coupled with broad experience in the health care industry, as well as the experience gained through the acquisition of Ethix Risk Management, positions GHS as the choice provider for managed care initiatives concentrated on improving the health status of the employer's workforce. Providers seeking to increase their direct contracting business with local employers should take note.

A description of the HTI program and its results follows.

Case Study: HealthTrust, Inc.

HTI was founded in 1987 and was acquired by Columbia/HCA Health System in 1995. The HTI wellness program originated from an analysis of its medical claims from 1991–1993. The analysis showed significant findings: approximately $9.3 million was spent on circulatory-related claims for the three-year period, $9.0 million was spent on digestive claims, $7.0 million on prenatal, and $7.0 million on mental nervous/substance abuse. The results of this program helped support the creation of several health management programs, such as a wellness program, a prenatal program, and an employee assistance program.

The wellness program was implemented in 1994 within its then 84 facilities (and later in 32 acquired facilities). At the onset of the program, 16 percent of the 23,621 eligible insureds chose *not* to participate in the program. Increased premiums collected from the nonparticipants more than paid for the cost of administering the program. Of the 17,220 who did participate, 2,628 were monitored under the high risk management program. At the end of the first six-month period, 50 percent of the monitored group met their goals.

After one year, HTI experienced a $1.1 million reduction in lifestyle-related medical claims. Total medical claims expenses were in excess of $5 million below the prior year.

New Business Venture: ETHIX Risk Management

ETHIX Risk Management (ERM) was incorporated in 1991 as a wholly owned subsidiary of the ETHIX Corporation. ETHIX Corporation, established in 1985 as an Oregon-based holding company for several PPO health plans, had successfully developed a reputation for effective, innovative managed care products. ERM was founded to create a managed care product which could positively impact group health plan costs via consumer incentives for personal health management. Prior to its acquisition by Gordian Health Solutions, Inc., ERM had been a part of the Sanus Corporation, a subsidiary of New York Life Insurance Company.

Since 1991 ERM has helped employers, such as HealthTrust, Inc., British Airways, and BRIM, to reduce their health care costs by offering employees programs and incentives for personal health management. This has been accomplished through health risk assessments, physician referral programs, and risk intervention programs. ERM also offers a Wellness Resource Network, providing clients with wellness-related resources such as a newsletter, discounts at health clubs, and toll-free access to wellness counselors.

ERM has experienced health promotion, systems, and administrative staff to service existing and new clients.

Description of HTI Products and Services

Medical Claims Analysis

Gordian will work with each client to analyze historic medical claims data for incidents of lifestyle related claims that help justify the need for health management program implementation. This analysis will help establish a baseline for long-term measurement of the success of the program implemented, and the results can be incorporated into employee communications material during the program implementation. The base information can usually be obtained from the company's third party administrator for medical claims administration.

Participation Incentives/Medical Benefit Program Integration

GHS promotes the use of monetary incentives as part of the medical benefit program premium structure to encourage active involvement of all insureds in the program, especially those with high risk lifestyle behaviors who are (or will be) at risk for high cost claims. The participation incentive program allows the employer the opportunity to recover short-term costs of program implementation and management through the collection of increased premiums from individuals who choose not to participate in the program.

Health Management Program Design

Gordian offers many products and services that can be tailored to meet the specific needs identified by the employer. Due to the program's flexibility, a corporation can "pick and choose" products and services which best meet their budget, demands, health management goals, benefit design philosophy, and corporate culture.

Health Risk Assessments (Including Health Fairs)

GHS offers a variety of health risk assessments (HRAs). Each HRA varies in levels of comprehension and price. All contain computerized answer sheets and meet GHS's high standards of critical data elements and data quality and integrity. Once the appropriate HRA is determined by the client, GHS will negotiate with local providers to conduct health fairs to collect required biometrics measures (e.g., cholesterol, blood pressure, etc.).

High Risk Identification and Analysis

From data collected and analyzed, GHS will identify categories of risk factors found within the corporation and work with the employer to determine risk factors which need special attention. For each risk factor identified, GHS will developed custom-tailored programs for the corporation (e.g., high risk management, physician referral option, etc.) to manage these risk factors on an individual, yet confidential basis.

High Risk Management

High risk programs deal with specific "high health risk" problems identified through the health risk identification process. Under this program, GHS identifies the individuals with high risks and then works with them on an individual, confidential basis to reduce their health risks. This process begins by working with each individual to establish a 6-month action plan of planned behavior changes and activities, providing follow-up by mail and telephone,

CASE STUDY

WELLNESS PROGRAMS PAY DIVIDENDS

Health promotion programs in the workplace are achieving greater acceptance. Many indicators show that they yield improvements in employee behavior and health status. Some companies have also looked at the relationship between such improvements and reductions in healthcare costs and absenteeism.

Working with the University of Alabama at Birmingham (UAB) and Wellness South, a Birmingham consulting firm, the city launched a wellness program for its 4,200 employees. It also implemented a self-insured, self-administered health plan, utilization review, incentives to direct employees to hospitals with favorable outcomes and lower rates, and an HMO option. (It has since abolished its self-funded indemnity plan.)

The wellness program, operated since 1991 by the UAB School of Nursing, includes on-site medical screening and a health risk appraisal. Participation in the screening and appraisal is a prerequisite for entry into the health plan. After the screening, intervention programs are provided in weight loss, stress management, smoking cessation, blood pressure control, cholesterol reduction, fitness, and back care. Incentives—such as department store coupons, T-shirts, and gym bags—are offered to encourage participation.

In the last five years, the city's healthcare costs have been essentially flat (see graph). The cost of medical benefits went from $2,047 per employee in 1985 to $2,075 in 1990, an increase of 1.4 percent over the five-year life of the study. By 1993, the per-employee cost of $2,609 was still well below the $3,262 average for southern states. For the year ending in June 1994, the per-employee cost was $2,762. Some analysts point out that other employers that used the same HMOs as the city health plan saw average annual medical cost increases of 11 percent to 14 percent during the same five years.

and by making available Gordian Wellness Counselors (health educators) for consultative services through a 1-800 telephone service. Confidentiality is maintained throughout the process which is necessary for legal, as well as employee acceptance, reasons.

Physician Referral Option Program

An option to the high risk monitoring program is to simply require individuals who are identified as "high risk" to consult with their primary care physician. GHS would monitor the receipt of physician referral forms and provide follow-up services, as deemed appropriate by the client.

Concluded

The city is also enhancing the health of high-risk employees by providing them with individual professional assistance. Participating employees must first undergo a health status assessment. Then, by following the recommendations of their providers to reduce risk factors, they can receive benefits that include lower health plan premium contributions and a waiver or reduction of co-payments for treatment and medication.

Another element of the program seeks to ensure that physicians encourage and manage preventive measures. "There are a host of recommended clinical practices to maintain and improve the health status of individuals," says Birmingham personnel director Gordon Graham. "But most physicians are not in the prevention and health promotion mode. They are trained to care for you after you become sick or injured. We're trying to shift that focus to keeping people well and preventing injury and disease." The pilot program, funded by a grant from two HMOs, is a partnership between the city of Birmingham and the UAB.

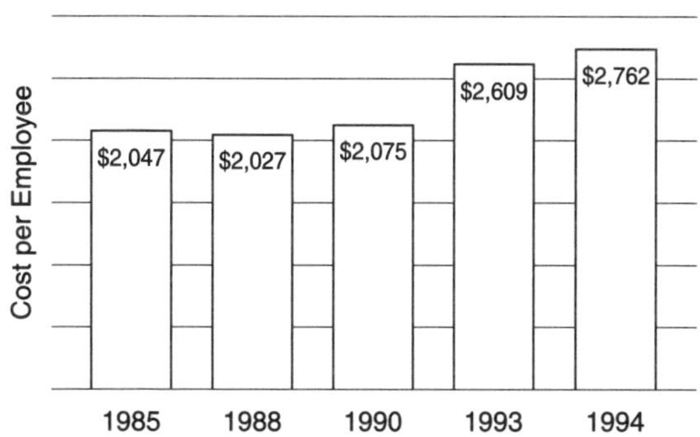

Lifestyle Improvement Programs

To help employees achieve or maintain lifestyles, that is, weight management programs, smoking cessation, back care programs, etc., Gordian offers multiple types and levels of support. Many programs are incorporated into the high risk management program to continually encourage monitored individuals to make lifestyle changes. Programs range from low-cost approaches (American Heart Association programs, American Cancer Society programs, programs developed in-house by GHS, etc. — all of which can be administered via "long distance") to more intensive lifestyle management programs (e.g., on-site Wellness Coordinators, health center management, etc.). GHS will work with each client to design a program which best fits their budget and goals.

Communication Program Development

GHS offers multiple communications tools for use by the client throughout the administration of the program. In the event that the client wants to customize communications campaigns, we will provide management tools and resources to facilitate this process.

Health Center Management

Gordian offers comprehensive health center services to employers and hospitals with existing health facilities. Health center management includes assessment of existing and needed fitness equipment (based on available space), lifestyle management programs, such as weight management programs, smoking cessation, etc., individual program development, post-surgery care (e.g., post-cardiac surgery fitness program), physician referral for high risk cases, etc.

Data Collection & Management

Data management and analysis provide an essential role in all phases of health management efforts. Through the collection of medical claims data and health risk data, GHS can establish baselines for analytical purposes for current and future periods to track the effectiveness of health management program efforts. Through the GHS comprehensive database, employers can make informed decisions on benefits plan design, efficient delivery systems and providers, and cost management issues.

THE FUTURE

Preventive services are already playing a pivotal role in the way healthcare is being organized to respond to purchaser needs. Activity in the employer sectors is evidence that there is a market for primary health prevention when it is based on long-term cost-effective analysis. Whether providers decide to make or buy primary health prevention services will depend on available resources and resident talent. Regardless of the approach, the future will require that efforts to expand preventive care and health promotion activities become central to every hospital's strategy for expanding a primary care base of business.

ENDNOTES

1. Phycor, Inc. "1994 Annual Report," p. 4.
2. "Boom (and Bust) in the Physician Management Market," *Hospital & Health Networks* (December 20, 1995), p. 47.

3. LeRoy, L. & Solkowitz, W. "Case Study #16: The Costs and Effectiveness of Nurse Practitioners." (Washington, D.C.: Office of Technology Assessments, 1978); Lawrence, D. "Physician's Assistants and Nurse Practitioners," *Health & Medical Care Services Review, pp.* 1–2; and Record, J., et al. "Primary Care Staffing in 1990," *Physicians Replacement and Cost Savings* (New York: Springer Verlag, 1981).
4. Sackett, D. L., et al. "The Burlington Randomized Trial of the Nurse Practitioner: Health Outcomes of Patients," *Annals of Internal Medicine*; Spitzer, W. O., et al. "The Nurse Practitioner Revisited," *New England Journal of Medicine,* vol. 310, no. 16.
5. Lewin, K. *Resolving Social Conflicts* (New York: Harper & Row, 1984).
6. Sullivan, J. A. "The Rural Nurse Practitioner: A Challenge and Response," *American Journal of Public Health,* vol. 68, p. 972.
7. Greenfield, S., et al. "Efficiency and Cost of Primary Care by Nurses and Physician Assistants," *New England Journal of Medicine,* pp. 298–305.
8. Sultz, H. A., et al. "Nurse Practitioner: A Decade of Change," *Nursing Outlook,* 32(3), Par. IV, 1984, p. 158.
9. Aburdene, Patricia and John Naisbitt. Megatrends for Women: From Liberation to Leadership (New York: Ballantine, 1992) p. 180.
10. "Currents: Continuum of Care," *Hospital and Health Networks* (December 20, 1995), p. 21.
11. Aburdene, Patricia and John Naisbitt. Megatrends for Women: From Liberation to Leadership (New York: Ballantine, 1992), pp. 180–181.
12. Martin, M. Caroline. "Working Out for the Best," *Healthcare Forum Journal* (November/December, 1993), p. 59.
13. Pelletier, Kenneth R. "A Review and Analysis of the Health and Cost-Effective Outcome Studies of Comprehensive Health Promotion and Disease Prevention Programs at the Worksite: 1991–1993 Update," *American Journal of Health Promotion,* pp. 50–51.
14. Smith, Gloria, R., and Ruby L. Wesley. "Health Promotion: Public Policy Goal," *Prevention Across the Life Span: Healthy People for the 21st Century,* (American Nurses Publishing), p. 98.
15. Jones, Lynn. "Hospitals Finding Innovative Ways to Put Prevention Into Practice," *AHA News* (June 15, 1992), p. 6.
16. Currents, *Hospitals & Health Networks* (July 5, 1994), p. 22.
17. The Stanford Corporate Health Program descriptive is adopted from Pelletier, Kenneth R. "Healthy People—Healthy Business," *1995 Healthier Communities Summit.*
18. The Gordian Health/Health Trust, Inc., description is adapted from "New Health Benefits Program at HealthTrust Sets Standard for the Future," HealthTrust, Inc., news release.

13 CHAPTER

Creating an Integrated Model

Today's healthcare leaders are recognizing that the impact of rapidly evolving managed care dynamics requires a proactive response. Although capitation is not yet the standard in most markets, shifting reimbursement structures and increasing competition for market share are providing undeniable evidence that—for the provider community—the healthcare business of tomorrow will look very little like the healthcare business of the past. A shift away from a biomedical model of care where profit margins have been dependent on disease care and episodic treatment is imminent.

Today, healthcare providers are straddling an abyss. In markets still vested in the biomedical model of treatment, the fee-for-service cash register may still be ringing, whereas in more mature managed care markets, the financial incentives are inversely related to utilization. Financial incentives are already fostering the design of delivery systems characterized by a seamless continuum of care and an investment in health status improvement. As the reimbursement environment shifts more and more toward capitation, such large health systems as Columbia/HCA, Mercy Healthcare, and Bon Secours Health System are finding that the managed care marketplace is a catalyst for looking beyond old ways of being in business. New models that embrace the well-being of the whole patient will be required in order to effectively *enhance customer intimacy, evidence market differentiation, and own a continuum of care.* (See Figure 13–1.)

FIGURE 13–1

Moving Forward: The Evolution of an Integrated Model

- Capitation drives the fiscal reality of managing the health of a population
- Boundaries collapse between public and private health sectors
- Service delivery characterized by a continuum of care, ease of access, seamless processes
- Impact measurements: "what works/what doesn't" is analyzed and reported
- Patient care begins to be characterized by a blending of mainstream medical and complementary approaches to address both the biomedical and psychosocial factors impacting health

- Independent Hospitals
- Autonomous Physicians
- Full beds; long waits in physicians' offices
- Unsophisticated consumers
- Fee-for-service

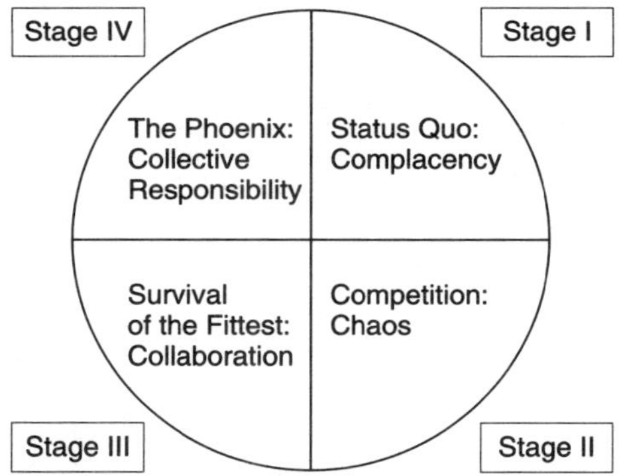

- HMO/PPO(s) consolidate
- Providers rapidly merging, acquiring, organizing, and looking at systems for integration
- The price window narrows
- "Report Cards" emphasize quality and patient satisfaction, *not just cost*
- Reimbursement continues to shift; primary care services capitate, global pricing more common
- Information technology is recognized as a cornerstone for designing continuums of care
- Organizational structure begins to try new ways for building consensus, committing to action
- Private and public health sectors come to the table to address primary care access, prevention, and education issues
- Physicians and clinical caregivers begin to look beyond the medical model for non-traditional approaches to patient-centered care in order to differentiate themselves in the marketplace.

- HMO/PPO/POS(s) enter the market like popping popcorn
- Alphabet soup: PHO, MCO, MSO, IPA, etc.
- Reimbursement shifts from FFS to per diem to global pricing
- Profit margins erode
- Organizational re-design: hospitals "slash and burn"
- Physicians begin to meet in groups, call lawyers
- Loose networks form
- Managed care emerges as a replacement product
- Consumer choice is restricted
- Customer intimacy and continuums of care become "back burner priorities"

Source: © Copyright 1995. Genie James, Integrated Healthcare Consultant/*Auscultа*

When viewed from the economic dimension, the emerging interest in an integrated approach to comprehensive service delivery must correlate with issues directly related to staying in business at the local level. This investigative chapter looks at a biopsychosocial approach to primary care, as well as at the application of specific therapies defined by complementary fields of practice. In order to ensure that the output of the work would have pragmatic value for those decision makers driving new business development, the potential benefit of an integrated approach to patient care has been assessed across several critical dimensions:

1. Can an integrated model of care expand or augment the existing delivery model and continuum of care in a way that appropriately *reflects the intent of our mission, enhances patient care, and contributes to community service*?
2. Can the addition of biopsychosocial approaches or complementary therapies to a continuum of care positively impact market share and contracting leverage via the value purchasing equation: *Value = Cost + Quality + Patient Satisfaction?*
3. In considering the development of an integrated model in the context of local market dynamics, how can a *contribution analysis* provide the basis for evaluating how well the vision and marketing and production objectives mesh?
4. How can an investment in a *new way of being in business* be aligned with more *immediate operations and performance concerns* at both the individual hospital and system levels?
5. What is the process for developing a *business plan* that can serve as a rational structure for the strategic roll-out of new programs or services?

WHAT IS A BIOPSYCHOSOCIAL APPROACH TO CARE?

The Collaborative Family Health Care Coalition (CFHCC) in Washington, D.C., first introduced the term *a biopsychosocial approach* to health and well-being to the industry. The CFHCC was conceived in 1993. Its inception sprung from the premise that the treatment of illness and the nurturance of health require close collaboration among physical and mental health practitioners, consumers, and healthcare administrators. According to the CFHCC, collaboration of this sort differs radically from the usual "diagnose and refer" pattern in which physicians, having ruled out biological factors, send patients to psychotherapists. In the collaborative model, biologically and psychologically-oriented professionals work in concert, sharing a frame of reference, a working space, and ongoing conversation.

The need for collaboration follows from two observations. First, approximately 80 percent of symptoms presented in primary care medicine have either no clear etiology or a psychosocial etiology and often require psychosocial intervention. Second, since most illness today is chronic illness, families are the major caretakers. After initial diagnosis and biomedical treatment planning, both the course of illness and the utilization of healthcare services depend significantly on adherence to medication schedules, diets, and exercise programs, and on such psychological factors as resilience and stress reduction.

Psychosocial health professionals, skilled in the mobilization of patient and family resources must be included in healthcare from the start. At the same time, the position of patients and families must be shifted from passive recipients to active, respected participants—members of collaborative healthcare teams.[1] A biopsychosocial approach, then, is a collaborative model for care that includes physical and mental health professionals, as well as the family.

Experts put the overall cost of stress to the economy as high as $150 billion a year—almost the size of the federal deficit. A recent National Ambulatory Medical Care Survey found that at least 75 percent of the 600 million office visits made to physicians in the United States are for stress-related symptoms.[2] Dr. Robert Cochran, a Nashville, Tennessee, internist and neurologist, sees many patients who have a combination of physical problems that extend to psychiatric illness. Dr. Cochran says that depression is actually several diseases, including bipolar disorder, seasonal affective disorder, atypical depression, and major depression. Atypical depression is characterized by a lot of somatic (bodily) symptoms. Dr. Cochran admits that he feels frustrated with society's inability to grasp the prevalence of depression and the fact that a precise cause for it cannot always be determined. In his work with workman's compensation cases, he has observed that some companies do not understand depression and pain at all. They want specific answers as to the causes of these problems; however, depression-related cases are complex and it is not always possible to pinpoint the cause.[3] In essence, Dr. Cochran recommends an approach to care that looks beyond the symptoms and integrates the mental and physical dynamics of health and well-being.

Alternative Therapies: Are You Kidding?

Although alternative therapies are still thought to be somewhat abstract, the evidence suggests that individual patient-consumers are accessing complementary therapy—and are willing to pay. In 1993, Dr. David Eisenberg published a groundbreaking article in the *New England Journal of Medicine,* entitled "Unconventional Medicine in the United States." Several primary findings have gotten the attention of both mainstream medical providers and business healthcare decision makers. For example:

- In 1990, Americans made an estimated 425 million visits to providers of unconventional therapies. This number exceeds the number of visits to all U.S. primary care physicians (388 million).
- Expenditures associated with use of unconventional therapy in 1990 amounted to approximately $13.7 billion, three quarters of which ($10.3 billion) was paid out of pocket.
- Roughly 1 in 4 Americans who see their medical doctors for a serious health problem may be using a complementary therapy in addition to conventional medicine for that problem, and 7 of 10 such encounters take place without patients telling their medical doctors.
- The use of complementary therapies is not limited to the person's principal medical conditions. From an analysis of survey results profiling the respondents' utilization patterns, Dr. Eisenberg inferred that a substantial amount of complementary therapy is accessed for nonserious medical conditions, health promotion, or disease prevention.[4]

When viewed from the economic dimension, the emerging interest in an integrated approach to comprehensive service delivery is quite understandable. Alternative therapies are now being experimented with and scrutinized by patient consumers, managed care payors, academic medical science communities, and government-funded research programs. The truth is that these treatment options should not be regarded as alternative; they should be considered for their potential to augment—or complement—existing systems of care. Patient consumers *know they are a customer, have the money to pay, and are going outside the system to purchase complementary care.* Asking the "What can this mean to me?" question presents a contemporary challenge for healthcare leaders directing new business development.

For the hospital moving toward strategic prioritization of community health initiatives, *there is a missed opportunity if complementary therapies are not a component of any utilization or health status profile. It makes sense—and takes little effort—to weave the current use of, desire for, and potential value of incorporating complementary therapies into a spectrum of care.* Existing surveys can be expanded to include questions probing for consumer purchasing patterns and preferences. Quantitative assessment can include state data regarding the licensing and regulatory issues associated with the availability of complementary therapies, as well as a local demographic and psychographic analysis of supply and demand. Local market analysis should also incorporate resource mapping tools that provide a comprehensive profiling of the scope of complementary therapists currently practicing within a community, as well as their existing base of business, referral routes, and fee schedules. A quick peripheral sketch of complementary providers can be obtained by looking in the local yellow pages, asking health food stores if they have a listing of area therapists, and beginning a word-of-mouth process of inquiry.

As with any strategic initiative involving the reshaping of service delivery, it is critical that the market be diligently analyzed for its receptivity to complementary therapies, as well as the potential barriers to market entry that may need to be addressed. Consumer focus groups discussing healthcare purchasing attitudes and access issues can be excellent forums to learn firsthand from the target customers. At this stage of market analysis, it is also very important not to neglect profiling the payor community. Obviously, the reimbursement environment is a critical variable when factoring a potential return on investment.

Provider health systems are faced with many difficult decisions. Most pregnant is the question of how best to strategically move into the future and invest in new ways of being in business without cannibalizing existing sources of revenue. If the addition of certain therapies or approaches can corner a market of self-pay dollars, then it is possible that this "investment" could pay for itself and make an additional positive contribution to the bottom line. Within this reality of a new market opportunity, it is important to first understand when, where, and how an integrated model for care delivery could positively enhance patient care or impact community health status. The next step is critical: The development of an integrated model must be strategically aligned with existing financial incentives and market dynamics.

ADDING VALUE

The Catholic Health Association (CHA) is leading a movement toward a new integrated model for health service delivery. Recognizing the need for a radically different focus, the CHA recently convened two thinktanks.[5] The first, in June 1994, brought together 12 leaders of health programs and services in CHA member institutions. The following October, the CHA convened 17 experts in a variety of disciplines—including insurance, government, traditional and complementary medicine, managed care, architecture, spiritual healing, and outcomes measurement. The CHA asked the thinktank participants to discuss the National Wellness Institute's six dimensions of health and well-being. They analyzed these dimensions—the physical, spiritual, emotional, intellectual, social, and environmental—as they envisioned the future healthcare system. Participants painted an intriguing picture of healthcare in 2005 and described what the healthcare system—and CHA members—must do to achieve the vision. In the future they described, Catholic healthcare organizations lead in creating a new system, drawing on the values they have always professed: *the common good and the intrinsic worth of each human being.*

The following observations reflect the output of the CHA thinktank effort:

- Complementary medicine has a cost-effective and healing place in healthcare, but education and dialogue between providers of conventional and complementary care have not yet taken place.
- Spirituality contributes to healing and needs to become an important component of holistic care. A healthcare system that deemphasizes the biomedical model should address patients' emotions, perceptions of meaning in their life, and awareness of a connection to a Higher Power. Clinical professionals need education to help them integrate spirituality into their clinical practice. Spirituality needs to be part of the core curriculum in all preparatory programs for caregivers so they can identify and address spiritual despair as a source or contributing factor of disease.
- The health system should enable people to take responsibility for their own health and participate in their own healing. Complementary approaches help patients use to the fullest extent their inner resources for healing. Most healthcare dollars are spent on chronic conditions related to lifestyle. Thus, the healthcare system must influence people's health behaviors through education, and identify the spiritual and emotional blocks that inhibit individuals' from choosing healthy habits.
- Two factors in particular are inhibiting the use of preventive measures: (1) uncertainty about how frequently and at what age services should be delivered, and (2) lack of financial incentives to provide preventive services. Also, preventive services should be delivered in less costly ways—for example, immunizations at schools instead of in physicians' offices.
- The "built environment," which includes lighting and places for reflection, color, sound, and artwork, must be recognized as a contributor to holistic care. In the next few years, the arts will become an important component in helping individuals develop their inner spirit. The Society for Arts in Health Care encourages using the arts

> as part of healing programs. Providers should enhance people's positive emotions—joy, love, enthusiasm—and humor is an effective way to do this. They should also encourage people to express other emotions."

These factors should be considered and evaluated by hospitals and health systems as to their value in moving a biomedically oriented system toward one that is community-based, emphasizing health prevention and promotion. The question that must be addressed within the boundaries of each local market is: Can an integrated approach expand or augment the existing delivery model and continuum of care in a way that appropriately *reflects the intent of our mission, enhances patient care, and contributes to community service?* In other words, can it *add value* to the services we deliver and *strengthen our position in the marketplace?*

In response to both questions, managed care payors, health systems and hospitals are answering with a resounding *yes!* New primary care delivery systems are narrowing the gap between consumer choice, behavioral lifestyle change/management, preventive holistic health, biopsychosocial approaches, complementary therapies, and health education. Consumers want access to providers that address their physical, mental, emotional, and spiritual concerns; conversely, healthcare providers need to offer realistic, cost-effective, and outcome-driven treatment modalities at first point of access.

THE COST OF INTEGRATED CARE

Managed care has shifted the emphasis from highly technical specialty care to primary care services. The theory is that routine medical care combined with an increasing emphasis on self-regulation can be first steps towards cheaper, more effective healthcare services delivery. In addition, the concept of a "gatekeeper" has been built on the thought that although it costs money to give everyone access to a family doctor, routine medical care can help quell the demand for higher-priced services. For instance, it costs $600 to provide prenatal care for a pregnant woman versus $2,500 a day to keep a premature baby in intensive care. Eight dollars will buy a measles shot, but treating a serious case of the disease can cost $5,000.[6] By reaching beyond hospital walls with a network of community-oriented primary care services, the economically driven functions of demand reduction and enhanced self-regulation appropriately shift away from the hospital.

There is ample evidence that integrating mental healthcare into primary care services has a payoff. In her testimony before the legislative implementation committee for TennCare, Dr. Elsbeth Freeman, PhD, President of the Tennessee Psychological Association, stated:

> The cost effectiveness of accurate diagnosis and appropriate treatment of psychological, emotional, and behavioral disorders is evident in studies demonstrating that psychological interventions can reduce outpatient medical utilization by 50 percent to 65 percent and can reduce medical–surgical hospitalization by 60 percent to 75 percent. These figures are based on reports from the Kaiser-Permanente HMO in San Francisco, which has a 25-year history of providing mental health services. These figures support other research indicating that people with psychological problems make twice as many visits to their primary care physicians as do people without mental health problems. A reviewer of the Kaiser-Permanente Health Insurance Plan data concluded that only one to four sessions of psychotherapy returned an average $2.59 for every $1.00 invested in therapy. If you could invest the state's money and get a 259 percent return on that money, would you not go for the investment? Another reviewer estimated that the cost of confirming diagnoses where there was no medical problem—the cost of ruling out medical diagnoses—could pay for up to six months of psychotherapy."[7]

What happens when mental health services are deliberately designed and provided to high medical utilizers? Numerous studies have shown the high cost of depression. One study, presented with great fanfare by Tipper Gore in 1993, found that depression costs the U.S. economy $43.7 billion a year in lost productivity, absenteeism, and treatment costs.[8] Results from a recent study of the Medicaid population in Hawaii also demonstrate significant cost savings. More than 1,000 high-utilizing Medicaid patients were followed over a 3½-year period. The group initially used medical services at a rate 2.5 times greater than an employed comparison group. If only the patients receiving the focused mental health treatment are compared to those receiving no mental health treatment, the difference in medical costs is 44 percent at 18 months. The costs of providing the special, focused mental health treatment were recovered in terms of reduced medical costs in just the first six months.[9]

Addressing the correlates of emotional distress and mental health concerns to medical utilization and costs can result in a fundamental change in the financing of medical care. When one views the bottom line and the dollars saved, a biopsychosocial approach suddenly has a magnetic attraction. This type of cost-savings data should motivate healthcare administrators to design operational models that drive closer collaboration between physicians, mental health professionals, patients, and their families.

As pressures increase to eliminate high-cost healthcare, once-suspicious providers and insurers are beginning to emphasize these lower-priced alternatives and make them a legitimate part of the healthcare system.

The American Holistic Center is a joint venture between Columbia/HCA and Grant Hospital in Chicago, Illinois. Its medical research director, David Eidelberg, MD, states, "Holistic Centers work in a cost-conscious system. Instead of referring upward to a specialist, you're referring laterally to a holistic practitioner where your costs are a fraction of what they would be." As an example, Eidelberg cites a $40,000 surgery to cure chronic back pain. Meanwhile, the same patient could have chiropractic and acupuncture care that would cost $400 for a four-week treatment. "An insurer looking at those kinds of savings can't help but offer alternative therapies as part of their health plan menu," said David Harrington, a healthcare consultant with Karen Zupko & Associates, a Chicago-based firm. "Bringing holistic care into the mix provides a value-added benefit to a health plan."[10]

The current healthcare cost crisis is primarily a crisis of treating chronic disease and a preview of the financial burdens incumbent in caring for a rapidly graying America. Today almost 33 million Americans are functionally limited in their daily activities by chronic, debilitating conditions such as arthritis, allergies, pain, hypertension, cancer, depression, cardiovascular disease, and digestive problems. More than 9 million, or almost one-third, of these individuals have limitations so severe that they cannot work, attend school, or maintain a household. The U.S. Public Health Service (PHS) estimates that 70 percent of the current healthcare budget is spent on the treatment of these individuals, as the population grows older, such conditions will continue to consume an even larger proportion of national healthcare expenditures. Furthermore, the worldwide pandemic of AIDS is threatening to completely overwhelm the healthcare delivery systems in certain areas of the United States.

While the dominant system of healthcare in the United States—often called biomedicine—is extremely effective for treating infectious diseases and traumatic injuries, it is often not sufficient to handle complex, multifaceted chronic conditions. Physicians frequently report that, even with the best of their clinical training, they feel frustrated at their inability to do more when working with a patient suffering from chronic pain, AIDS, cancer, or coronary artery disease. While the physicians' expertise lends itself to the treatment of the physical symptoms, these chronic concerns also require that their biopsychosocial ramifications be addressed. Behavioral lifestyle changes, prevention, education, counseling, and teaching require focused energy from qualified health professionals. In the interest of both time and money, the outcomes associated with the treatment may very well be enhanced by moving beyond a one-dimensional model to an integrated approach involving a team of health professionals.

With markets rapidly moving toward capitation, increasing pressures for cost containment are causing many former skeptics within the provider community to reexamine their view of complementary therapies. Although the outcomes data is limited at this time, champions of incorporating mind–body therapies like yoga, meditation, and visualization are bolstering acceptance by tracking their impact on *length of stay* and *resource demand.* The data support the claim that with the introduction of some complementary approaches, patients recover more quickly post-operatively and request fewer pain medications.

Complex chronic conditions require multifaceted treatment approaches. Furthermore, it is far less expensive to prevent them from occurring in the first place than to attempt to treat the symptoms and consequences with surgery and expensive drugs, which often offer only short-term solutions. For example, coronary artery disease affects approximately 7 million Americans and causes about 1.5 million heart attacks and 500,000 deaths a year. Approximately 300,000 coronary artery bypass graft operations are performed in the United States each year at a cost of about $30,000 each, or $9 billion total. Yet coronary artery bypass surgery prevents premature death in only a few patients with the most serious main coronary or multiple-vessel heart disease.[11]

On the other hand, Dean Ornish, MD, has recently made headlines by demonstrating the efficacy of integrating biomedical treatments and complementary approaches to lifestyle change for heart patients. Three studies published by Dr. Ornish and his collaborators have shown that lifestyle changes of a low-fat vegetarian diet, moderate exercise, stress management techniques, smoking cessation, and group support can dramatically improve the clinical status of patients with moderate to severe coronary heart disease. Medical colleagues who once poked fun at the contention that yoga and meditation might affect heart disease via a behavioral and psychosocial approach are now rethinking their objections as managed care payors cast their votes regarding the value of such programs. Both Mutual of Omaha and Blue Cross Blue Shield of California have endorsed Dr. Ornish's program as a clinical treatment alternative to bypass surgery and angioplasty for selected heart patients, and have accepted the cost of the program ($5,000 vs. the $30,000 cost of bypass surgery) as a standard benefit at hospitals where it is available.

In integrated models of care delivery, the cost benefit of other complementary approaches is being recognized. The value of *an increased focus on nutrition* can be recognized when one examines the negative impact of poor nutritional status on utilization costs associated with the treatment of the elderly or with the care of low-birthweight babies. Programs emphasizing nutrition and diet can be integrated across a continuum of care and incorporated into community health initiatives with a minimal financial investment.

Armed with research citing the cost efficiency and the clinical efficacy of *acupuncture, nutritional supplementation, vitamin therapies, homeopathic regimens, or herbology,* some providers are reworking their inpatient formularies. Others are piggy-backing on their success in developing more natural inpatient formularies and are finding that the mail-order business can be a potential source of revenue that also extends a continuum of care beyond hospital walls. Some of the presenting concerns most often mentioned include sinusitis, otitis media, chronic pain, women's health concerns, and gastrointestinal disorders.

In the marketplace, financial tensions and a renewed commitment to employee satisfaction are creating fertile ground for innovative interventions involving complementary therapies. Employers are not altruistic when determining where and how to spend their healthcare dollars. They want healthcare plans that reduce the days lost from work, get people back to work in better shape, and lower disability costs. Programs that have been most easily embraced are those that use complementary approaches such as acupuncture in the treatment of back pain or psychosocial therapies to decrease the incidence of stress-related illnesses. If considering a package that integrates approaches, employers are demanding increasingly sophisticated means of tracking health and cost outcomes. The emphasis on wellness, health promotion, and improved health outcomes at lower costs can be an advantage.

While talking dollars, most healthcare system administrators need to step back, look at the facts, and recognize a potential retail opportunity for medicine. If self-pay dollars are involved, then an integrated model may be a potential source for replacement revenue. Take the example of Sierra Tucson. It was once a Cadillac of substance-abuse centers—and a company-provided Cadillac at that: Employee health insurance routinely covered most of the costs of the standard 30-day stay there. Today, however, Sierra Tucson is a different place. Where there used to be 313 beds for people with a host of mental health problems, now there are only 70. Management has added to its offerings Miraval, a holistic health spa along the lines of the nearby tony Canyon Ranch. Some of those who still visit Sierra Tucson to cope with addictions do much of their therapy in short, intensive workshops. And more than three-quarters of them now pay the $650-a-night tab out of their own pockets.[12]

THE QUALITY OF INTEGRATED CARE

Do integrated approaches work? The data are being harnessed and the story is beginning to unfold. Many alternative medicine practitioners are primarily clinicians rather than researchers, and medical practice is their primary priority. Therefore, case studies and anecdotal reports are often their only evidence that a practice is effective.[13]

In response to this increasing public pressure, in 1992 Congress established the Office of Alternative Medicine (OAM) in the Office of the Director of the National Institutes of Health (NIH). OAM's mandate is to facilitate the evaluation of alternative medical treatments that might offer promise for addressing a number of serious health problems that afflict the nation. OAM also was mandated to establish an information clearinghouse to exchange information with the public about alternative medicine. In addition, OAM was charged with supporting research training in topics related to alternative medicine that are not typically included in the training curriculums of mainstream physicians and other health professionals.

OAM's mandate is not to be an advocate of any particular alternative medicine treatment (or complementary therapy), but rather to advocate the fair, scientific evaluation of alternative therapies that are found to have *potential* for improving the health and well-being of a significant number of people. In doing so, OAM has positioned itself as an intermediary between the alternative medical community and the federal research and regulatory commissions, in order to help reduce the barriers that may keep promising alternative therapies from coming to light.[14]

The following treatment components are already being recognized for their ability to enhance a spectrum of care: psychosocial approaches, diet and nutrition/lifestyle changes, herbal medicine, manual healing, and acupuncture. Let's take a look at each component.

Psychosocial Approaches

Research from the fields of neurology, internal medicine, and psychiatry has begun to illuminate an area of intersection between the physical symptoms and the psychological states associated with certain diseases. The new field of psychoneuroimmunology has emerged, and projections are that it will have a significant impact on medical care. Even in its embryonic stage of scientific development and acceptance, the field of psychoneuroimmunology is providing insight into the mind–body connection. It is also beginning to suggest some new strategies and illuminate some very old strategies for maintaining health and treating acute as well as chronic conditions.

Within the theory that mind–body therapies should be regarded as integral components of any spectrum of care is the hypothesis that the mind can influence the responses of the autonomic nervous system. The autonomic nervous system regulates life-sustaining inner-body processes, or visceral responses. These responses include heart rate, breathing, and blood flow. Proponents of the mind–body approach to healthcare contend that the responses of the autonomic nervous system are entirely trainable—as trainable as the somatic nervous system that controls the skeletal muscles.

In approaching the field of mind–body interventions, it is important that the mind not be viewed as if it were dualistically isolated from the body, as if it were doing something *to* the body. Mind–body is always mutual and bi-directional—the body affects the mind and is affected by it. Mind and body are so integrally related that, in practice, it makes little sense to refer to therapies as solely "mental" or "physical." For example, activities that appear overwhelmingly "physical," such as aerobic exercise, yoga, and dance, can have healthful effects not only on the body but also on such "mental" problems as depression and anxiety. Conversely, "mental" approaches such as imagery and meditation can benefit "physical" problems such as hypertension and hyper-cholesterolemia, as well as have salutary psychological effects. Even the use of drugs and surgery has its psychological side. The use of these methods often requires placebo-controlled, double-blind studies to estimate and factor out the physical effects of patients' beliefs and expectations.

Psychotherapy consultants and pastoral care professionals are the most readily accepted into case management teams serving patients with medical crises, somatic illnesses, or chronic concerns where stress is recognized as an underlying disease factor, that is, hypertension, cancer, AIDS, infertility, and others. Individual analysis and session work is often combined with social support groups.

If the patient has a physical illness, the psychotherapist's or mental health professional's role within a case management process is to focus on short-term treatment dealing with the emotional state directly related to the physical condition. According to a study by James J. Stain, an average of "one of every five people in the United States has a psychological disorder every six months—most commonly anxiety, depression, substance abuse or acute confusion."

Diet and Nutrition/Lifestyle Changes

Because of the recent rapid rise in chronic illness related directly or indirectly to diet, the focus of nutrition research has shifted away from eliminating nutritional deficiency to dealing with chronic diseases caused by nutritional excess. Another concern among nutrition researchers is the accumulation of evidence indicating that less-than-adequate intake of some micronutrients over a long period may increase the risks of developing coronary heart disease, cancers, cataracts, and birth defects. A variety of diet alternatives with or without nutritional supplementation have been combined with lifestyle choice programs in the treatment of cancer, cardiovascular disease, rheumatoid arthritis, male infertility, insulin resistant syndrome (IRS), depression, and hyperactivity.

Some alternate dietary lifestyles are believed to offer a greater resistance to illness. These include several variations of the vegetarian diet, the macrobiotic diet, and certain cultural eating patterns such as those characteristic of Native American, Asian, and Mediterranean populations. With the repeated documentation that nutrition is a significant variable in lowering the risk factors for heart disease, certain forms of cancer, elderly health concerns, and diabetes, the medical community has become increasingly concerned with the role nutrition can play in minimizing disease progression and optimizing health and wellness.

Herbal Medicine

The recent revival in the interest in herbal therapies stems from the general public's concern about the side effects of pharmaceutical drugs, a desire to self-doctor naturally, and an increasing recognition of the unique benefits of many forms of herbal medicine. In general, herbal medicines work in much the same way as do conventional pharmaceutical drugs. Because herbs and plants use an indirect route to the bloodstream and target organs, however, their effects are usually slower in onset and less dramatic than their synthetic, commercial counterparts.

Manual Healing

Manipulative treatment is commonly used, especially by osteopathic and chiropractic family physicians, as adjunctive care for systemic illness and for various neuromusculoskeletal problems, such as low back, head, and neck pain. In this context, a wide variety of hands-on and—in some situations—"energy" applications are used in a range of disciplines, including family practice, pediatrics, geriatrics, physical medicine, surgery of all kinds, physical medicine and rehabilitation, neurology, rheumatology, pulmonology, and sometimes behavioral medicine and psychiatry.[15]

Acupuncture

Acupuncture is a form of primary healthcare based on traditional Chinese medical concepts. It involves the direct manipulation of the network of energetic meridians, which are believed to connect not only with the surface or structural body but also to influence the deeper internal organs. Western-style research has demonstrated acupuncture to be an effective therapy in the treatment of chronic pain. In addition, acupuncture is well-recognized as a proactive approach to the treatment of addictive disorders.[16]

Today the challenge for providers moving toward the development of an integrated model is to develop innovative indicators to demonstrate the efficacy of new interventions. Improving health status will demand that providers collect data on how both biomedical and complementary treatments affect patients' quality of life, functionality, and overall sense of well-being.

PATIENT SATISFACTION

The biomedical model revolutionized medicine and the way health and illness are viewed, but it is becoming increasingly expensive. An integrated model of care, with an emphasis on preventive medicine, may have much to offer in further controlling healthcare costs. Although in most instances in which an integrated model is tested, there is some trade-off between the desire for immediate revenue and the need to invest in new techniques as a loss-leader if the resources of talent and skills are available, the integration of large financial rewards may potentially be reaped when the paradigm shifts and providers are incented for wellness. Some health systems—like Mercy Healthcare, Catholic Healthcare West, and Sharp Medical Center—are making million-dollar investments in the research and design of integrated models. Still, the good news is that you don't have to build a swimming pool to test the waters. Hospitals like St. Charles Medical Center in Bend, Oregon, California Pacific Medical Center in San Francisco, California, or Griffin Hospital in Derby, Connecticut, have found that it is often the simple, low-cost things—like art, music, and patient resource centers—that enhance their image and increase patient satisfaction.

The practice of Steve Hines, MD, an innovative Vanderbilt University-trained internal medicine specialist with commitment to an integrated approach, presents another example of "it is the little things that count." Dr. Hines has chosen to remain autonomous in his practice in Nashville, Tennessee, despite increasingly seductive offers from Columbia/HCA, Saint Thomas Hospital, and Baptist Medical Center. Dr. Hines reports that he will only be able to hold the market forces at bay for so long, but his concern in joining a group is a little different from that of other doctors considering giving up their solo practices. Dr. Hines differentiates his practice in two ways:

1. He has created within his office a clinical environment that is differentiated by the use of light, art, and music. According to his patients, the office itself creates a context for healing.

2. He works with exercise physiologists, nutritionists, and mental health professionals to foster a multidisciplinary team approach to patient care.

How Dr. Hines operates does not cost a lot more, but it does add up in terms of increased patient satisfaction and functional outcome.

Hospitals and health systems embracing and manifesting a healing philosophy within their own walls anecdotally report some impact on corporate culture, as well as an *indirect, yet financially significant, impact to their bottom line.* Anecdotal reports indicate that employee productivity is up, recidivism is down, and the seamless flow of patients throughout the system is more finely tuned. In addition, the output of qualitative assessment tools and informal discussion groups both appear to reflect the same theme: Individuals working within a "healing environment" feel that they have rediscovered their original mission within healthcare. They view themselves as patient advocates and members of care-giving teams that can make a difference. These implications regarding the integration of complementary therapies are likely to become more salient in the foreseeable future, given the simultaneous convergence within acute and sub-acute care delivery systems of cost-containment pressures and patient-satisfaction measures.

In creating a healing environment, one primary caution emerges: ***Ask your patients what they want!*** What "feels like home" to one person might be anything but soothing to another. For instance, gospel music may be perceived as healing by some communities of patients, whereas others may prefer classical harp and flute renditions. Similarly, preferences for certain kinds of art, color schemes, and textures may vary according to geographic region, race, age, sex, and psychographic profile. Remember to incorporate questions into consumer focus group discussions and to probe deeply into the question What would this look, feel, sound, smell like to you? in order to design an environment where your patients feel welcome, comfortable, supported, and nurtured.

Of course, an intensive market analysis is required to obtain a valid understanding of local customer segments, current utilization patterns, perceived needs, and supply/demand issues. It is possible that to consider that an integrated model of care could add density to a hospital's or health system's objective to *enhance customer intimacy.*

LEARNING FROM OTHERS

The following lists provide some examples of existing models that could be considered as learning laboratories (this is a beginning list and should by no means be considered to be a complete index of existing models).

Biopsychosocial Models

1. **The Vine Hill Clinic:** The Vine Hill Clinic in Nashville, Tennessee, is exemplary in that it moves beyond the biomedical model of physical fitness and incorporates mental health as integral to a new definition of well-being. Begun in 1991 by the Vanderbilt University School of Nursing and a grant from the Kellogg Foundation, the Vine Hill Clinic is a model that may illuminate nursing centers as a practical fulcrum for change in this era of health reform. The concept of nurse practitioners running a satellite primary care center is not new. What is new is a biopsychosocial approach to care that is getting the attention—and the contracts—nursing centers are receiving from the managed care payors. In Tennessee, the Vine Hill Clinic successfully competed for the TennCare business and tripled its patient volume to more than 10,000 patient visits in 1995.

   What is especially potent about the Vine Hill Clinic model is its three-pronged approach to fulfilling its role as a primary care services provider: traditional clinical services, mental health services, and community outreach. By definition, the nurse practitioners' clinic model is recognized for its emphasis on teaching and counseling. This is a plus in a system that is becoming vested in enhancing individual responsibility. For the purposes of this discussion, however, I would like to highlight the mental health triage component. The Vine Hill Clinic is a model that is bringing mental health into the center of the primary care arena. By bridging the gaps between physical and psychological health, the Vine Hill Clinic is making important strides toward creating a model in which the context of care is social well-being.

2. **Booker T. Washington High School Adolescent Program:** Emory University's Nell Hodgson Woodruff School of Nursing, in collaboration with the Washington Cluster of the Atlanta Project, has opened the Booker T. Washington High School Adolescent Health Care Station at Washington High in Southwest Atlanta. This new venture goes beyond physical illness in adolescents to deal with psychosocial "distress signals," particularly in early adolescence. These distress signals, which may include increasing absenteeism, apathy, confusion, or mild depression, may eventually lead to more serious problems in later adolescence, including school failure, pregnancy, drug abuse, or violent behavior. The healthcare station provides a comfortable environment in which students can come to discuss personal issues. The nurses refer

students to the West End Clinic, also located at Washington High, for problems of physical illness.

Adolescents are giving us early distress signals, but we are not listening, says Nell Hodgson School of Nursing Dean Dyanne D. Affonso, PhD. And because these early symptoms are not being addressed by our educational and healthcare systems, millions of children nationwide are drifting into depression, substance abuse, pregnancy, violence, and suicide. Waiting until these problems already exist is waiting until it is too late, Dr. Affonso believes. And using established healthcare programs to address the physical ailments of teenagers while ignoring their mental health is asking for trouble.

The nursing school has a five-year commitment to the health station. Emory nurses work with students referred by teachers, the school nurse, counselors, or the students themselves. Medical problems are referred back to the school nurse or the West End Clinic. Since Washington High is a magnet school for the health sciences, the nurses also teach health classes during school, which is a way of marketing their program. Additionally, Emory nursing school students can become more involved by volunteering for an advisory committee to help plan the program or by helping develop seminars and health fairs and leading programs for younger students. "Our model is one of a health continuum," one of the nurses explains. "One end of the continuum is the illness state. A lot of interventions are geared to actual problems which occur at the end of the continuum. We want to identify symptoms before the students have problems. Once they are on drugs, or become pregnant, or have dropped out of school, it's almost too late, like falling off a cliff."[17]

3. **Care Oregon:** John Saultz, MD, Medical Director of Care Oregon, the state's third-largest managed care company, is a convinced and convincing advocate of what he calls integrated care. His model enacted a partnership among rural health centers, the university health center, and the State Department of Health. Dr. Staultz thinks that in 10 years, all care will be integrated and that the Medicaid population will lead the way because medical systems are going to become responsible by law for the whole person. Apparently the Oregon Health Plan, which covers 100 percent of the poverty level population (instead of the 53% cutoff for most states), will mandate employers to cover mental health benefits beginning in 1997. What is most unique is that Oregon's prioritized list of services will include three new categories: the mentally or

physically disabled; the chemically dependent; and the deinstitutionalized, chronically mentally ill.[18]

4. **Collaborative Care Center, NYU Medical Center:** At the Collaborative Care Center at NYU Medical Center, directed by Anthony Grieco, MD, a family "care partner" lives in with the patient during acute hospitalization. The care partner and patient share a room, each with their own bed. There is a laundromat on the floor and the nursing stations are one floor down. The care partner learns to provide care and is thus trained to do home care. The educationally intensive experience encourages full patient and family involvement in care, increases patient satisfaction, improves compliance, and reduces subsequent use of high-cost healthcare resources such as rehospitalization. The hospital can provide excellent service for one-third less than the cost on traditional units. And, apparently, no one cares for a person as well as a family member who is empowered by the system to do so.[19]
5. **Early Start Project, Kaiser Permanente:** In Oakland, California, the Early Start Project at Kaiser Permanente has been so successful in reducing newborn ICU days and increasing abstinence rates among mothers that it has been expanded to three other sites. The project places chemical dependency counselors in OB\GYN offices to assist in screening for substance abuse in early pregnancy.[20]

Complementary Therapies

1. **Hospital and Health System Ventures:** All of the following are evidence that respected, financially stable, and strategically aggressive health systems are investigating complementary therapies as working components of a continuum of care. Joint ventures between hospitals and health systems include:
   - Beth Israel Hospital and Harvard Medical School's Center for Alternative Medicine Research (Boston, Massachusetts).
   - New England Deaconess Hospital and Harvard Medical School's Mind/Body Institute and affiliates (Boston, Massachusetts).
   - Mercy Healthcare's Arizona Center for Health and Medicine (Phoenix, Arizona).
   - Columbia/HCA and Grant Hospital (Chicago, Illinois).
   - St. Charles Medical Center's Healing Healthcare Project (Bend, Oregon).
   - California Pacific Medical Center's Institute for Health and Healing (San Francisco, California).

- Sharp Medical Center and Deeprak Chopra's Center for Mind/Body Medicine (San Diego, California).

2. **Managed Care Programs:**
   - Mutual of Omaha has embraced Dr. Dean Ornish's diet and lifestyle modification program as a cost-effective means for reducing the incidence and subsequent costs of heart disease.
   - American West Life has set up a naturopathic triage model, fostered the formation of complementary medicine provider panels, and created the Wellness Plan as an alternative to the traditional HMO or PPO.
   - Kaiser-Permanente has funded studies to examine the economic consequences of moving beyond the accepted medical case management processes to address the psychological and behavioral needs of their membership.
   - Harvard Community Health Plan is researching therapeutic interventions that include the elicitation of the relaxation response as an integral part of the treatment program.
   - Blue Cross of Washington and Alaska launched a pilot alternative care program, Alternpath, which covers services of homeopathic and naturopathic physicians and acupuncturists.
   - Memorial Healthcare System is piloting a behavior modification program that provides employees financial incentives to change high-risk behaviors.
3. **Universities and Academic Medical Centers:**
   - Andrew Weil, MD, has founded the Division of Social Perspectives in Medicine at the College of Medicine, University of Arizona, where he teaches about alternative medicine, mind–body interactions, and medical botany. A pilot program for training in integrative medicine is now being initiated within the medical school.
   - The University of Maryland at Baltimore School of Medicine, in connection with the Laing Complementary Medicine Project, has established the Division of Complementary Medicine. Brian M. Berman, MD, and his staff—trained in the treatment of chronic pain—are attempting to develop interdisciplinary programs for pain management. The goal of their work is to shift away from the anesthesiology pain center setting into a family medicine milieu, which allows access to alternative/complementary therapies.
   - Stanford University School of Medicine's Center for Research in Disease Prevention is using baseline health status measures to

design creative approaches to health risks and disease management. Program evaluation includes utilization, patient satisfaction, an economic dimensions.

- Columbia University is the site for Indo-Tibetan Medical Project of the Dharam Hinduja Indic Research Center.
- The University of Colorado Center for Nursing Research has established the Center for Human Caring to foster the development, application, and analysis of caring–healing praxis models.
- Several medical schools such as those at Harvard, Georgetown, and Emory universities are making arrangements to provide education in unconventional methods to medical students.

4. **Independently Owned Clinics:**
   - The Health Institute of Dallas (Dallas, Texas).
   - The Lamat Corporation/Lamat Healthcare Centers (Minneapolis, Minnesota).
   - The Alternare Group (Portland, Oregon).
   - The Upledger Institute, Inc. (Palm Beach Gardens, Florida).
   - Steve Hines, MD, Internal Medicine Specialist (Nashville, Tennessee).
   - Women's healthcare clinics and birthing centers, e.g., Spence Center for Women's Health (Cambridge, Massachusetts), Feminist Women's Health Centers (Northern California), and Women's International Pharmacy (Madison, Wisconsin).
5. **Non-Profit Consumer Health Organizations:**
   - Planetree Hospital's model units and affiliates.
   - Commonweal (Bolinas, California).
   - The Health Communications Research Institute (Sacramento, California).
6. **Health Information, Decision Support, and Telemedicine Services:**
   - Planetree Health Resource Centers (San Francisco, California).
   - H.E.A.L. (Louisville, Kentucky).
   - Direct Medical Knowledge (Sausalito, California).
   - IBIS (Portland, Oregon).
   - Home Medical Advisor (American West Life Insurance).
   - Health Decisions, Inc. (Golden, Colorado).
   - CIGNA and the Foundation for Informed Medical Decision Making (Bloomfield, Connecticut/Hanover, New Hampshire).

7. **Research, Education, and Funding:**
   - National Institute of Health's Office of Alternative Medicine (OAM).
   - The Fetzer Institute and the Pew-Fetzer Foundation.
   - The Institute of Noetic Sciences.
   - The James Irvine Foundation.
   - The National Cancer Institute.
   - Collaborative ventures with other countries.

INVESTING FOR A VIABLE FUTURE

In today's competitive marketplaces, there are no cookie-cutter solutions. Health systems are forced to take calculated risks when they make business decisions that will directly impact their future. When moving into a totally new arena where there are no established track records for what works or what doesn't, it can be difficult to assess the potential contribution of a new approach to a hospital's overhead or profitability. The development of an integrated model for healthcare delivery is really an investment in research and development (R&D). The methodology for evaluating such an R&D strategy is contingent on the objectives for the effort.

In beginning to consider the potential benefits of incorporating biopsychosocial approaches and complementary therapies into a continuum of care, *it is critical that each individual hospital clearly identify what it hopes to gain.* Decision makers should use market analysis information to identify the point of intersection between financial objectives, R&D goals, public relations efforts, and goodwill investments. In some instances, the hospital may see the establishment of an integrated clinic model for primary care services as a strategic move to capture market share. In other markets, the hospital may identify a need for market differentiation and decide to formalize its commitment to customer intimacy.

The important point is that investments in R&D represent costs to a hospital. These investments, therefore, should be tied to the achievement of some objectives, either in the short or long term. In considering the development of an integrated model in the context of local market dynamics, should a *contribution analysis* provide the basis for evaluating how well the vision, marketing, and production objectives mesh?

As stated previously, the purpose of R&D is to maintain or improve a hospital's competitive position. Sometimes the development of new programs or services will create immediate sources for new revenue streams. One example would be strategy to capture a self-pay customer base by expanding a continuum of care to include complementary therapies already being accessed in the market by the individual consumers. More often, however, R&D activities may initially be lower-contribution services. Community health initiatives, for instance, are more long-term investments. Their payoff will not be realized until the market is impelled to decrease utilization by improving health status, that is, capitation.

Given the more long-term nature of the investment, a R&D strategy that involves the development of an integrated model is probably best evaluated on a qualitative, rather than a quantitative, basis. Further, it should be developed and evaluated in the context of the findings from the *external market analysis* and the *internal diagnosis of cultural readiness*. The following questions can be a useful *framework for measuring the effectiveness of a research and development strategy leading to new business development:*

- What are the current *managed care market pressures and financial dynamics* that would cause a hospital to consider developing an integrated model of care as a proactive business development strategy?
- Can a move toward developing an integrated model for service delivery enhance a hospital's and/or system's competitive position by either expanding its existing customer base or by improving its reputation for providing cost-effective and quality products and/or services? In other words, will it establish *market differentiation?*
- Is the hospital and/or system ready to be a *leader in innovation?* Can it *sustain the cost of investment* without immediate return?
- How do the hospital's and/or system's R&D strategies and capabilities compare to trends and *emerging competitor developments* in the external environment?
- Is a move toward developing an integrated model, or incorporating complementary therapies in any way across a spectrum of care, *indicative of the intersection between mission, values and performance objectives?*

Within the context of developing an integrated model for the delivery of healthcare services and the question of when, where, and how to expand a continuum of care to appropriately incorporate complementary therapies, the following question sets a framework for initiating the process of inquiry and moving consciously and strategically towards new business development.

WHAT IS YOUR BASE OF BUSINESS TODAY . . . AND TOMORROW?

Look at your revenue streams. If a hospital's book of business is still primarily fee-for-service, then that hospital is still making money on treating episodes of illness. In such a market it would be difficult to convince a CEO to "stop the cash registers from ringing" by beginning to invest in programs impacting health status and a mind–body–spirit approach to well-being. Conversely, hospitals in more mature managed care markets are probably feeling the squeeze as the price window of negotiations narrows. In such cases, a CEO might look favorably on the idea of integrating complementary therapies into a continuum of care—if the consequences include more cost-effective delivery of services, enhanced patient satisfaction, and market differentiation.

The key is to understand the relationship of current revenue streams to the old way of being in business and to anticipate the rapidity with which those dollars could be subtracted from the bottom line. Such an analysis will allow for proactive planning. Integrating complementary therapies into the biomedical model should not cannibalize the existing sources of revenue. Instead, the integration of complementary therapies should be tightly synchronized with strategies for managing the shift from fee-for-service to capitation, while at the same time developing sources for replacement revenue. See Figure 13–2 and 13–3. In order to strategically step into the future, you must first know where you stand today:

- Analyze the managed care environment: percentage of penetration, trends, and momentum.
- Define market economics and current reimbursement scenario.
- Understand legislative/regulatory issues.
- Identify market risks and areas of financial tension.
- Recognize competitive dynamics: opportunities and threats.

In your own market, it is important to start *with what you are already doing* and to target conditions an integrated model of care. This makes the most ethical and business sense.

FIGURE 13–2

Moving Forward with an Integrated Model: Opportunities/Strategies

Low Risk ←——→ **High Risk**

Expand or enhance **pastoral care** programs; recognize **spiritual health** as a key component of case management processes. **Models:** ■ **California Pacific Medical Center** ■ **Griffin Hospital** ■ **St. Charles Medical Center**	Educate internal and external customers via educational forums and resource library; emphasize that the **environment & physical plan** can create the context for healing. **Models:** ■ **Planetree** ■ **St. Charles Medical Center** ■ **Arizona Center for Health & Medicine**	Align with respected **academic center of research** to develop pilot program/ demonstration project; target patient populations where physicians recognize the limitations of the biomedical model, i.e., chronic pain, AIDS, oncology, cardiac disease. **Models:** ■ **The Mind/Body Institute, Harvard Medical School & New England Deaconess Hospital** ■ **The Laing Complementary Medicine Project, Dept. of Family Medicine – Univ. of Maryland at Baltimore**	Integrate complementary therapies into **existing service lines** in order to enhance customer intimacy or to leverage cost/quality/value of service delivery. **Models:** ■ **Commonweal/ Oncology** ■ **Selected Acupuncture & Detoxification Centers/ Substance Abuse and Addiction** ■ **The Upledger Institute/Brain & Spinal Cord Dysfunction Program** ■ **Physicians Plus/Sports Medicine** ■ **Center for Mind–Body Medicine, Washington DC/Community Health** ■ **Hospice Programs American Hospice Management** ■ **The Spence Center for Women's Health**	Create a **referral network of local complementary medicine providers** in order to expand primary care services to include: traditional Chinese medicine; acupuncture; homeopathy; nutritional therapy; Ayurvedic medicine; psychological counseling; Trager and Feldenkrais body awareness techniques; therapeutic massage; therapeutic touch; osteopathic manipulation; guided visual imaging; herbal therapy; yoga and t'ai chi classes; aroma therapy; color, dance and art therapies. **Models:** ■ **American Holistic Centers** ■ **The Institute for Health & Healing, California Pacific Medical Center**	Use complementary therapies/integrated approaches as a strategy for **market differentiation and managed care contracting**; consider creating a PPO or direct contracting with employers. **Models:** ■ **Stanford Center for Research in Disease Prevention, Stanford Univ. School of Medicine** ■ **Vine Hill Clinic, Vanderbilt Univ. School of Medicine** ■ **Arizona Center for Health & Medicine** ■ **American Holistic Centers** ■ **Center for Mind–Body Medicine, Sharp Healthcare System** ■ **Preventive Medicine Research Institute, Dean Ornish MD** ■ **Alternare Clinic of Natural Medicine** ■ **American Western Life**	**Expand base of primary care business** beyond hospital walls; create a stand-alone clinic model. **Models:** ■ **Vine Hill Clinic, Vanderbilt Univ. School of Medicine** ■ **Arizona Center for Health & Medicine** ■ **American Holistic Centers** ■ **The Health Institute** ■ **King Co. Clinic**

FIGURE 13–3

Moving Forward with an Integrated Model: Opportunities/Strategies

← Stages of Managed Care Evolutions →

High Risk ↕ Low Risk

Stage I	Stage II	Stage III	Stage IV
■ Assess legal and regulatory issues/constraints. ■ Involve pastoral care departments. ■ Emphasize the value of incorporating and expanding easily understood services: nutrition, health promotion, relaxation therapy. ■ Look at opportunities to enhance *customer intimacy* by focusing on caring philosophy and healing environments (i.e., Planetree, Center for Caring, Healing Healthcare). ■ Begin a peripheral sketching of the number and types of complementary health professionals practicing in your market. ■ Incorporate questions regarding use of complementary therapies into patient survey. ■ Conduct internal audit: What is already being done? ■ Informally assess disposition of medical staff. ■ Offer educational forums. ■ Remember that the patient is multidimensional: Mind–body–spirit.	■ Conduct comprehensive market analysis: Get ready for what's coming. ■ Direct contract with large self-insured employers; health promotion, education, lifestyle change programs. ■ Participate in community health initiatives; include questions on use of complementary medicine information and health status/needs summary. ■ Look for opportunities to expand services in order to "own the continuum" (i.e., community-oriented primary care, workplace wellness, hospice programs, etc.). ■ Identify opportunities to enchance cost competitiveness via incorporating lower-cost biopsychosocial approaches and complementary therapies into service delivery when appropriate. ■ Build case management processes with teams of health professionals working together. ■ Stay close to physician champions. ■ Become the fulcrum for education and reference information on complementary medicine and integrated care models, create a resource center/library.	■ Include complementary treatments in outcomes tracking efforts. ■ Incorporate complementary medicine approaches into managed care contracting strategy (i.e., "Dean Ornish, MD type" programs, acupuncture, detox, herbal formularies, etc.). ■ Tailor integrated programs to meet specific market needs (i.e., holistic promary care centers, women's health programs, sports medicine, chronic pain programs). ■ Make community health a strategic priority; invest in programs that have the potential to reduce utilization and resource demand. ■ Become a community resource for health information pertaining to lifestyle choices, biomedical treatment options and potential complementary approaches (i.e., develop a library, database, and/or local resource directory). ■ Focus on market differentiation via emphasis on *customer intimacy*.	■ Include complementary healthcare providers in risk pool. ■ Provide seamless care across a continuum; relational databases. ■ Complementary medicine fully integrated into biomedical model.

TABLE 13–1

Where Would You Start?

- Serious, chronic, debilitating, or terminal illness, especially when conventional medicine has limited success in controlling symptoms or disease processes. (Examples: HIV disease, chronic fatigue syndrome [CFS], multiple sclerosis [MS], autoimmune disorders, cancers)
- Acute or chronic conditions for which conventional medicine has little or nothing curative to offer. (Examples: headache, persistent back pain, various skin conditions, colds, allergies, fatigue, weight control, asthma, rheumatic diseases, pain syndromes)
- Conditions for which a person prefers non-drug, non-invasive approaches, and which have popular reputations for nonmedical management success. (Examples: insomnia, allergies, colitis and other disorders of the digestive system, pregnancy and childbirth, asthma, headache, back pain, arthritis.)
- Desire to replace recommended medical therapies that are offensive or impair quality of life, or with which a person disagrees. (Examples: invasive therapies, drugs with significant toxicity, disfiguring treatments, drugs with mood-altering or sense-altering side effects, extended or lifelong regimens)
- Need to control side effects of conventional medical therapies (while not wishing to discontinue the therapies).
- Dissatisfaction with treatments, outcomes, or personnel and attitudes of conventional medicine.
- Failure of conventional therapy.
- Inability of physicians to arrive at a diagnosis, especially after lengthy efforts or exhaustive testing.
- Diagnoses that are too vague, that are offensive to the patient, or with which the patient disagrees. (Examples: persistent "fever of unknown origin" [FUO], illnesses in which mental illness or psychosomatic processes are considered to be sole or contributing factors)
- Illnesses that conventional medicine does not recognize as diagnostic categories. (Examples: folk illnesses, new diseases, e.g., Chronic Fatigue Syndrome)
- Instances in which conventional medicine is considered to be addressing symptoms, but not underlying causes. (Examples: allergies; digestive disorders; illnesses in which spiritual or supernatural causal factors are implicated, from the patient's point of view)
- Instances in which conventional medicine is felt inadequate to address a person's health concerns. (Examples: nutrition, prevention, health maintenance or promotion of "wellness," preference for natural rather than synthetic medicaments, preference for high patient involvement in determination of therapeutic course)
- Whenever a particular health belief system is part of a person's cultural heritage or identity-group culture, or part of a consciously chosen lifestyle.

Source: From Bonnie Blair O'Connor, *Healing Traditions: Alternative Medicine and the Health Professions,* 1995.

TABLE 13–2

How Would You Start?

- **Begin an informal audit of internal readiness.** It *is not recommended* that you begin with a formal medical staff survey. Instead, initiate some one-on-one discussions to determine physician's and health professional's current attitudes and level of interest.
- **Create a resource map** identifying any existing pockets of service delivery already integrating complementary therapies. It is always easier to move into the future if you *start from where you already are.*
- **Initiate a process of inquiry** by offering seminars and educational forums with the concept of integrated medicine as the focus. Survey participants after the forums, not before.
- **Get a feel for the scope and volume of services already being accessed** beyond the biomedical model. (Note: Even without a formal market analysis profiling supply and demand, it is possible to get a quick read simply by looking in the yellow pages or calling a local health food store and requesting a listing of complementary health professionals.)
- **Look at the areas where the hospital could be at risk,** i.e., revenue, market share, and reputation, and consider the possibility of integrating complementary therapies as part of a proactive strategy to ensure market strength.
- **Review models of care and match market characteristics** in order to develop criteria to determine which ones could have local benefit.
- Move forward with comprehensive **quantitative and qualitative market analysis.**
- Use analytical information to **create a framework for new business development** within the context of integrated medicine.

TABLE 13–3

What are Common Characteristics That Should Be Present Before Moving Forward to Integrate Approaches into a Continuum of Care?

Internal Readiness

- **Educational forums** introducing the concept and initiating a process of inquiry as to the potential value of complementary therapies to an integrated model and expanded continuum of care.
- **Physician Champion(s).**
- **Medical staff buy-In** and clinical professional support.
- **Existing programs/services** already integrating approaches (i.e., pastoral care, cardiac rehab, women's health, worksite wellness, hospice, etc.).
- **Corporate culture** emphasizing customer intimacy.

External Market Drivers (Note: Will require a market analysis)

- **Legal/Regulatory Issues** impacting patient access.
- **Supply and Demand:** Local availability of complementary providers.
- **Purchasing Patterns/Trends:** Patient/customer going outside the medical model and self-referring to complementary therapists.
- **Utilization:** Volume of self-pay, fee-for-service business going outside the hospital's existing continuum of care.
- **Competitive dynamics:** Are other hospitals within your market getting into this business?
- **Percent managed care penetration:** How rapidly is the market transitioning from FFS to capitation? Can complementary therapies provide opportunities to enhance cost performance or create opportunities for replacement revenue?
- **Reimbursement environment:** Will the payor pay?

TABLE 13–4

What Are Important Elements of an Integrated Model of Care, Stated in Terms of Results Produced for Customers?

- **Enhanced customer intimacy:** An emphasis on the whole person and an expanded definition of health.
- **Expanded spectrum of service offerings:** Patients do not have to go outside the system to access desired complementary treatments when the hospital "owns" the continuum of care.
- **Opportunities to improve provider performance:** Cost, quality, and patient satisfaction.

TABLE 13–5

How Should the Hospital Develop a Positioning Strategy and Marketing/Communications Plans?

- **Position biopsychosocial approaches and complementary therapies** so as to *enhance—not replace*—the biomedical model.
- **Work closely with physician champion(s)** and medical staff. All new approaches to clinical care should be either physician supervised or approved, as appropriate.
- **Begin with existing "footholds"** within current service lines, i.e., start by reinforcing those programs already integrating biopsychosocial approaches and complementary therapies.
- **Communicate** how an integrated model of care is congruent with, and adds practical density to, the organization's vision/mission/purpose.

TABLE 13–6

What Infrastructure Is Required to Move Toward an Integrated Model of Care?

- **Operations:** Must have *physician support,* no new initiatives should ever be done in contest with the medical staff.
- **Financing:** Must be clear regarding objectives associated with services. Is the hospital looking for opportunities for *replacement revenue, R&D* or *demonstration projects* that respond to imminent shifts in reimbursement or *a "hook" for market differentiation?* The answer to that question should dictate the dollars committed.
- **Human Resources:**
  Resource Mapping: Existing health professionals already practicing complementary therapies within the hospital systems of care, i.e., nurses, pastors/spiritual directors.

  Supply and Demand: Availability of credentialed/licensed practitioners.

  Panel Selection: Ability to pull together a panel of providers outside the physician community that is respected by the medical staff.

  Cross-Training: Opportunities to further the education of interested physicians in complementary therapies.

TABLE 13–7

What Features Will Need to Be Addressed/Put in Place to Ensure the "Fit" of an Integrated Model within a System of Care?

- **Credibility:** All professional caregivers associated with any practice of complementary medicine must be respected by the medical staff. The integration of specific therapies should be supported by empirically sound data and the output of scientific research.
- **Case management:** The use of complementary therapies must fit within a framework addressing the health needs of the whole patient, i.e., a biopsychosocial/spiritual approach to case management.
- **Outcomes Tracking:** Information systems and relational databases will be required to fit complementary therapies into a matrix measuring impact and tracking performance indicators.
- **Market Differentiation:** Need to determine when/how the integration of complementary therapies can add leverage to service value or cost performance.

ENDNOTES

1. Sollee, Diane. "Working Together," *The Collaborative Family Health Care Coalition Newsletter,* vol. 2, no. 2, (Winter 1995).
2. Moskowitz, Reed. "Establishing Health Insurance Coverage for the Treatment of Stress-Related Disorders," *Advances,* vol. 5, no. 4, p. 61.
3. Eisenberg, David. "Pain and Depression Common Ailments in Neurologist and Internist's Office," *Mental Health Today* (June 1994).
4. "Unconventional Medicine in the United States," *New England Journal of Medicine* (1993), p. 246–51.
5. The following paragraphs on The Catholic Health Association's think tank findings are adapted from: "Create a Healthy World—Health and Well-Being: Lessons From the Experts." Executive Summary of Two Think Tanks Convened by the Catholic Health Association of the United States.
6. Cowley, Geoffrey. "What High-Tech Can't Accomplish," *Newsweek* (October 4, 1993), p. 63.
7. Freeman, Elsbeth. *Testimony Before the Legislative Implementation Committee for TennCare* (October 29, 1993).
8. Neus, Elizabeth. "Depression Possibly Mistreated," *The Tennessean* (Jan. 21, 1996), p. 12A.
9. "Mental Health Treatment Reduces Medical Costs," *Mental Medicine Update,* vol. IV, no. 2 (1995), p. 7.

10. Japsen, Bruce. "Cost Conscious Providers Take to Holistic Medicine," *Modern Healthcare* (Aug. 21, 1995), pp. 138, 142.

11. "Alternative Medicine, Expanding Medical Horizons," A Report to the National Institutes of Health on Alternative Medical Systems and Practices. Prepared under the auspices of the Workshop on Alternative Medicine in Chantilly, VA, September 14–16, 1992, p. ix.

12. Glieck, Elizabeth. "Rehab Centers Run Dry," *Time* (Feb. 5, 1996), p. 44.

13. "Alternative Medicine, Expanding Medical Horizons," A Report to the National Institutes of Health on Alternative Medical Systems and Practices. Prepared under the auspices of the Workshop on Alternative Medicine in Chantilly, VA, September 14–16, 1992. p. xlii.

14. ibid., p. xlvi.

15. Reynolds, H. M., M. C. Beal, and R. C. Hallgren. "Quantifying Passive Resistance to Motion in the Straight Leg Raising Test on Asymptomatic Subjects," *Journal of the American Osteopathic Association,* vol. 93, pp. 913–920; Sleszynski, S. L., and A. F. Kelso. "Comparison of Thoracic Manipulation with Incentive Spirometry in Preventing Postoperative Atelectasis, *Journal of the American Osteopathic Association,* (1993), pp. 834–845.

16. "Alternative Medicine, Expanding Medical Horizons," A Report to the National Institutes of Health on Alternative Medical Systems and Practices. Prepared under the auspices of the Workshop on Alternative Medicine in Chantilly, VA, September 14–16, 1992, pp. 74–75.

17. "Washington High School Health Station Addresses Early Adolescent Distress Signals," *Emory Health Sciences News* (Jan. 2, 1996).

18. "Around the Network," *CFHCC Newsletter* (Winter 1995), p. 3.

19. ibid.

20. ibid.

PART FIVE

MAKING COMMUNITY HEALTH A STRATEGIC PRIORITY

14 CHAPTER

Shaping the Hospital's Role

Why do hospitals and health systems want to get involved in community health? For some, it is a matter of mission. For others, financial risk is the motivator. Regardless of their reasons, smart administrators recognize that they can't change their business overnight. Fundamentally changing hospital operations requires systematic planning for new product development. Also, sick care will always be a component of a healthcare delivery system, even if there is a need for replacement revenue with capitation.

So how do you as a local healthcare leader get involved with community health in a way that works for you? First, recognize that just because health is the key vocabulary word in some task force's label, you are not responsible for taking ownership for community health initiatives. You probably can't afford it, and even if you can, it won't work if you do. By definition, a community health initiative requires the buy-in of local healthcare purchasers and consumers. To work, community health initiatives must touch individuals where they live, work, eat, sleep, play, and worship. The provider community cannot single-handedly foster enhanced individual responsibility for health or modify behavioral response. Although the monkey is not off the hospital's back because it plays a key role in any effort to impact community health status, success does demand a coordinated effort.

Next, look at this whole burgeoning issue of community health as a catalyst for new product development. Getting into the wellness and health promotion business needs to happen at the same time as a streamlining of existing services. Hospitals can choose a segment of the community and pilot programs designed to impact health status. This allows time for the testing of innovative approaches, the training of staff, and the integration of a new component into a continuum of care. By having a chance on a small scale to really see what works and what doesn't, providers can get primed for capitation without committing in a big way to a focus that, under most current reimbursement schemes, yields inadequate profit margins.

COLLAPSING BOUNDARIES

Collapsing the boundaries between competitive players should begin by addressing how best to *merge cultures, not assets.* To address the barriers existing between the public and private health sectors, *look at functions first.* Moving past discussion to implementation requires that short-term survival needs be openly addressed. For instance, few providers will be willing (or able) to readily relinquish revenue streams associated with primary care services. Public health officials will argue that primary care is legitimately more in their realm of prevention and education. Community service agencies may struggle with new measures of accountability as they try to demonstrate their value in the health status, cost/benefit equation. Competing agendas and conflicting incentives can dilute the potency of new partnerships. More often, and more pervasive, anxiety can displace passion, which renders the entire collaborative process sterile.

Collective responsibility characterizes more sophisticated managed care markets. The definitions between adversaries and advocates often become blurred. This collapsing of boundaries can be attributed to the fact that the market has moved beyond multiple players chaotically competing on price to a more secure market characterized by payor and provider consolidation. Collaboration stories are each unique because they have evolved locally and because they incorporate a multiplicity of market pressures, political issues, and social factors.

At this point, the key determinants of longevity for new collaborative ventures appear to be the following:

- Commitment to being in the future with a new social contract for collective responsibility and community health.
- Constancy of purpose.
- Shared ownership of objectives.
- Education at the hub of all activities.
- Solid local market data.
- Awareness of the subtle and "sexy" political land mines.
- Willingness to merge cultures and blend assets.

- Increased communication and systematic dissemination of salient information.
- A system for shared decision making, process management, impact measurement, reporting, and continuous improvement.
- The design of a community partnership in which visions are aligned with market realities and constancy of purpose is supported by immediate and pragmatic, doable steps.
- The emergence of a new environment and new leaders.
- New aggressive and creative strategies to promote health and well-being.
- A willingness to be a living laboratory.

Community health objectives must be translated into a real-life experience that has meaning for each player in this new initiative. Robert Sandler, associate vice president of the Connecticut Hospital Association, shares the following example of how a high risk health concern—teen pregnancy—can impact across the board of community constituants. (See Figure 14–1.)

CASE STUDY

TEENAGE PREGNANCY

Teen pregnancy is a problem that cuts across all levels of the community. Unless we are directly involved, however, we tend to ignore the problem or think it is someone else's problem. The fact is, we all are impacted one way or another whether we recognize it or not. In Connecticut in 1993 there were 1,559 deliveries to teenagers aged 13 to 17 years old. This number represents a conservative estimate of teenage pregnancies because it does not include terminated pregnancies. I would like to share with you an actual story of one of these teenagers. A cursory review of the information in the flowchart that spans from p. 212 to 215 reveals:

- We have a 15-year-old teenager who was first pregnant in 1985.
- She delivered 5 babies between 1985 and 1991.
- Each box represents a stay in the hospital.

When we look at the data in detail we see that the teenage mother:

- Delivered all her babies by Caesarean section.
- Probably had an untreated sexually transmitted disease.
- Probably was involved in drug and/or alcohol abuse.
- Had little or no prenatal care.

Continued

- Had poor nutrition.
- Probably did not take vitamins or receive medications.

When we look at the babies delivered we see:

- Baby #2:
  had 18 hospital stays between 1987 and 1991.
  is a low birth weight baby (1,303 grams—a little under 3 lbs.)
  is blind, paralyzed, and brain damaged, and has kidney problems, respiratory problems, and infantile cerebral palsy, has a permanent tracheostomy and feeding tube.
- Baby #3 also had problems, although not as severe.
- Babies #4 and #5 are twins. They were born pre-term, weighing at 2,070 grams—approximately 4.5 lbs—each.
- The total *hospital* cost for this teenager and her five babies through 1992 was approximately $200,000.

What we are looking at here is a real tragedy. It is a tragedy for the teenager, the babies, and the community. Where was the community support system? Why did this teenager fall through the cracks? Assuming we could *not* prevent the pregnancy, even with appropriate parenting and education, this teenager should have been identified and picked up after the delivery of her first baby.

This teenage pregnancy impacts negatively on all segments of the community. Consider that:

- The quality of the teenager's life is drastically reduced and a childhood is lost.
- The quality of life for at least one of the babies has been significantly diminished.
- Family life and relationships are impacted.
- The neighborhood is changed—values are challenged, issues of adequate housing are raised, living conditions diminish, and teenager and babies may not be accepted as members of the community.
- The school system is impacted—distractions/disruptions/values are challenged and in the future there may be special education issues for the children.
- The government is impacted—the services provided to the teenager are paid for by Medicaid, a publicly supported program.
- In addition, taxpayers, hospitals, social service agencies, businesses, the police department, and the church community are all impacted in some way.

Continued on pg. 216

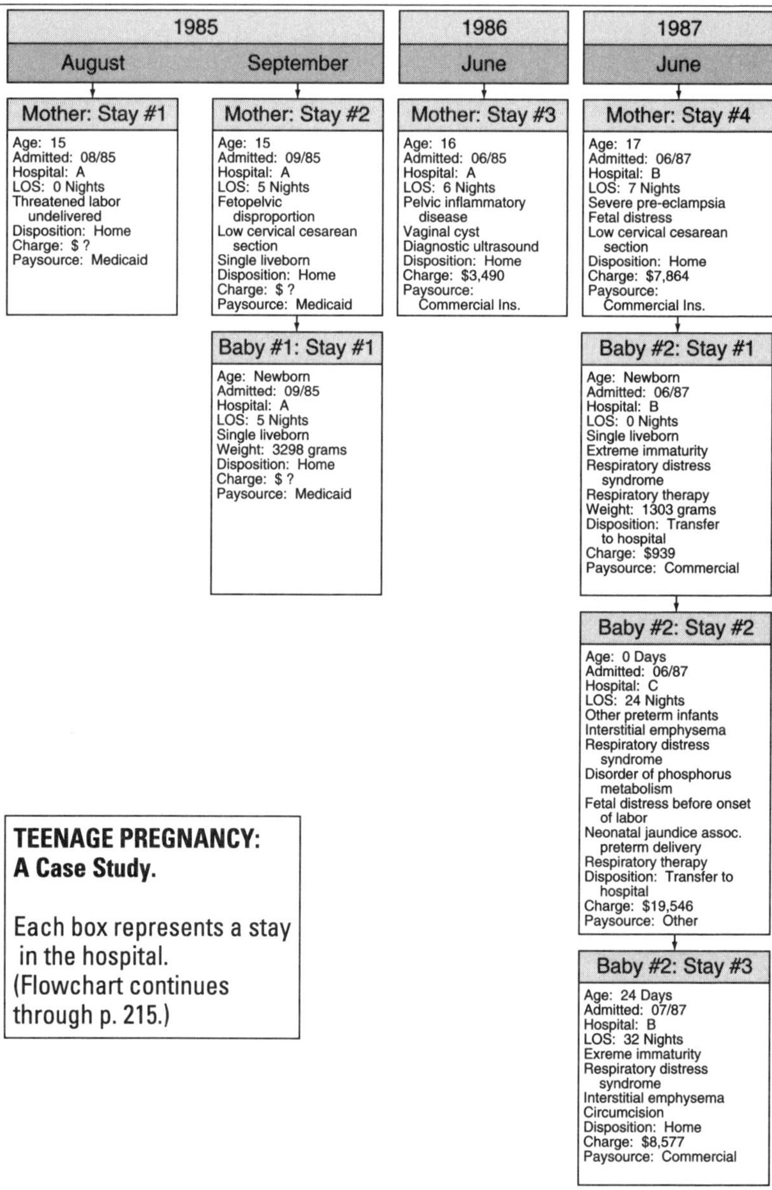

Source: Connecticut Healthcare Research and Education Foundation.

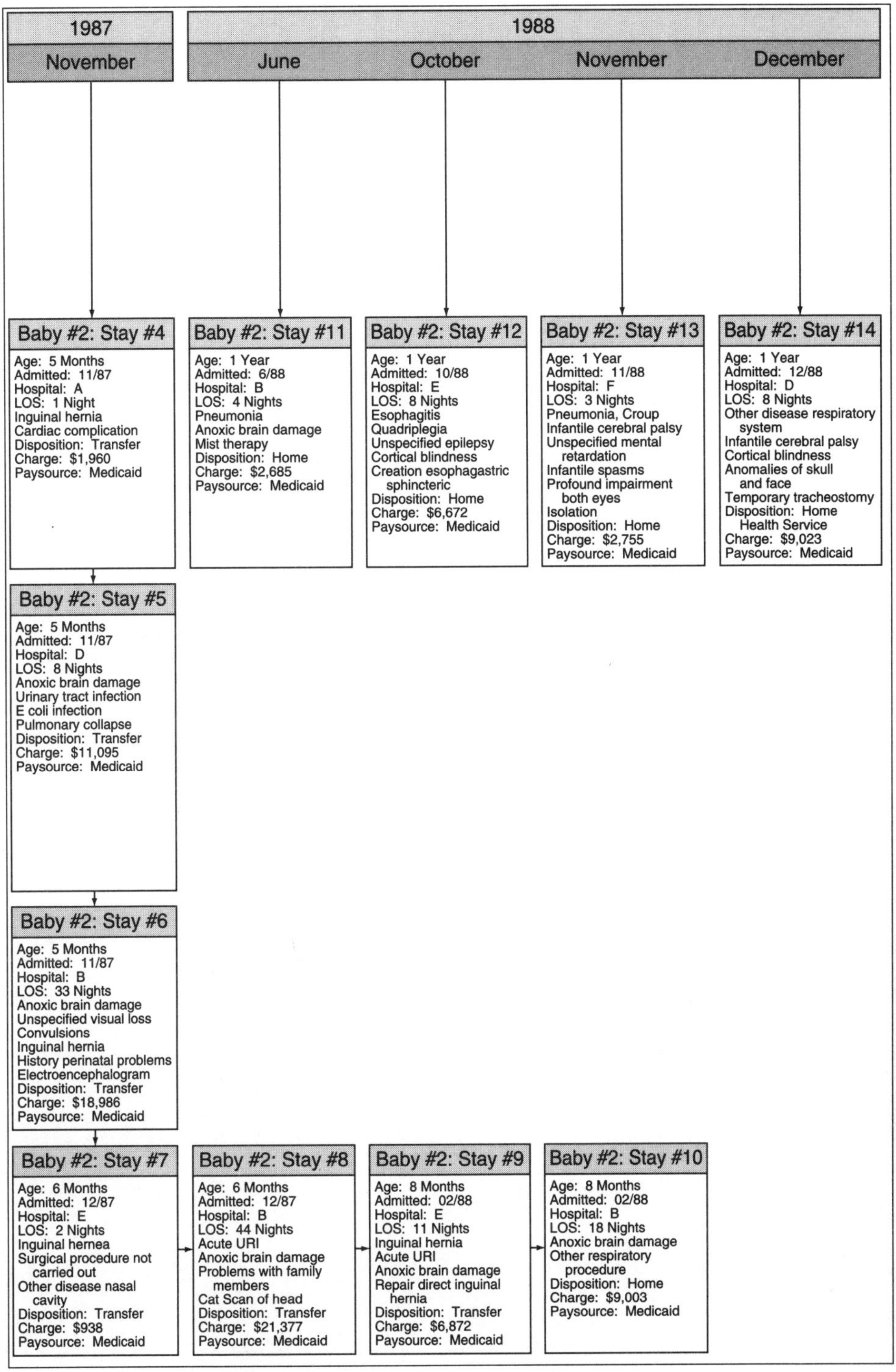
1987
November
1988
June
October
November
December
Baby #2: Stay #4
Age: 5 Months
Admitted: 11/87
Hospital: A
LOS: 1 Night
Inguinal hernia
Cardiac complication
Disposition: Transfer
Charge: $1,960
Paysource: Medicaid
Baby #2: Stay #11
Age: 1 Year
Admitted: 6/88
Hospital: B
LOS: 4 Nights
Pneumonia
Anoxic brain damage
Mist therapy
Disposition: Home
Charge: $2,685
Paysource: Medicaid
Baby #2: Stay #12
Age: 1 Year
Admitted: 10/88
Hospital: E
LOS: 8 Nights
Esophagitis
Quadriplegia
Unspecified epilepsy
Cortical blindness
Creation esophagastric sphincteric
Disposition: Home
Charge: $6,672
Paysource: Medicaid
Baby #2: Stay #13
Age: 1 Year
Admitted: 11/88
Hospital: F
LOS: 3 Nights
Pneumonia, Croup
Infantile cerebral palsy
Unspecified mental retardation
Infantile spasms
Profound impairment both eyes
Isolation
Disposition: Home
Charge: $2,755
Paysource: Medicaid
Baby #2: Stay #14
Age: 1 Year
Admitted: 12/88
Hospital: D
LOS: 8 Nights
Other disease respiratory system
Infantile cerebral palsy
Cortical blindness
Anomalies of skull and face
Temporary tracheostomy
Disposition: Home Health Service
Charge: $9,023
Paysource: Medicaid
Baby #2: Stay #5
Age: 5 Months
Admitted: 11/87
Hospital: D
LOS: 8 Nights
Anoxic brain damage
Urinary tract infection
E coli infection
Pulmonary collapse
Disposition: Transfer
Charge: $11,095
Paysource: Medicaid
Baby #2: Stay #6
Age: 5 Months
Admitted: 11/87
Hospital: B
LOS: 33 Nights
Anoxic brain damage
Unspecified visual loss
Convulsions
Inguinal hernia
History perinatal problems
Electroencephalogram
Disposition: Transfer
Charge: $18,986
Paysource: Medicaid
Baby #2: Stay #7
Age: 6 Months
Admitted: 12/87
Hospital: E
LOS: 2 Nights
Inguinal hernea
Surgical procedure not carried out
Other disease nasal cavity
Disposition: Transfer
Charge: $938
Paysource: Medicaid
Baby #2: Stay #8
Age: 6 Months
Admitted: 12/87
Hospital: B
LOS: 44 Nights
Acute URI
Anoxic brain damage
Problems with family members
Cat Scan of head
Disposition: Transfer
Charge: $21,377
Paysource: Medicaid
Baby #2: Stay #9
Age: 8 Months
Admitted: 02/88
Hospital: E
LOS: 11 Nights
Inguinal hernia
Acute URI
Anoxic brain damage
Repair direct inguinal hernia
Disposition: Transfer
Charge: $6,872
Paysource: Medicaid
Baby #2: Stay #10
Age: 8 Months
Admitted: 02/88
Hospital: B
LOS: 18 Nights
Anoxic brain damage
Other respiratory procedure
Disposition: Home
Charge: $9,003
Paysource: Medicaid

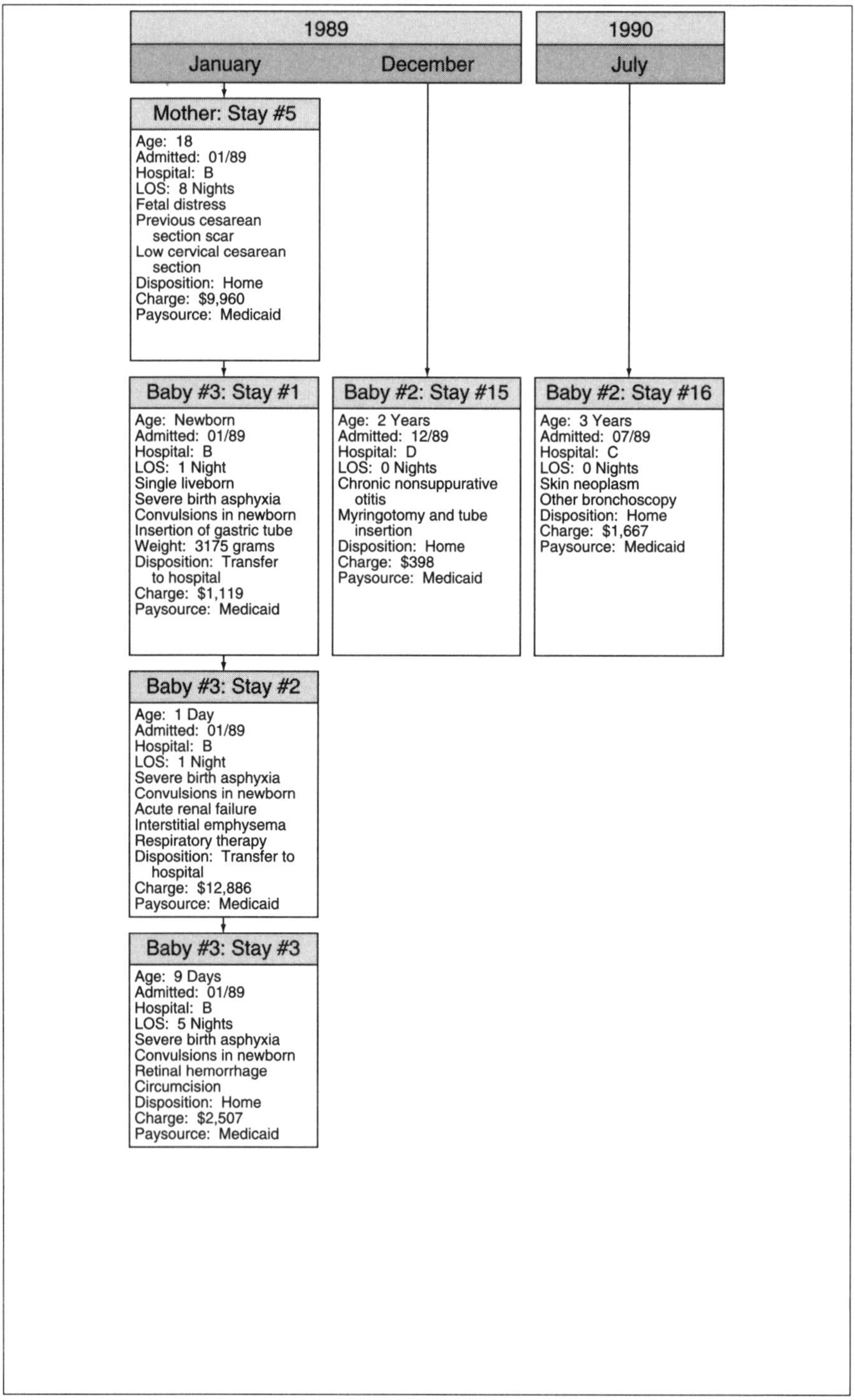
1989
January
December
1990
July
Mother: Stay #5
Age: 18
Admitted: 01/89
Hospital: B
LOS: 8 Nights
Fetal distress
Previous cesarean section scar
Low cervical cesarean section
Disposition: Home
Charge: $9,960
Paysource: Medicaid
Baby #3: Stay #1
Age: Newborn
Admitted: 01/89
Hospital: B
LOS: 1 Night
Single liveborn
Severe birth asphyxia
Convulsions in newborn
Insertion of gastric tube
Weight: 3175 grams
Disposition: Transfer to hospital
Charge: $1,119
Paysource: Medicaid
Baby #2: Stay #15
Age: 2 Years
Admitted: 12/89
Hospital: D
LOS: 0 Nights
Chronic nonsuppurative otitis
Myringotomy and tube insertion
Disposition: Home
Charge: $398
Paysource: Medicaid
Baby #2: Stay #16
Age: 3 Years
Admitted: 07/89
Hospital: C
LOS: 0 Nights
Skin neoplasm
Other bronchoscopy
Disposition: Home
Charge: $1,667
Paysource: Medicaid
Baby #3: Stay #2
Age: 1 Day
Admitted: 01/89
Hospital: B
LOS: 1 Night
Severe birth asphyxia
Convulsions in newborn
Acute renal failure
Interstitial emphysema
Respiratory therapy
Disposition: Transfer to hospital
Charge: $12,886
Paysource: Medicaid
Baby #3: Stay #3
Age: 9 Days
Admitted: 01/89
Hospital: B
LOS: 5 Nights
Severe birth asphyxia
Convulsions in newborn
Retinal hemorrhage
Circumcision
Disposition: Home
Charge: $2,507
Paysource: Medicaid

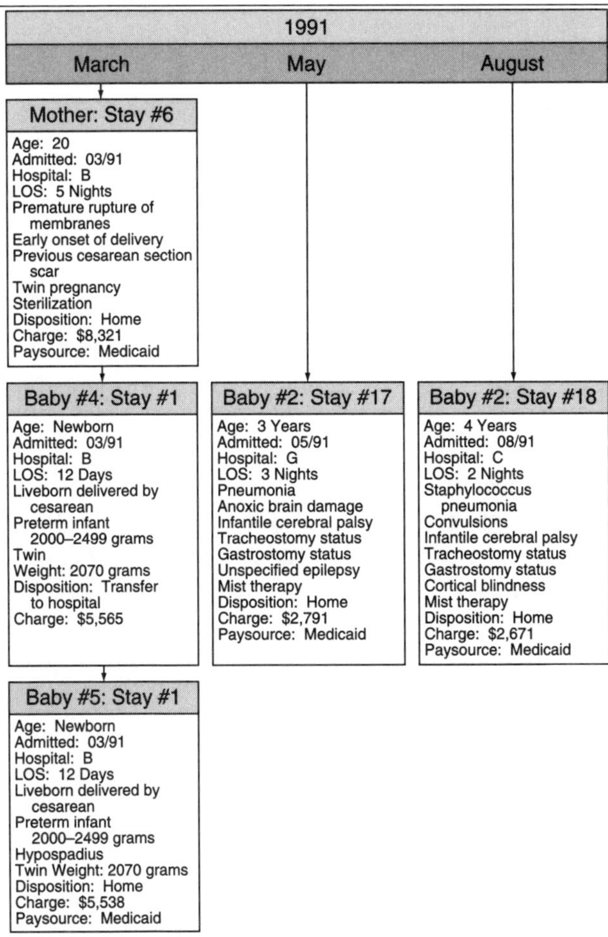
1991
March
May
August
Mother: Stay #6
Age: 20
Admitted: 03/91
Hospital: B
LOS: 5 Nights
Premature rupture of membranes
Early onset of delivery
Previous cesarean section scar
Twin pregnancy
Sterilization
Disposition: Home
Charge: $8,321
Paysource: Medicaid
Baby #4: Stay #1
Age: Newborn
Admitted: 03/91
Hospital: B
LOS: 12 Days
Liveborn delivered by cesarean
Preterm infant 2000–2499 grams
Twin
Weight: 2070 grams
Disposition: Transfer to hospital
Charge: $5,565
Baby #2: Stay #17
Age: 3 Years
Admitted: 05/91
Hospital: G
LOS: 3 Nights
Pneumonia
Anoxic brain damage
Infantile cerebral palsy
Tracheostomy status
Gastrostomy status
Unspecified epilepsy
Mist therapy
Disposition: Home
Charge: $2,791
Paysource: Medicaid
Baby #2: Stay #18
Age: 4 Years
Admitted: 08/91
Hospital: C
LOS: 2 Nights
Staphylococcus pneumonia
Convulsions
Infantile cerebral palsy
Tracheostomy status
Gastrostomy status
Cortical blindness
Mist therapy
Disposition: Home
Charge: $2,671
Paysource: Medicaid
Baby #5: Stay #1
Age: Newborn
Admitted: 03/91
Hospital: B
LOS: 12 Days
Liveborn delivered by cesarean
Preterm infant 2000–2499 grams
Hypospadius
Twin Weight: 2070 grams
Disposition: Home
Charge: $5,538
Paysource: Medicaid

Concluded

We all pay for this problem and will continue to pay for years to come. Because of cost shifting, the final burden placed on the community could run into the millions of dollars. I think the point is clear: The problem is everyone's, not just the teenager's and her babies'. In addressing teenage pregnancy, the issues are numerous: self-esteem, education, peer pressure, access, prenatal care, and cultural diversity, to name a few. It is not always easy to change behaviors; however, the opportunity exists to make a difference, to improve and save lives by bringing all segments of the community together.

Source: Robert Sandler, Connecticut Hospital Association.

The example just presented represents a medical and social problem that can be positively impacted by collapsing the boundaries between public and private sectors. Collective responsibility for community health concerns like teenage pregnancy, elder care, or environmental concerns begins when the individual operating units within a community look at their bottom lines and recognize the negative effect of doing nothing. Understanding the "What's in it for me?" question can dramatically increase the momentum behind key players coming together to address shared concerns. Generally, *awareness dawns* when community health concerns are made to correspond to dollars and jobs. *Collaboration begins* with the collapsing of organizational boundaries. *Collective responsibility* occurs when cross-functional systems are put in place to make all players accountable for the outcomes of the shared ventures.

The new bottom line for the 1990s is that *health care is a local issue and a collective responsibility*. Federal and state reforms or public policy initiatives will not be sufficient for genuinely *discovering what is and is not working, what new systems work best, and what the patient needs and wants*. The new reality is that when we transpose the original intent of managed care and the motivating concept of community health, we discover the same future.

PILOTING NEW PRODUCTS/SERVICES

While capitation provides the financial incentives to promote the health of a base of covered lives, intense price competition does not allow providers to take on the responsibility for the well-being of the community at large. Still, providers can play a key role in shaping broad-based community health initiatives by contributing staffing and resources to newly formed coalitions. For one, often a hospital can make a significant contribution to the community simply by sharing its demographic and psychographic data. Similarly, by first determining a dollar amount that is feasible to contribute or invest, a hospital can support the community health agenda by hiring an on-site program director or by contracting with a consulting agency to facilitate process management. The crux of the opportunity for the hospital is to become a stakeholder in, but not an owner of, all community health improvement efforts.

"Any provider investing in the health of the community will likely be at a short-term disadvantage," says Leanne Kaiser Carlson of Kaiser & Associates in Brighton, Colorado. "A number of communities have offset this problem by agreeing to collaborate in the area of wellness and health promotion and compete in other areas," she explains.[1]

This is not an easy process or a "quick fix." Delivering services in a capitated environment requires that providers define a whole new way of conducting business. Aggressively shifting focus from inpatient services to ancillary care requires a multifaceted strategy. Indeed, providers that recognize the fact that their new business line will include wellness and health promotion are:

- Already identifying the population groups that pose the greatest financial risk.
- Analyzing those populations' utilization patterns according to a high risk/high cost equation.
- Designing specific interventions to positively impact health status to result in long-term cost benefits as a component of research and development strategy. (**Note:** These high-risk = high-cost populations could be Medicaid/Medicare population subsets; chronic disease groups such as AIDS, oncology, chronic pain, or cardiovascular disorders; or employee groups with a high percent of risk factors.)

Pilot programs can be a tangible means of testing out approaches that could eventually reconfigure the delivery system. Needless to say, the provider community cannot just simply agree that it would be a good idea to be in the wellness business, and then just close up shop for all its acute care business. Nor can a health system afford to invest in a single-thrust R&D effort that will absorb all of its existing resources (i.e., money, manpower, energy, and creativity). Even with capitation in place, a focus on health promotion and wellness services alone will not guarantee enormous revenues or turn around an inefficient system. For long-run profitability, a good first step is to simulate a capitated environment and try out health promotion/wellness as a new service line *before* capitation becomes a reality in your marketplace.

By being proactive and taking the time to plan and test, a hospital or health system can develop a service line that can be introduced—quickly and effectively—to all customer groups as soon as the reimbursement environment shifts. One way to do this is to pilot a health promotion strategy to your own employees first. You definitely have a captured group to work with, and you have a base of quantitative claims data and qualitative information against which to measure what works and what doesn't.

Regardless of how you choose to do it, the scope and approach of a pilot program for health promotion should include the following:

- A defined population or community.
- A measurement of the baseline health status of the population.
- An analysis of the population's current utilization patterns and trends.
- An identified set of root causes of illness and injury.
- Designs for health promotion and educational programs, as well as innovative approaches to proactive primary care service delivery (which may require "new partners").
- A viable mechanism to track impact and communicate results.

Figure 14–1 outlines one way a hospital might begin to test the concept of health promotion as a service line without cannibalizing the revenue streams still in place for providing "sick care."

Again, today's providers cannot be made solely responsible for comprehensive community health initiatives. Providers can, however, shape new roles for themselves as the industry metamorphoses. In addition, providers have an opportunity to pilot health promotion activities that could serve as a new base of business under capitation. For the local hospital, playing a key role in community health initiatives is not just *being nice;* it is a proactive strategy for future business.

MANAGING THE PROCESS

Healthcare reform is occurring locally in every marketplace. Intense competitive pressures and shifting reimbursement trends are creating a challenge to ***simply stay in business***. Hospital leaders are in the unique position of creating a new model for healthcare service delivery as they attempt to respond to market pressures in a professional and fiscally responsible manner. The hospitals or health system you represent has an incredible opportunity to reap significant benefit as they look to the community as a new partner.

The challenge is how to define and champion a process that will effectively result in moving beyond traditional roles to strengthen the civic infrastructure required to sustain health improvement as a community-wide objective. Because providers have been saddled with the blame for the high cost of healthcare and a system that is not working, whatever you do will be noticed and scrutinized. An approach rooted in the value of *education* and

FIGURE 14–1

A Sample Pilot Program

I. OBJECTIVES

A. Customer Base

1. As a product/service line, population-based health status management is beginning to emerge as a trend in the "new world" of capitated service delivery. If this works for the hospital's own employee group, then potential customers include:
   a. other provider partners
   b. large employers
   c. managed care organizations
   d. community health coalitions

2. Because this concept is still considered to be developmental and because the scope of the work is so intensively integrated throughout many levels of operations within the customer organization, the launch of a pilot program requires a commitment to relationship building and educational processes.

B. Revenue Potential

1. This product/service line has the greatest potential to be *significantly revenue producing* if it is viewed as a *model.* This model could be tested in local markets and be refined as a *first-move strategy for providers leading the transformation of our industry* from a business of treating sickness to one promoting wellness.
2. Potential *revenue could also be derived from the sale of support systems, data base development and maintenance, health education and promotion materials.*

II. METHODOLOGY

Phase 1: Baseline Data Capture

A. Project Goals and Objectives

1. Establish explicit statement of purpose for project consistent with overall mission statement and market positioning.
2. Obtain support of CEO and top management team and identify a "champion" at a senior level who will drive and support the process.
3. Determine organization's self-interests, goals, objectives.
4. Assess organizational readiness and profile culture and environment for communication.
5. Identify barriers to change.
6. Form a steering committee representing internal and external "players," i.e., management, employees, local government, physicians, community constituents, employer groups, regional coalitions, managed care representatives, and consultants.
7. Determine short-term (1st year), intermediate (2–3 years), and long-term (3–5 years) goals and objectives.
8. Establish annual budget/project costs.
9. Identify technical expertise needed in addition to steering committee on an ad hoc basis (internal expertise, vendors, and/or consultants).

Continued

B. Market Dynamics and Environmental Profile

1. Key state policy issues and trends affecting local healthcare.
2. Local social, economic, and political trends impacting health and well-being.
3. Local, regional, and state resources mapping of providers, community services, and public health agencies; include analysis of workload/capacity.
4. State, local, and organizational resources for data capture and information sharing.
5. Managed care market dynamics and other provider-competitive profile factors contributing to market condition.
6. State, regional, and local profile of employers and industry

C. Baseline Health Status Profile

1. Utilization profile:
   a. demographics
   b. current and projected utilization drivers
   c. managed care plans/options
   d. steering mechanisms/benefit plan incentives and disincentives
   e. morbidity/mortality rates by cause
   f. financial impact of healthcare services
2. Consumer profile
   a. demographics
   b. psychographics
   c. health and lifestyle behaviors
   d. cultural and ethnic influences
3. Health risk factors analysis:
   a. stress
   b. tobacco use
   c. body weight
   d. blood pressure
   e. family history
   f. current knowledge of risk factors
   g. environmental threats
   h. other factors

D. Organizational Communications Profile

1. Quantitative review and analysis/interpretation of:
   a. audit of existing communications systems and tools
   b. number of employee grievances by month
   c. employee opinion surveys
   d. job performance surveys
   e. absenteeism
   f. turnover rates by department
   g. exit interviews data
   h. number of job applications

Concluded

2. Qualitative organizational satisfaction review and analysis/interpretation (focus groups, interviews, surveys):
    - *a.* worker and co-worker satisfaction
    - *b.* communications climate
    - *c.* information accessibility/load/dispensation
    - *d.* readiness for change

III. ACTION STEPS

Phase 2: Implementation & Evaluation

A. Program Implementation

1. Detailed timetable and specific measurable objectives.
2. Training and/or orientation of external and/or internal staff.
3. Recruiting and/or screening of employee participants.
4. Selection criteria for employee participation in high-risk programs.
5. Ongoing quality assurance and supervision.

B. Evaluation

1. Quantitative outcomes—short-term (1–2 years) and long-term (3–5 years):
    - *a.* analysis of specific risk factors in each high-risk program
    - *b.* change in morbidity and/or mortality in the targeted risk areas
    - *c.* measurement of claims costs in specific program target areas
    - *d.* change in overall risk status of targeted groups and overall employee population
    - *e.* cost–benefit analysis
2. Qualitative outcomes—short-term (1–2 years), intermediate term (2–3 years), to long-term (3–5 years):
    - *a.* knowledge and awareness of health risk factors
    - *b.* change in employee psychological status
    - *c.* change in employee attitudes
    - *d.* work group morale
    - *e.* increasing program dissemination among active work force
    - *f.* program delivered to dependents
    - *g.* employee satisfaction with health promotion policies
    - *h.* management satisfaction with health promotion

information sharing is one strategy for fostering a shared vision and sense of joint ownership and accountability.

Managing the process means:

- Creating a shared vision of a healthier community.
- Within the framework of that vision, defining the hospital's role as a caregiver, service provider, and community leader.
- Recognizing the challenges associated with remaining financially viable while managing the transition from operating in a system

where the *cash register rings every time someone gets sick to one where there is a pot of gold for keeping people well.*

- Committing to a strategy that reflects an awareness of the critical importance of *educating, listening, inquiring, and testing* at every level.

In the initial stages of any community health initiative, I recommend that a project coordinator be assigned to serve as "the arms, legs, eyes, ears, and voice" of hospital administrators and community leaders. As a designated roving leader, the project coordinator is accountable for interconnecting project goals, community outreach needs, and administrative objectives. In other words, this person is "on first" to lead by carrying the vision, sharing information, educating, listening and probing for areas of confusion or concern, assuming responsibility for aligning processes, encouraging innovative and coordinated action, and solving day-to-day problems in a manner that consistently supports the mission of a community health coalition.

Over the last few years, I have been brought in in the role of project coordinator by hospitals, YWCAs, and interested neighborhood groups to help move community health agendas from ideas to action. Regardless of who brings me in, I always recommend an aggressive and interactive communications strategy. Strong foundations begin with harnessing market intelligence information, profiling sound empirical data, and prioritizing appropriate educational themes. Using information-sharing as a pivot for demonstrating the hospital as a new kind of leader within your community, I recommend concentrical education across organized forums or a "bull's eye" approach. For instance, sample educational themes might include: "Healthcare Reform Is A Local Phenomenon . . . What Is Your Role?"; "It Takes A Whole Village To Raise A Child and Honor The Old"; "Managed Care: From Mania To Miracles"; and "Healthy Communities: From Visions To Realities."

In my work with communities, I have developed a three-pronged educational strategy that works:

1. Go to the places where your community members are already convening. Churches, schools, employer groups, civic organizations, and neighborhood groups are ready-made community forums.
2. Call together special town hall meetings for community-wide health education, visioning, and celebration. These forums can create the stage for profiling the needs of your local communities. At the same time you can share success stories from across the country to help create a new and shared vision of what community health can mean in your own future.

3. Identify, educate, and train key persons within the community to be accountable for sharing the message in the streets. In other words, invest in the value of community leadership and develop local champions who will have ownership in realizing sustainable and tangible output from a project espousing the importance of community health.

In addition to communication with the greater community, it is critical that internal education within the hospital does not get overlooked. Often those entrenched in the realities of a changing industry do not realize that there are many people within the hospital walls who are confused and frightened by rapidly changing rules and regulations. For those caregivers who are resisting change and worried about whether or not they will have a job tomorrow, community outreach may seem like a waste of time and a diffusion of resources. However, you must remember that your own management teams, physicians, board members, and employees already exist as roving leaders within their communities. As such, they must have the information they need to understand the changes themselves so they can help you communicate with the community. Moving beyond the hospital walls first requires an intensive commitment to internal information sharing and education in order to move out credibly with consistent themes and maximum momentum.

In sum, managing the process of any grassroots initiative requires that someone be dedicated to act as a roving leader, facilitator, liaison, and process manager. An emphasis on community education and information dissemination is key to cultivating joint ownership of the process and collective responsibility for the outcomes. The analytical process of compiling community-specific data should feed into a comprehensive strategic planning process. For the hospital, playing a key role in building a healthier community is one way to move slowly into a new business model; that is, a model of health promotion and wellness.

Figure 14–2 is a synthesis of several community education proposals I have submitted recently. I am including it here because I believe it outlines an emphasis on education and exemplifies an approach to interconnecting processes that will translate to almost any market.

In response to a high volume of requests for assistance from member hospitals, the Connecticut Hospital Association (CHA) began to explore how it might offer technical support to those who wanted community health initiatives to be more than fluff. First the CHA researched the different methodologies currently being touted as the new wave of scientific formulas for health status assessments. The CHA discovered that although national and state data are readily available, it is problematic in terms of its application

FIGURE 14–2

Sample Community Health Proposal Emphasis

Community Education

The best results will come if I work in partnership with you, your project leadership team, the hospital administrators, and the steering committee (once it is in place). At the onset, I would view my most critical charge to be to *design and implement an aggressive educational strategy* tailored to the needs of your local community. As we move forward, I would be qualified and equipped to assume responsibility for *preparing analytical analyses, identifying project options, developing financial models, building consensus, communicating with the project stakeholders, and developing action plans.* In working with you, I require that the following elements be mutually agreed upon as central to the fostering of a project approach that will have meaningful and long-term impact:

- Commit to a process of *education and information sharing* as a pivot for fostering collective responsibility for a shared vision of community health.
- Involve business leaders, community members, and payor/customers from the onset.
- Provide a framework for teamwork and collaboration.
- Provide adequate resources and support, i.e., people and money.
- Harness objective data to guide identification of priorities and processes.
- Develop a comprehensive health promotion strategy.
- Create a framework for using data and applying tools for feedback and program improvement.
- Evaluate the impact on the root causes of preventable illness and injuries.
- Turn data into information via a strategic communications plan.

Phase One

I. COMMIT RESOURCES TO COMMUNITY EDUCATION

A. *Designate roving leaders*
1. consultant(s)
2. internal representative(s)

B. *Build team*
1. roving leaders
2. employees already interfacing with the community
3. physician(s)
4. board member(s)

C. *Define educational themes and identify target audiences*
1. continue to educate regarding the impact of managed care
2. begin to educate regarding "how a community health status methodology can be the most critical strategic foothold for the future"

Continued

3. be consistent in communicating themes intertwining quality of life concerns and fiscal realities
4. move concentrically from the hospital into the community
5. consider sponsoring a community-wide forum profiling working community partnerships "in your backyard and around the country"
6. initiate/champion a community partnership approach to improving local health status

D. ***Educate as a stepping stone towards implementation***

1. begin by prioritizing most acute needs
2. analyze the correlation between identified needs, community awareness/readiness, and financial impact
3. recognize the need for empirically sound baseline data
4. evaluate the benefits of championing a community partnership approach to health status assessment
5. define measures of accountability (i.e., timelines, checkpoints, tools for impact measurement)

II. DEVELOP MARKET-BASED COMMUNITY HEALTH PROFILE

A. ***General market assessment***

1. define geographic community
2. create a local resource map
   - *a.* providers
   - *b.* community service agencies
   - *c.* public health agencies
   - *d.* churches
   - *e.* neighborhood groups
   - *f.* schools
   - *g.* local service clubs
   - *h.* others
3. interview parties/agencies regarding needs and/or concerns
   - *a.* hospital management team
   - *b.* physicians (representative sampling)
   - *c.* Chamber of Commerce leader
   - *d.* business coalition director (if any)
   - *e.* top 5 employers (by number of employees)
   - *f.* elected officials (mayor, city manager)
   - *g.* public health agencies

B. ***Patient utilization***

1. demographic profile
2. current and projected utilization drivers
3. managed care scenario/trends
4. analysis of uninsured population; effect of any current or anticipated state initiatives

Continued

5. percent outmigration by service line
6. analysis of mortality rates by cause
7. financial impact of health care services

C. *Provider community*

1. analysis of provider specialties, services, needs, access
2. assessment of provider corporate culture (i.e., readiness for change)
3. nature and scope of health-related organizations, services and agencies
4. analysis of workload/capacity
5. interagency "partnerships"
6. referral patterns/process
7. average healthcare delivery costs by service
8. economic impact study, i.e., measure hospital's role in sustaining the infrastructure of the local community

D. *Consumer profile: focus groups and surveys*

1. health behaviors
2. lifestyle behaviors
3. psychographic descriptors; i.e., income, education, family unit, tenure, etc.
4. perceptions of, preference regarding, and satisfaction with existing healthcare services

E. *Written report and presentation of findings and opportunities to project leadership team*

III. CREATE COMMUNITY PLANNING STEERING COMMITTEE

A. *Composition*

1. healthcare professionals
2. public health leaders
3. business leaders
4. public and private payors
5. local government representatives
6. educators
7. ministers
8. law enforcement officers
9. neighborhood leaders
10. consumers at large

B. *Charge*

1. represent cross-section of population needs
2. provide leadership and direction to the project
3. foster collaborative problem solving
4. communicate output, build consensus, and increase community "buy-in"

Concluded

C. *Introductory steering committee meeting and presentation*

1. involve in the education and information-sharing process
2. identify community health needs
3. align intervention goals with community resources
4. solicit "buy-in" from committee members
5. present action plan with time lines

Phase Two

I. DEVELOP A COMMUNITY HEALTH IMPROVEMENT ACTION PLAN

A. *Review data*

B. *Prioritize community health needs*

C. *Target opportunities for improvement and collaboration*

D. *Specify budgetary requirements, staffing needs, timeline, and performance milestones*

E. *Put appropriate infrastructure in place*

F. *Develop and implement monitoring and evaluation systems (process, outcomes, and community benefit)*

G. *Identify potential funding sources*

H. *Develop communications plan by audience*

II. INTEGRATE COMMUNITY HEALTH INITIATIVES INTO HOSPITAL STRATEGIC PLAN

A. *Recognize community health as a primary care intervention addressing root causes of illness and injury*

B. *Reduce the strain on hospital provider resources via collaboration*

C. *Include other health-related agencies in a defined network and continuum of care*

D. *Demonstrate to buyers a viable commitment to prevention, education, and long-term goals*

E. *Include measurements of impact and performance in outcome reports*

F. *Become a "hospital without walls"—move from a focus of inpatient to ancillary services*

G. *Invest in health promotion and wellness as new components of a managed care business development strategy*

because of inconsistency in the definitions that correspond to reported mortality rates. For instance, when stroke was identified as an indicator, it was not always clear whether or not the stroke occurred in conjunction with a myocardial infarction. Similarly, an AIDS patient who died of pneumonia might have pneumonia listed as the cause of death, not AIDS. Looking at the problems inherent with the information that was available, CHA decided the best way to support its member hospitals was to develop its own database with consistent definitions and town-specific profiles. Other providers need to take note: After examining available quantitative data, it may be necessary to look for additional information to substantiate preliminary conclusions or to redefine the population base to a smaller unit in order to discover meaningful patterns or trends.

NETWORK MARKETING

Providers need to become very creative when they consider how to promote community health as their new agenda. Enhancing individual responsibility for healthy lifestyle choices becomes a strategic priority when unhealthy choices erode profit margins. Getting the word out and creating behavior-altering momentum will not happen through an expensive advertising campaign. Perhaps providers can take a lesson from Amway and use a network marketing approach to create behavioral change. What can an organization like Amway teach the healthcare industry? Two very important lessons: (1) the power of the one-on-one sale, and (2) the exponential growth that can be achieved through network marketing.

How can you implement a network marketing approach? First identify and train health advocates. They might be primary care outreach coordinators who are on the hospital's or HMO's payroll. They might be parish nurses or home health workers. More often, they are loyal, culturally matched, trusted neighborhood or worksite leaders. Many lay workers are willing to champion the cause of health because they care about the people whose lives they touch. They—like providers—are incented to positively impact health. One-on-one teaching and counseling creates the opportunity for individual change. A network marketing approach can create the context or environment that can support new behaviors. It's like a buddy system for health. It works and *it doesn't cost much.*

Sales trainers emphasize that a customer must be given a message at least seven times before they actually hear it. Thus, providers can augment network marketing efforts with a theme blitz across their community. Healthy lifestyle choices can be the theme of radio and TV infomercials, billboards, printed reminders on grocery coupons, newsletters, and materials distributed through churches and schools. This is not simply another twist on an advertising campaign. It is a very simple phenomenon that human beings don't hear and internalize a message until they've heard it at least seven different ways. Just as in any other community health initiative, the provider can choose to support—not own—the process. By limiting investments and sharing responsibility, providers can actually win more. With more people chanting the health mantra, the voice for change may be loud enough to be heard.

ENDNOTE

1. "Measuring and Improving Community Health," *The Quality Letter for Healthcare Leaders,* vol. 6, no. 5, (June 1994), p. 10.

15 CHAPTER

Making a Go of It

When I first began to research who was doing what in community health, it seemed that healthcare reform was pitting the virulent against the virtuous. Eroding profit margins contaminated the willingness of providers to move the concept of community health from esoteric discussions to strategic decision making. I unearthed several consultants who claimed to be architects of a new system of care, but few of them appeared to be moving their clients beyond visions shared over coffee and muffins.

I soon discovered that those who are "making a go of it" are generally too busy in the streets with their operations to be at conferences singing their own praises. By probing deeper, interviewing project coordinators, and making work-site visits, I met many pragmatic idealists . . . who are convinced that systems thinking and related disciplines will lead to significant consequences for their business.

The following real-life examples are profiled because of their unique approach to facilitating incredible changes at the local level. The feature that differentiates each is highlighted. By sharing with you parts of their stories, I hope to plant a seed of conviction that transformative change is not only possible, it is happening!

A BROADER DEFINITION OF HEALTH

Successful prevention models show that responsibility for youth and family health promotion and alcohol/drug prevention should be shared by the entire community. In 1989, four United Way agencies collaborated on a needs assessment survey in South Lake Tahoe, California. In the category of problems facing youth and families in the area, respondents overwhelmingly identified illicit use of drugs and alcohol; poor family management practices; family disruption; and the lack of food, clothing, and housing as the greatest problems. Further, the collaborative group discovered that an uncoordinated community response had produced a disjointed and overlapping system of youth services. In 1990, the membership of the group was expanded from 4 to 20 organizations, as the need for wider community participation became obvious. The group effort culminated in the fall of 1990 with the submission to the Office of Substance Abuse Prevention a proposal for a Community Partnership Program. The community partnership proposal was approved under the auspices of the El Dorado County Public Health Department, which formed the Tahoe Prevention Network to coordinate the project in South Lake Tahoe.

The framework of the Tahoe Prevention Network is based on the risk reduction resiliency strategies of the community partnerships pioneered by Hawkins and Catalano at the University of Washington and further promoted by the Center for Substance Abuse Prevention (CSAP). The basis for the Tahoe Prevention Network is to promote a "Community for Healthy Living" by using local resources to meet the health and social service needs of the community. As John W. Gardner states in his book, *Building Community:*

> Families and communities are the ground-level generators and preserves of values and ethical systems. No society can remain vital or even survive without a reasonable base of shared values and such values are not established by edict from lofty levels of society. They are generated chiefly in the family, school, church, and other intimate settings in which people deal with one another face to face. The ideals of justice and compassion are nurtured in communities.

In small towns, major cities, and rural areas across the nation, people are joining together in unprecedented efforts to build and rebuild community, joining together to tackle the arduous tasks of cleaning up our environment, saving our oceans, ozone, and alpine lakes. They are joining together to build better structures to withstand the ravages of earthquakes and hurricanes; to house the homeless and feed the hungry; to cure the incurable, from AIDS to the plague of alcohol and other drug abuse. The Tahoe Prevention Network (TPN) is one of those community-building efforts. Schools, business, social services, churches, law enforcement, government, and individuals from every segment of the society are working together to reduce those things which place our children and families at risk, and to develop resiliency skills for all those who reside in the community.

Between 1990 and 1994, the Tahoe Prevention Network grew into an organization of more than 1,800 groups from all parts of the community. In all, over 10,000 persons have participated in TPN activities. The purpose of the Tahoe Prevention Network is to provide collaborative solutions to the health, mental health, alcohol/drug, and economic problems that face the residents of the South Lake Tahoe area through widespread community member planning, project design, and implementation.

In that period a wide range of community services were developed or improved, including a latch-key program, construction of a Boys and Girls Club building out of used tires, an AIDS/HIV prevention program, a tobacco prevention program, school-based health and alcohol/drug prevention programs, child abuse and neglect prevention programs, a family advocate program, and a multitude of community health events. In addition, the Tahoe Prevention Network actively pursued improvements in the existing social service system by increasing interagency client coordination in an effort to make service more available, appropriate, culturally sensitive, and non-duplicated through the United Project.

The target population for prevention activities in South Lake Tahoe is the entire community, with special emphasis on the needs of the area's large migrant/transient, Latino, and Anglo populations. Because of low socioeconomic status, mental health, and substance abuse problems, the transient/migrating lifestyle often produces risk factors in children and families such as language barriers, lack of school enrollment/attendance, abused and neglected children and families, and dysfunctional family systems.

The approach the Tahoe Prevention Network took in providing solutions to these problems stemmed from the following beliefs: The first belief was that the resources needed were contained in the community and that community advice in service planning and implementation was essential. Second, TPN members believed that increased networking among service providers and community members would produce services more in line with community needs. Third, they believed that interagency management of programs would produce increases in networking and services, and decreases in duplication of services and administrative expenses. Finally, TPN members believed that prevention efforts needed to focus on family issues in recognition of the fact that many disruptive behaviors evident in youth are the result of dysfunctional home environments.

Between 1990 and 1994, the Tahoe Prevention Network developed resources exceeding $12,000,000 in response to community program needs. TPN has legitimatized its activities and was seen as the major force behind coordinated health and social service activities in the South Lake Tahoe area. By working to address family issues of food, clothing, and housing, the Tahoe Prevention Network impacted root causes of illness and injury within a *broader definition of health.*

ENLIGHTENED SELF-INTEREST

Michael Felix, founder of Felix, Burdine and Associates, Inc., a consulting firm based in Allentown, Pennsylvania, has led a movement in which public health principles are the centerpoint of healthcare delivery. When I first began to investigate working community health initiative models, I discovered an article describing the Partnership for Community Health in Pennsylvania's Lehigh Valley. I found this partnership particularly intriguing because since 1992 it had developed several sustainable programs, including a Medicaid HMO. The work in the Lehigh Valley turned out to be one of Felix, Burdine and Associates' flagships.

Mr. Felix was gracious enough to respond to my query and even invited me to observe his firm facilitating a town meeting for a new project in Augusta, Georgia. Attending that meeting were representatives of seven hospitals, the public health department, an additional 33 healthcare providers, and representatives from churches, civic organizations, schools, and area businesses. What presented itself was a radically different partnership approach to community health.

Felix, Burdine's partnership approach used the idea of community capacity building to give a practical focus to the concept of health status management. In addition, each community health task force member was required to enter into a social contract specifying what he or she would be willing to contribute and be responsible for doing. From the very beginning, the issues of Why would I? and What's in it for me? were on the table. Complex political, social, cultural, and economic pressures impacting the representative players were not ignored. Multiple hidden agendas associated with revenue streams and jobs were uncovered. By first identifying individual and institutional *self-interests* and then openly incorporating those into partnership strategies, Felix, Burdine effectively set the stage for action. (See Table 15–1.)

PARTNERS WITH PUBLIC HEALTH

A couple of years ago, I had the privilege of working with Marshall Hospital in Placerville, California, to begin a process of community resource mapping. Community health had catapulted to the top of a list of the hospital's strategic concerns when non-capitated Medicaid patients could no longer be seen in state clinics. All of a sudden it seemed there was a neon sign over Marshall Hospital's emergency room door which directed these displaced patients inside. The increased utilization was costing the hospital money and the CEO realized that community health was not just something you did with old marketing people you were putting out to pasture.

TABLE 15-1

Enlightened Self-Interest Can Lead To:

- Restructuring and/or the integration of local healthcare and human services systems through mergers, acquisitions, joint ventures, and memoranda of agreement.
- Creating community-based primary care systems, including managed care organizations for low income and uninsured persons, and community-oriented primary care in schools, churches, and other community organizations.
- Health status interventions to improve child health through schools, churches, and community organizations for primary care, adolescent pregnancy prevention, substance abuse prevention, domestic violence and homicide prevention.
- Conducting population-based community health status assessments and resource inventories as well as community health benefit analyses.

Source: Felix, Burdine & Associates, 1995

Market analysis revealed that most of these non-capitated Medicaid patients who were using the emergency room as their "doc-in-a-box" resided in the nearby community of Georgetown, California. Because Georgetown did not have a primary care provider, the El Dorado Public Health Department and local social service agencies were also concerned with the health needs of this community. Marshall Hospital's and the El Dorado Public Health Department's shared interest in serving this population prompted conversations and, before long, they had formed a partnership—the Divide Wellness Center—to address the special health needs of this low income population.

Marshall Hospital and the El Dorado Public Health Department had always been friendly; in the past, however, they had segmented their activities without too much overlap. With a commitment to establish The Divide Wellness Center, they became business partners in a joint venture. First, they jointly pursued grant funding and, ultimately, received start-up seed money from the Office of Rural Health Services. Next, Marshall Hospital contributed the bricks and mortar for the clinic, as well as the salaries for both a resident nurse practitioner and a rotating physician supervisor. Similarly, the Public Health Department committed a full-time staff person to serve as coordinator, along with a public health nurse. Area social service agencies were involved and an interdisciplinary approach to case management and outreach services was implemented.

Were there any areas where competitive structures did not easily reconfigure into collaborative activities? Sure. A prime example is the fact that neither Marshall Hospital nor the Public Health Department felt that it could afford to lose the revenue associated with its laboratory services. Therefore, for an identified period of time they agreed that this service would be duplicative and that the scope and cost efficiency of both contenders would be evaluated.

From the perspective of the Georgetown community, the Divide Wellness Center is a godsend. Local consumers have participated in creating a local definition of health through educational forums, town meetings, and visioning sessions. Everyone—from the individual to the school to the volunteer fire department—is viewed as a partner with something to offer and has been asked to get involved. Community-oriented primary care is happening in Georgetown. The result is that the Divide Wellness Center is a working example of how financial risk can have the power to collapse boundaries and build new programs. This new venture exists because the hospital was open and willing to *partner with public health.*

SETTING THE STAGE FOR ACTION

As director of strategic planning for Saint Thomas Hospital in Nashville, Tennessee, Joanne Pulles identified an opportunity to focus the community on the objective of developing a system of care that would (1) help people lead longer, more productive lives and (2) spend less money on healthcare services. Because her passion for community health would not abate, Joanne left Saint Thomas in 1992, did her homework, met with over 100 community leaders—including an influential member of the Nashville city council and several hospital CEOs—then knocked on the mayor's door with a business plan.

The product of that meeting was the Nashville Healthcare Partnership, a unique public/private partnership which involves government and business, as well as local providers and neighborhood health centers. The mission of the partnership is to focus resources to improve the health of the Nashville community, reducing costs through the prevention of disease and promotion of health. (See Figure 15–1.)

Because of her marketing and strategic planning background, Pulles realized that the partnership's success would have a lot to do with how it was packaged and presented to the community. The first tactical decision was to locate the partnership in the Nashville Chamber of Commerce. This positioning strategy immediately alleviated the risk that the partnership would, by association, be linked with the ills of the provider community. Instead, the business community assumed a greater sense of ownership. Local providers were challenged to participate and commit to an action-oriented agenda in partnership with some significant healthcare purchasers—or explain why they would not.

FIGURE 15–1

Nashville Healthcare Partnership

The Mission of the Nashville Healthcare Partnership is to improve the health of the Community, reducing costs through the prevention of disease and promotion of health.

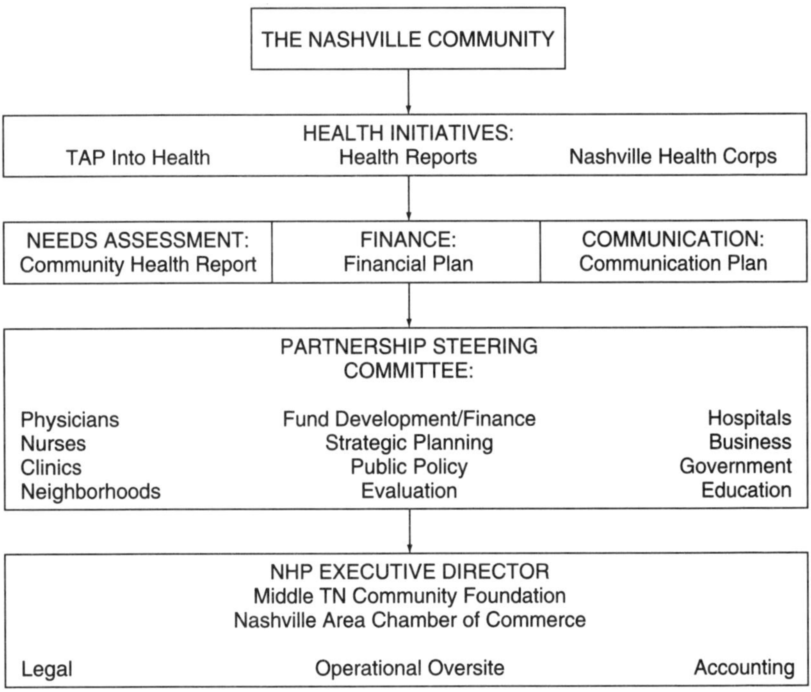

By locating the partnership in the Chamber of Commerce and using the business community as a foothold, Pulles set the stage for action. Primary results to date include the following:

- Through the AmeriCorps Program for National and Community Service, the Nashville Healthcare Partnership has spearheaded grant preparation and presentations leading to the successful award of a competitive national grant of $1.5 million to fund the Nashville Health Corps, a 40-member local health corps, for three years.
- Working in partnership with public health nurses, the Nashville Health Corps is improving the health of over 5600 at-risk children and families through home visits. Sixty percent of the health corps'

clients are teens. Initial outcomes after one year and 5,589 home visits include:
— 97 percent of visited children now have up-to-date immunizations;
— the majority of low birthweight children have tripled their weight by their first birthdays;
— there has been a 25 percent increase in parenting knowledge and skills.

In addition, over 85 percent of the teen clients are now attending school, pursuing their GEDs, or working outside the home.

- Working with the State of Tennessee and the Metro Department of Education, the Nashville Healthcare Partnership has developed TAP Into Health, a technical assistance panel for teachers of a new wellness course. Additionally, 50 volunteer consultants have been recruited to work with 80 teachers and 6,000 students in nine metropolitan Nashville high schools.
- Finally, with support from the Nashville Chamber of Commerce, the partnership has spearheaded communications with public relations activities that have resulted in significant media coverage.

The Nashville Healthcare Partnership has increased community leaders' ownership for local health concerns. In addition, the Partnership entered the market and immediately earned respect by demonstrating an active grasp of the basic business disciplines. One of the first steps Ms. Pulles took was to initiate a comprehensive study of all of Nashville's health services. This provided an accurate inventory of current resources and also illuminated unmet areas of need.

Today, because of the TennCare program, the Nashville Healthcare Partnership is operating in a new type of competitive environment that could impact the longevity of its current structure and function. Now everybody is considering health status management part of their business and private sector providers are in competition to care for TennCare enrollees. With the shifting of this low-income patient base away from the public health system, the role of Metro's health department is also changing.

Beginning in mid-1996, funding for Metro Public Health Department will be 5 to 7 percent less than the current budget of $29.5 million, said Dr. Stephanie Bailey, Director of Metro Public Health. However, some of this money is earmarked for community health assessments. The department has brought in an epidemiologist to help analyze data, is consulting with companies proficient in gathering medical data, and upgrading its computer hardware and software. In short, the public health system will monitor the health of all residents.[3]

The good news is that Nashville has turned up the volume in its conversation about public health. Now that area providers and the public health department are stakeholders, it will be worth tracking the future of The Nashville Healthcare Partnership to see if it can successfully foster mutually reinforcing, dependent relationships. The sharing of health status data could be what helps everyone realize that cooperation can ultimately enhance competitiveness. *The stage is set for action.*

RUNNING LIKE A BUSINESS

In Atlanta, Saint Joseph Hospital's Mercy Care Services deserves a standing ovation for both its missionary success and its strides in developing impactful, community-oriented primary care services. This program has been a favorite of mine since I worked with Saint Joseph's Hospital in 1990 to package its mobile mammography services and heart attack risk screening programs for direct contracting with large employers. I realized then that Mercy Care's flagship program, Mercy Mobile Health Care, was a model for the future. Mercy Mobile is an example of value because it effectively applies secular norms to stewardship. It is *running like a business.*

For over 10 years, Mercy Mobile Health Care has helped break down the economic, cultural, and linguistic barriers that prevent low-income and uninsured individuals from accessing primary care services in greater Atlanta. In 1995, teams of outreach workers, educators, case managers, nurses, and doctors used five vans and two mobile clinics, a community center, and a fixed-site clinic to deliver primary care to 18,000 individuals excluded from the mainstream health system. Services are provided in three languages (English, Spanish, and Vietnamese) at over 100 sites each month by a staff of 95 and a volunteer corps of 356.

Mercy Mobile Health Care offers a full spectrum of care that fully meets the objectives for the primary care component of a continuum of care. Of all the models I have reviewed in action, this one really meets community needs and, most importantly, runs like a business.

Mission, Vision, and Values

The mission of Saint Joseph's Mercy Care Services is to improve the declining health status of the medically underserved. This entails a multipronged approach which combines outreach, health promotion, social services, and clinical care to address the needs of body, mind, and spirit. These programs integrate the philosophy of the Sisters of Mercy and the clinical excellence of

Saint Joseph's Health System with the dedication and leadership of talented staff and volunteers. Together a unique, effective, affordable model of care has been created.

History

Saint Joseph's Mercy Care Services had its beginning in two volunteer-initiated programs based at Saint Joseph's Hospital of Atlanta. In 1984, a small group of healthcare professionals from the hospital was preparing a meal at a downtown Atlanta shelter as part of an outreach program. The group observed the significant health problems of the homeless—including foot and skin problems, nutritional deficiencies, and respiratory conditions—most of which went untreated. The volunteers recognized the need for ongoing care and began to take doctors, nurses, and medical supplies to various shelters. At about the same time, the hospital's emergency room was experiencing a huge increase in the number of Hispanics seeking treatment. Only a few physicians on the staff spoke Spanish and they were not always available as interpreters when clients presented. A group of Spanish-speaking volunteers organized to provide interpretation services. Just as in the case of the homeless, the needs and problems were more serious than first realized.

From these simple attempts to provide care and comfort, Mercy Mobile Health Care was created. A grant from the Saint Joseph's Mercy Foundation, along with some encouragement from the Sisters of Mercy and the community at large provided the impetus to create a sustainable, flexible system of primary care. In 1996, Mercy Mobile Health Care has an operating budget of $7 million, $1.6 million of which is funded by Saint Joseph's Health System.

In a decade, Mercy Mobile Health Care has grown from a grassroots effort offered by volunteers into a community-wide program. Many facets of Mercy Mobile's culture have made this odyssey possible. Key among them are:

- Channeling hospital system resources to care for the underserved.
- Developing a mobile, primary care delivery system that responds to emerging needs of culturally diverse communities.
- Collaborating with others to develop and implement innovative approaches to community-based primary care.
- Garnering grant funds of $2.5 million in 1995.
- Involving clients with community residents in every facet of needs assessment, program planning, and evaluation.
- Recruiting bilingual and culturally aware health promoters to work within their own neighborhoods to deliver culturally sensitive health services to their peers.

Mobile/Community Based

One of our country's most pressing concerns is how to provide healthcare to the poor, elderly, and underserved. In spite of the fact that we spend more than other industrialized nations on health services ($2,900 per person in 1991), an estimated 39 million persons lack insurance. In Georgia, 22 percent of the population (1.3 million persons) is uninsured. Access to healthcare was perceived as the major need of community residents in a survey of 20 low-income communities conducted by the Atlanta Project.

Mercy Mobile Health Care's success in meeting this need can be measured by steep increases in the clients served and services provided between 1992–1995. The greatest increase is in community health promotion, an indicator of the program's ability to reach those who are most isolated. Access to services of Mercy Mobile and other providers is facilitated by a sustained, predictable presence in targeted communities. As needs are identified, mobile teams are dispatched to specific geographic communities to canvass neighborhoods, offer health promotion classes, and set up health fairs or primary care clinics.

Community health promoters, case managers, and other staff members also maintain relationships with churches and service providers. Services are coordinated whenever possible to eliminate the need for clients to travel to multiple locations *even when rescheduling is inconvenient for Mercy Mobile's staff.* Cooperative letters of agreement between agencies allow for the exchange of appropriate information and facilitate intra-agency referrals.

Defining Primary Care and Measuring Results

A cross-functional team of staff members at Mercy Mobile Health Care is responsible for outcomes measurement. Their first task was to define primary care. An adaptation from the definition of the Institute of Medicine reads as follows:

> Primary care is the provision of integrated, accessible health care services by teams who are accountable for addressing holistic healthcare needs; developing a sustained partnership with clients; practicing in a collaborative context with family and community; and consistent with the mission and values of Mercy Mobile Health Care.

Then standards, rationale, and measurable indicators were created for access, integration, accountability, holistic care, partnership, collaboration, and values.

As an example, the access standard says, "Mercy Mobile Health Care provides medically underserved clients with information, referral and/or direct services which contribute to health and well-being." Indicators of accessibility include: points of entry into the system; linguistic and cultural appropriateness; transportation; interpretation locations and services; provision of transportation, child care and interpretation; distribution of services; after-hours coverage and utilization; waiting times; number of walk-ins served versus those turned away; and executed follow-up/return visits. The organization cannot create access by operating in a defined way at a particular location. It must continually flex to meet the needs of clients and respond in a nimble fashion. (See Table 15–2.)

The organization also monitors clinical outcomes. In the case of HIV infection, seropositivity has declined from 12 percent to 5 percent between 1991 and 1994. During this period, Mercy Mobile mounted an intensive HIV outreach and risk reduction initiative. The organization recognized that the homeless community had an urgent need for HIV services due to an alarmingly high rate of HIV infection. Through creative partnerships and the effective use of grant funding, a continuum of services was built that now includes: outreach, risk reduction, and education for African Americans and Hispanics as well as the homeless; a multi-site HIV testing and counseling program that services 3,000 persons per year; Street Home, a one-stop shopping program of HIV primary care, case management, and nutritional support; and the Edgewood, a 46-unit residence for homeless and low-income persons with HIV/AIDS who are in recovery from substance dependency.

Mercy Mobile also responded to the problem of poor access to women's and children's health services. Grady Memorial Hospital reported that one quarter of its unregistered patients had little or no prenatal care, a factor contributing to its high infant mortality rate. Grady and Mercy Mobile joined together to address this problem by stationing nurse midwives and a social worker at mobile sites to identify high-risk pregnant women, initiate care, facilitate access to Grady for delivery, and establish a system for ongoing communication. Prenatal and parenting classes are provided in English and Spanish. Eighty-two percent of the clients identified by trained resource mothers are enrolled in their first trimester. Bilingual health promoters seek out underserved Hispanic, African American, and Asian women, offering cancer screening. Twenty-nine percent of the women have never had a Pap test and 87 percent have never had a mammogram.

Multicultural

Mercy Mobile Health Care is committed to creating an organization reflective of the communities it serves. Prenatal and parenting classes are provided in English and Spanish. Mercy Mobile Health Care has also responded to the

TABLE 15–2

Mercy Mobile Health Care 1996 Services

Outreach	Information & Referral	Prevention	Social & Pastoral Care Services	Clinical Services	Community Services
Client & Community Surveys	Health Hotline	Infectious Disease Risk Reduction	Mental Health & Substance/Dependence Assessments	Adult Medicine:	Health Fairs
Transportation	Assessment & Intake,	Substance/ Dependence Risk Reduction	Case Management	■ Primary Health Care	Charis House Construction in Summerhill
Posters & Displays	Service Referrals	Immunizations/	Pastoral Support & Reassurance	■ Chronic Disease Management	Speaker's Bureau
Brochures & Flyers	Translation &	Flu Shots	Child Care	Pediatric Care	Volunteer Recruitment & Coordination
Network Newsletter	Interpretation,	Tuberculosis Therapy	Psychotherapy	Maternal Services:	Advocacy for Medically Underserved
Home Visits	Cultural Assessment,	Injury Prevention/ Car Seat Program	Mental Health & Substance/Dependence Recovery	■ Prenatal Education	Collaboration
Outreach to:	Service Schedule Distribution,		Financial Aid	■ Childbirth Preparation	Community Health Planning
■ Churches	Telephone Support & Followup	**Screening**	Housing Assistance	Prenatal Care & Delivery	Professional Consultation :
■ Youth Groups		Breast Exams	Medicaid Enrollment	Infectious Disease Services:	■ Mobile Healthcare Delivery
■ Labor Pools	**Health Promotion**	Mammography	Food & Clothing	■ STD Testing & Treatment	■ Multicultural Health Svcs.
■ Soup Kitchens	Hygiene Kits	Pap Smears &		■ HIV Early Intervention	Internships:
■ Shelters	Health Promotion Handbooks	Cervical Cancer Screening	**Education**	■ PPD Testing	■ Pastoral Care
■ Laundromats	Substance Dependence Recovery Groups,	HIV Testing	Parenting Classes	■ Directly Observed Therapy/TB	■ Nursing
■ Jails/Courts	HIV + Counseling & Support Groups,	Pregnancy Testing	Healthy Women Series	Colposcopy	■ Medicine
■ Parks	Well Child Checks,	Tuberculosis Screening	Healthy Men Series	Laboratory	■ Social Work
■ Neighborhood Meetings	Nutritional Counseling/WIC	Blood Pressure, Glucose & Anemia Monitoring	Violence Prevention Training	Pharmacy	
	Diabetic Counseling		Immunization Education	Radiology	
			Family Planning Education	Dental Care	
			Resource Mothers Training	Medicinal Case Management	
			English as a Second Language		

needs of rapidly growing communities of culturally and linguistically isolated Hispanics and Asians, by providing bilingual medical clinics, education, and screening and translation assistance at health department hospitals. The composition of Mercy Care's staff demonstrates the importance of ethnic sensitivity when attempting to impact health concerns that are linked to lifestyle and rooted in culture. In addition to staff diversity, the board of directors is also comprised of 50 percent racial or ethnic minorities. (See Table 15–3.)

Coordinated across a Continuum

Mercy Mobile Health Care relies heavily on collaboration and partnerships to create a continuum of care for the medically underserved. The organization began with over 20 public and private agencies forming a coalition. Presently the organization has 12 partnership grants which focus on providing care to women and children; prevention and treatment of infectious diseases; cancer screening and prevention; substance dependence recovery; and healthcare for the homeless and others. In each case, a consortium of churches, non-profit

TABLE 15–3

Saint Joseph's Mercy Care Services : Staff Diversity Profile

Ethnic Origin			*Country of Origin*		*Language Other Than English*		
	No.	%		No.		No.	%
African American	27	28	USA	68	Spanish	26	30
Asian	5	5	Peru	1	Vietnamese	4	5
Caucasian	41	42	Puerto Rico	2	Iranian/Persian	1	1
Hispanic	21	22	Argentina	2			
Other	1	1	Colombia	5			
			Cuba	2			
			Chile	1			
			Nicaragua	2			
			Iran/Persia	1			
			El Salvador	1			
			Mexico	1			
			Vietnam	3			
			Dominican Republic	1			
			Cambodia	1			
			Korea	1			

organizations, public health departments, universities, and private providers join together and apply their expertise to address a particular need by embracing an opportunity to have an impact on community health.

As Mercy Mobile identifies changes in demographics, diagnoses, or acuity level of clients, the organization seeks partnerships and funding sources to support initiatives in each area of emerging need. Because of the multiple and extensive needs of clients, many collaborative efforts are required to ensure access to seamless care.

The collaboration with Grady Memorial Health System mentioned earlier is one example. Clearly, Grady's traditional approach to relying on pregnant women to initiate prenatal care in an appropriate and timely fashion was ineffective 25 percent of the time. Presently, a midwife works in mobile clinics to provide prenatal care through a method that is known to and trusted by low-income, isolated, and potentially high-risk women. Transportation, child care, and interpretation augment clinical and social services. Additional services are offered by a Women Infant Children nutritionist who is donated by the Fulton County Health Department and a full-time pediatric nurse practitioner who is funded by Scottish Rite Children's Medical Center.

Another successful collaboration focused local and national attention on the potential of partnership between healthcare providers and faith communities. Mercy Mobile Health Care joined with The Carter Center's Interfaith Health Program, the Georgia Nurses Foundation, and the U.S. Department of Health and Human Services, Region IV, to create a vision for transforming healthcare by exploring collaborative potential and best practices. Presently over 50 percent of Mercy Mobile Health Care's clinic sites are church-based, reflective of the philosophy of linking physical and spiritual well-being. A new mobile clinic is being donated by the Atlanta Billy Graham Crusade. In 1995, Mercy Mobile entered into a partnership with Central Presbyterian Church to operate its 75-year-old clinic called Central Health Center.

Mercy Mobile Health Care utilizes a computerized clinical record to track care provided to clients in a variety of mobile settings. The laptop computer-based system enables providers to access a client's history without having a paper record on hand. This system is currently being expanded to incorporate social services and clinical data to form an integrated record which will have greater applicability for coordinating care and exchanging information.

Publicly Accountable

In the community-wide survey referenced earlier, access to healthcare was identified as a top priority. Similarly, Georgia Health Decisions studied the healthcare priorities of citizens across the state and found access to care, including indigent care, to be a major concern.

By channeling the resources of Saint Joseph's Health System to Mercy Mobile (25 percent of the operating budget is funded by the health system), the organization is fulfilling its social accountability commitment to the community. Many financially successful not-for-profits have seen their tax exempt status challenged for not proactively addressing community health needs.

Based on community-wide studies and a comprehensive strategic plan, Mercy Mobile Health Care has focused on expanded access for the underserved and uninsured. Not only are free clinics offered, but working poor and underinsured persons receive care on a generous sliding fee scale with prices ranging from $20 to $50. By leveraging government grants; support from individuals, corporations, and foundations; donations of volunteer expertise and in-kind contributions, Mercy Mobile has created an affordable and accessible system of care.

Mercy Mobile produces newsletters and reports to keep the diverse group of shareholders who support the organization informed. Regular reports on results are produced which focus on scope of services, emerging needs, partnerships, cost of care, sources of support, outcomes, and case studies.

The organization is governed by a voluntary board of directors who have broad spheres of influence in the community.

Cost Effective

In the early 1990s, it became obvious that the program's dependence on federal and state grant dollars could threaten long-term sustainability. Like hospitals that recognized that imminent changes in federal and state funding of Medicare and Medicaid could rapidly escalate a position of vulnerability, Mercy Mobile saw the need to diversify revenue streams. The organization proactively committed internal resources and hired a business strategist to focus on development of patient service revenue. The investment paid off. In FY 1995, grant dollars accounted for 40 percent of total revenue versus 59 percent in 1994. Most importantly, Mercy Mobile plans to increase financial stability by securing approximately 23 percent of total 1996 revenues through a newly initiated Medicaid billing system (see Figures 15–2 and 15–3). This will be accomplished through billing of Medicaid for eligible clients in two fixed-site and five mobile clinics. While taking the new step of billing for service, Mercy Mobile will continue to provide free care to those in need, regardless of ability to pay.

Additionally, the Saint Joseph's Mercy Foundation has launched a major fundraising campaign to support Mercy Mobile Health Care. Three million dollars will be raised to support indigent care, capital purchases, and

FIGURE 15-2

Mercy Mobile Health Care
Sources of Support 1994

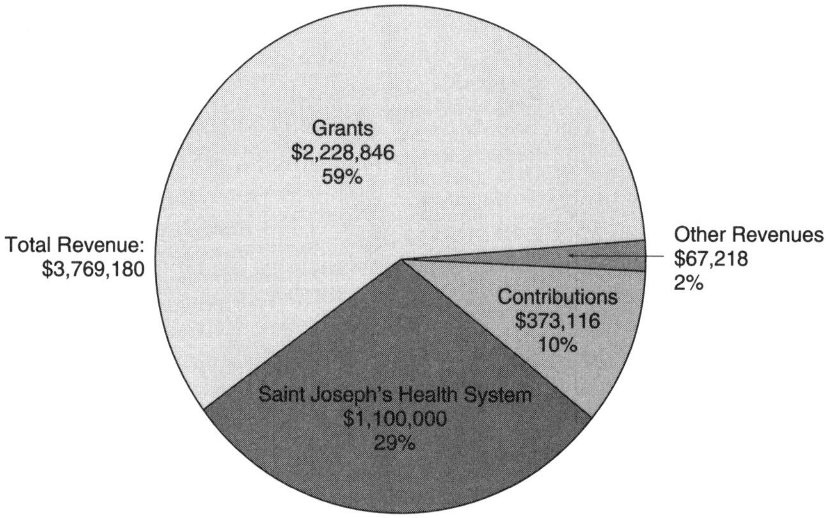

Source: Mercy Mobile Health Care.

endowment. Presently the organization's endowment is approaching $7.5 million. In addition to grants and donations, the organization enhances its cost effectiveness by relying on volunteer contributions and in-kind donations from suppliers. In 1995, the expertise of health professionals (doctors, nurses, pharmacists, and social workers) was valued at over $98,000. Although the program expended $160,000 on medicines in the same year, the retail value of the medicines was over $700,000, a result of an aggressive initiative to seek contributions from pharmaceutical companies. The Share the Care program of Pfizer, Inc., was responsible for $75,000 in donations.

In a period of budget cutbacks, Mercy Mobile Health Care's goal is to continue to advocate for an equitable health system. The organization has adopted a servant leadership approach to demonstrate that accessible, integrated, accountable, and collaborative care is possible by providing education, clinical, and social services to Atlanta's needy. Specific areas for future development include: making Central Health Center a viable resource for the working poor; improving housing options by providing supportive services at the Edgewood and the Imperial, residences for the homeless and working

FIGURE 15-3

Mercy Mobile Health Care
1996 Revenue Sources

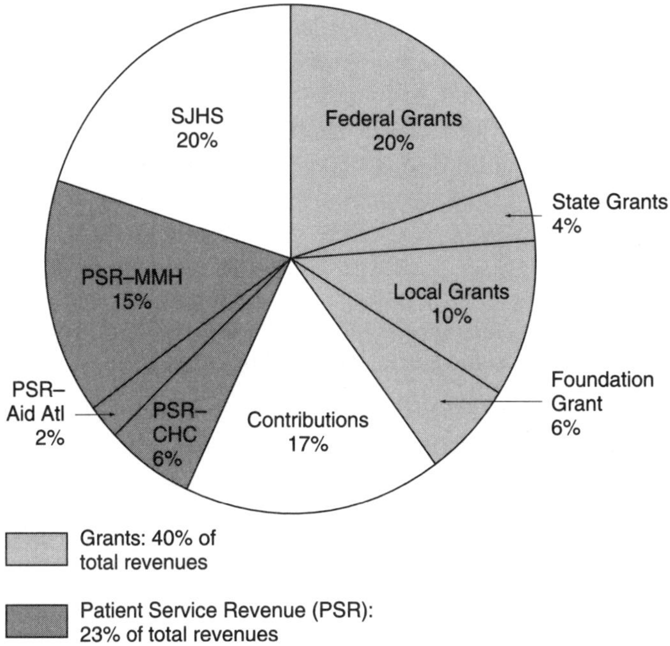

Source: Mercy Mobile Health Care.

poor; maximizing patient service revenues while ensuring access to care and continuing to build bridges between healthcare and faith communities. Most of all, Mercy Mobile will make its most dramatic contribution by continuing to successfully straddle the abyss between community health concerns and patient service revenue.

Working on a Shoestring

With budget cuts, changes in reimbursement, and a rather uncertain financial future, hospitals cannot afford to invest heavily in community health. Many providers are creatively financing new endeavors and are getting real results.

Community partnerships can pull together resources and dollars. With local businesses and city governments involved, the hospital does not become the sole underwriter. Grant dollars can provide a jump start but, though helpful when there are minimal cash reserves, grants should not be expected to sustain a program over time.

Some organizations, such as Memorial Health System in South Bend, Indiana, are developing a tithing approach to finance outreach programs. Under a tithing approach, a hospital chooses to reserve 10 percent of its previous year's surplus funds to insure a long-term commitment to community health that will not clash with an acute care budget. Charitable giving and volunteer commitment are also possible sources for revenue. When the assets of a community are combined, the opportunities for financial support can be exponential.

Conclusion

As I reviewed the real-life, in-the-street scenarios described in the chapter, the following scripture came easily into my mind:

> 'For I have plans for you,' declares the Lord, 'Plans to prosper you and not to harm you, plans to give you a hope and a future.'
>
> *(Jeremiah 29:11)*

Perhaps, then, it is fitting that the Catholic Health Association (CHA) is making a very overt effort to bridge service and solvency. In 1994 and 1995 the CHA was particularly outspoken regarding the need to turn the industry upside down. As I described in Chapter 14, the CHA convened two thinktanks to describe healthcare and the healthcare business systems that ***must*** ideally be in place by 2005. The thinktanks' output appeared in an executive summary. The following statements respond to the question of social responsibility:

> In a society with appalling rates of substance abuse, violence, heart disease, and infant mortality, healthcare providers are being called to take a new path. No longer is it sufficient for healthcare providers to concentrate on treating illness and injuries after they occur. No longer is it acceptable for them to continue current practices as our society spends more than any other on medical care and yet demonstrates no better health outcomes than countries that spend far less.

The Catholic Health Association recommends that providers making strategic decisions and investing dollars to catapult community health from a vision to a business "redefine organizational missions to emphasize serving community needs." This could require letting go of some current activities—perhaps even *standard inpatient care.* Social activists can be strengthened in this era of healthcare reform. Health policy may not be derived from social concerns, but it can definitely be fashioned from economic realities.

16 CHAPTER

Elder Services: The Sleeping Giant Awakens*

Much has been written about the "graying" of America and what will happen when the Baby Boomer generation reaches its senior years. Seventy-six million people were born in the United States between 1946 and 1964—approximately one-third of all living Americans. Baby Boomers have dominated American culture for four decades and will continue to dominate the social, political, and marketplace themes as they enter their elder years. Because the first of the Boomers are now entering their 50s, the time is quickly approaching when speculation will be replaced by experience. Those providers that have proactively planned to serve this burgeoning market base will soar to the top as new industry leaders. Those that have been too busy managing the day-to-day crises associated with an almost obsolete delivery system will be caught dangerously unaware as the sleeping giant of elder care awakens.

For the long-term care industry, questions are now being posed that require answers *before* experience becomes the teacher. What kind of services

*This chapter was written by Susan McBroom and Margo Caulfield. Susan McBroom has over 20 years' experience within the healthcare industry as a consultant and administrator. In these capacities, her chief mission has been to develop and help implement methods to improve service delivery, ameliorate barriers to improvement of quality of care, and design new services in response to changing needs, technology, and funding.

will the elder population require? What will be the form and function of service delivery? Most importantly, what are the implications for healthcare providers? This chapter will identify trends impacting service delivery for elders and describe the tools healthcare decision makers need to capture this exploding market.

The elderly are growing faster as a percentage of the population, and they are heterogeneous by ethnicity, age, socioeconomic, and health status.

TRENDS IMPACTING SERVICE DELIVERY

Advances in living conditions and medical care have enabled more Americans to live longer than ever before. The Census Bureau estimates that by 2000 the elderly population will be about 35 million, and it will increase to almost 40 million by 2010. The 85 and older group, of which approximately 50 percent will require some type of long-term care, is estimated to be 3.3 million at the turn of the century. The number of elderly needing nursing home care is expected to increase from about 1.8 million in 1990 to 4.3–5.3 million in 2030, depending on the projection assumptions. Census Bureau estimates range from a low of approximately 9 million persons age 85 and over to a high of approximately 18 million persons age 85 and over by 2040.[1]

Graying America is also heterogeneous by ethnicity, age, socioeconomic, and health status. The minority elder population is growing and will represent one-third of the elder population by 2050. Widows will continue to outnumber widowers. While the percentage increase in older minorities between 1990 and 2030 will be higher among people of color (247% among African Americans and people of other races and 395% among Hispanics), the percentage of elderly among white non-Hispanics in 2030 (24%) will still be higher than the percentage for African Americans and other races.[2]

The aging process is a reflection of our attitudes and beliefs. The health conditions experienced by the elderly today reflect the changes in lifestyle behavior and advances in medicine since 1950. Behavior in different age groups varies according to culture, gender, and values. The degree of sophistication we apply to differentiating the younger population by age must be applied to the elderly. While Dychtwald, in his book entitled *Age Wave: How the Most Important Trend of Our Time Will Change Your Future,* suggests breaking the age groups down to 50–64, 65–79, and 80 plus,[3] variations among cohorts will also exist because of geography, gender, marital status, religion, and culture. The diverse elder population, now and in the future, requires a higher level of vigilance and sophisticated analysis to understand the changing needs of these groups. If market data and demographic projections are analyzed in an elegant manner, health systems can have the opportunity to build a delivery system that will uniquely correspond to a growing market base.

Lifestyle changes will also impact the choices and decisions about how and where to live. According to Deepak Chopra, "A balanced lifestyle is one of the most important steps toward retarding the aging process."[4] Similarly, Eric Pfeiffer, a psychiatrist at Duke University, found that "people who age successfully are those who stayed in training throughout their adult lives in three major areas: physical activity, psychological and intellectual activity, and social relationships."[5] Consequently, health promotion and preventive medicine rise to the forefront of service delivery objectives targeting the elderly population.

According to the U.S. Census Bureau, since 1960 the number of elderly individuals living alone has increased from 7.3 percent to 30.3 percent.[6] Historically, women served as the caregivers for the elderly and the infirm; However, with 43.6 percent of women now working (1985), compared to 20.5 percent in 1915, women are less available to fill this role. The American Association of Retired Persons says 12 percent of caregivers have had to quit their jobs and 14 percent work part time so they can tend to the aged. In addition, some adults help their elders financially: 69 percent of adults provide up to $250 a month to parents, according a report in *USA Today.* "Elder care is one of the hottest new benefits issues because employees are desperate for practical help," says Dr. Daniel Thursz of the National Council on Aging.[7] What this means to the local health system is this: If you are viewing the large employer as a target customer, then you will need to include elder care.

Income not only determines access to care but also directly influences self-perception of health and health status for the elderly. Ken Dychtwald comments: "Americans over 50 now have a combined personal income of over $800 billion and control 70 percent of the total net worth of U.S. households—nearly $7 trillion of wealth."[8] Furthermore, those 65 years and older perceive their health in general as excellent, very good, or good, and tend to have better health habits than the non-elderly.[9] The wealth of this generation is a driving force in the development of new and unique services. In contrast, "elderly persons in families with incomes below $10,000 experienced more acute conditions and had higher rates of chronic and potentially costly conditions, such as hearing impairment, diabetes, heart disease, and hypertension, than elderly persons in higher income families."[10] While education and income appear to influence level of disability

Health care providers must move beyond the medical model and embrace business, service, and clinical expertise to capture the elder market.

among the elderly, income appears to be the more important of the two factors. In the Longitudinal Retirement History Survey, the non-poor had disability rates up to 80 percent lower than the poor, and disability was 42–67% lower for those with 16 or more years of education compared to those with 11 years or less.[11]

CHANGES IN LONG-TERM CARE

In the last 10 years, long-term care (LTC) has undergone a major change in (1) who provides the service and (2) its philosophy and utilization. In prior decades, LTC was predominately viewed as the nursing home industry. A sleeping giant that realizes there is much to gain by being awake, the industry is repositioning itself now to include a spectrum of services. These changes are not only occurring because of consumer demand but also in response to changing reimbursement, regulatory requirements, and the proliferation of business interest in this market segment.

Federal policy changes during the 1980s helped increase the demand for nursing facilities. For one, in 1983 Medicare's prospective payment system for inpatient hospital stays worked to shorten hospital stays and increase the number of referrals and admissions to nursing homes.[12] Second, legislation in 1988 established a minimum level of spousal asset and income protection for use when determining Medicare nursing facility eligibility. This also contributed to an increase in Medicaid program costs.[13] With the increase in demand came a corresponding increase in the costs of Medicaid and Medicare. States, in response, adopted policies to control Medicaid nursing facility demand, including Medicaid eligibility policies and preadmission screening programs. These policies may have had a constraining effect on demand and, consequently, the growth in nursing facility capacity.

While the demand for nursing home care increased from 1978 to 1993, the bed growth rate did not keep pace with the increase in the population 85 years or over.[14] In fact, a survey of state health planning officials in 1993 found that only seven states believed that they had an under-supply of beds. Twenty states were rated as having an over-supply, 22 were viewed as having an adequate supply, and 2 had no opinion.[15] With changes in Medicaid reimbursement and the elderly opting for care in alternative settings—that is, assisted living programs, comprehensive community retirement centers (CCRC), and home care—it is not surprising that nursing homes found themselves with empty beds. In an effort to fill vacancies, nursing homes are looking to physical medicine and rehabilitation and other forms of subacute care, as well as assisted living, hospice, and home care as ways to stay in the market.

While the nursing home industry has been central to the delivery of long-term care, it is now becoming a component part of a changing industry. With a battle cry of "aging in place," consumers and advocates are looking for a wide array of community-based programs to keep the elderly and disabled at home, or at the very least in a home-like environment. In recent years the reimbursement structure, in an effort to reduce the high cost of re-institutionalization, has also jumped on the "community based" bandwagon. The result has been an evolution of new or expanded services, featuring a combination of social and health-related programs. Briefly, these services include:

- **Assisted Living (AL):** "Homes" and facilities for elderly and physically challenged people have existed for many years; however, the concept of assisted living was formally acknowledged in the United States in the mid-1980s. Viewed as a cost-effective alternative to nursing homes, there are now estimated to be as many as 65,372 facilities, housing between 104,803 and one million residents.[16] The Assisted Living Facilities Association of America (ALFAA) defines AL as:

  > a special combination of housing, supportive services, personalized assistance and health care designed to respond to the individual needs of those who need help with activities of daily living and instrumental activities of daily living. Supportive services are available, 24 hours a day, to meet scheduled and unscheduled needs, in a way that promotes maximum dignity and involves the resident's family, neighbors and friends.

  Oregon has actively pursued the development of AL programs as a replacement for nursing homes. By offering incentives for developers and providing a reimbursement source for care components, Oregon has seen no growth in nursing home beds in almost a decade. According to Richard Ladd, in an interview for *Contemporary Long Term Care Magazine,* "There are 10,000 fewer people in nursing homes today in Oregon than there were 10 years ago. All the growth has been in either assisted living, foster homes or home care."[17] While Oregon has received a great deal of recognition for its program, it also has critics. These facilities can quickly become warehouses in an effort to reduce costs and serve as many people as possible, destroying the original intent of Assisted Living.

- **Continuing care retirement communities (CCRC):** Unlike the retirement communities of the 1950s and 60's, residents of CCRCs can obtain a full range of healthcare services, with the exception of acute hospitalization, without leaving the campus. Depending on the size of the facility these services can include: assisted living, primary care, home care, and nursing home care. To various degrees, CCRCs provide a bundle of housing, personal care, and nursing home services in exchange for varying combinations of prepayment at entry plus monthly and specific fees for services. The American Association of Homes and Services for the Aging (AAHSA) distinguishes CCRCs from other kinds of housing options for older persons by limiting use of the term to organizations that offer long-term contracts for a continuum of care spanning residence, personal care, and nursing care.

Continuing care retirement communities appear to be a good prospect for reducing institutional long-term care. In a study of CCRCs, those offering completely prepaid LTC coverage reduced use of nursing home care by 13 percent and personal care by 5 percent. It should be noted that prepaid LTC coverage did not use more stringent health screening at entry, so "cream skimming" does not appear to explain this result. The authors of the study believe that "proximity to residents in a CCRC setting permits supportive services to be provided in a timely manner so that services are tailored to residents' changing needs. Financial incentive to target services most appropriately may also be at work."[18] In addition, accessible living facilities help reduce the incidence of falls and injuries, while having a readily available peer group reduces social isolation. The latter also is supportive of caregivers, enabling residents to remain independent and not to require personal care or other services.

Industry giants such as the Mariott Corporation are competing in the CCRC market. With an established reputation for service and sophisticated use of information, companies like Marriott are better positioned to respond to the requirements of the elder population.

- **Adult day care (ADC):** The National Institute on Adult Daycare estimates that 3,000 adult day cares are currently operating in the United States. Most (90%) are operated on a non-profit or public basis and many are affiliated with larger organizations, such as nursing homes, hospitals, or multi-purpose senior organizations. ADCs, designed to meet the needs of functionally impaired adults through an individual plan of care, provide an array of services in a protective setting during any part of a day, but less than 24-hour care. Typical services include: transportation, nursing care, therapeutic activities, social services personal care, rehabilitation therapies, meals, and counseling.
- **PACE–On Lok Model:** Medicaid, in an effort to reduce the high cost of nursing home care, has been offering a waiver program since 1981 for community-based services which can demonstrate

that care in their programs is less costly than nursing home care. This waiver program has resulted in the development of services which address the full spectrum of elder needs by using a coordinated and integrated approach, combining community-based personal and medical services, as well as institutional care.

An excellent example of this community-based model is the PACE–On Lok Model. PACE is a fully capitated comprehensive care program that specifically targets the frail elderly. The program consolidates and integrates all services to this population by controlling the evaluation and delivery of services. The PACE model evolved from the On Lok program in San Francisco, "serving the very impaired and frail elderly who require ongoing care for the rest of their lives." The program's operating principles include:[19]

1. Comprehensive medical, restorative, social, and supportive services that together address the client's multiple, interrelated problems.
2. A fully integrated, coordinated response to the needs of the client.
3. Complete control by the service team of any and all services needed.
4. Emphasis on participants' continued community residence, and a risk management orientation."

In 1986 Congress passed P.L. 99–509, granting limited replication of the On Lok model through Medicare and Medicaid capitation financing. The law granted an initial waiver, for a period of three years, to provide comprehensive healthcare services on a capitated basis to the frail elderly at risk for institutionalization. The sites approved for replication share risk with Medicare and Medicaid during their first three years of operation, as provided by P.L. 100–203, section 4118. All sites must be prepared to assume full financial risk after three years. The Medicare and Medicaid waivers override normal benefit definitions and limitations and allow a "lock in." In other words, freedom of choice in selection of providers is suspended for enrollees.[20]

CHANGES IN THE REIMBURSEMENT STRUCTURE

Managed care reimbursement, a major thrust in healthcare over two decades, is now an influencer in the long-term care arena. Social HMOs (SHMOs), while still in the experimental phase, are financed at full risk through capitated payments from Medicare, Medicaid, private member premiums, and member co-payments for long-term care benefits. These HMOs provide all Medicare Part A and Part B benefits, prescription drugs, and other ancillary services. Eligibility is based on multidimensional assessments that state governments use for nursing home preadmission screening.

The first round of evaluations of SHMOs has been mixed. Shortfalls have included slow enrollment growth, frequent operating deficits, and limited LTC benefits. On the plus side, enrollment targets have been achieved, deficits were less for HMO sponsors than if all of their Medicare members were in their risk plan, and no other HMOs offer any LTC benefit. According to Walter N. Leutz, an associate research professor at the Institute for Health Policy, The Heller School, Brandeis University, the first round of experiences with the SHMOs has proved that these programs can be successful at maintaining individuals at home; being financed privately; and incorporating acute care services.

Long-term care insurance, a relatively new product in the insurance industry, was established to help people with the high cost of long-term care. While it has been estimated that up to 42 percent of the elderly population can currently afford a long-term care policy, only 4 percent of the population over 65 has made such a purchase. By 1990, more than 130 companies sold LTC insurance, a 79 percent increase from 1987. While 1.65 million policies are believed to have been sold from 1987 to June of 1990, a number of policies have lapsed, making the actual number of policies significantly lower. In 1990, premiums averaged $483 for people 50 years old; $1,135 for 65 year olds; and $3,841 for persons 79 years of age.[21]

While most policies (77%) have been sold to individuals, more and more employers are now beginning to offer the benefit. The average age of persons buying an individual policy in 1990 was 72. Another form of long-term care coverage, called accelerated death benefits, is also becoming widely available as a rider to a life insurance policy. These policies advance a portion of the death benefit to the policy holder each month to help with medical expenses.

Available LTC policies offer a wide array of benefits and costs. A typical policy includes coverage for nursing homes and home healthcare. Some policies carry benefits for adult day care or respite care. Policies normally pay from $40 to $120 per day for nursing homes and $20 to $60 a day for home healthcare. Newer policies include payment for case management services as well. Earlier generations of insurance products contain many limitations that can restrict a consumer's ability to receive coverage for needed benefits. These include requiring a prior stay in an institution to obtain home health benefits and the lack of coverage for Alzheimer's disease.

The current mood in Congress is not one that lends itself to an expansion of the Medicare or Medicaid program. Options such as tax-free medical savings accounts (MSAs), which would operate in a manner similar to an individual retirement account, or the expansion of SHMOs may become attractive.

GROWTH IN ELDER CARE ADVOCACY AND RESEARCH

The industry's growth is also mirrored in the growth of advocacy and special interest groups, academic research centers on aging, and specialty providers in gerontological services. In the last decade alone, participation in advocacy or special interest groups and exploration of aging research has exploded. The Leadership Council of Aging Organizations boasts some 35 member organizations that represent a variety of special interests about aging.

With the growth of academic centers, specialists have evolved in the field of gerontology to address the complex healthcare needs of this population. Specialists in psychiatry, pharmacology, psychology, nursing, nutrition, and the like understand the synergistic impact of interventions. For example, it is not unusual for a frail elder person to consume in excess of 10 medications. Often these medications are prescribed for specific symptoms and by more than one physician. The consequence for the individual is a potential decrease in level of awareness and activity, weight loss, dehydration, and skin breakdown. This process can happen very quickly and can necessitate further medical intervention.

TOOLS FOR CAPTURING THE ELDER CARE MARKET

The new order of business is a coordinated and integrated approach with case management at the center. The philosophy of this system is to enable the elder to "age in place" with maximum function in all domains. The case manager acts as the hub of the wheel, working with elders to obtain those services they need to achieve and maintain function. The case manager reviews the services and interventions, accessing specialists as necessary, to minimize untoward effects and institutionalization.

Effective services address the full spectrum of elder needs by using a coordinated and integrated approach. This approach combines community-based personal and medical services, as well as institutional care. Woven throughout this system of care is a distinct emphasis on service.

The spokes of this wheel reach beyond the traditional medical model. They include: community-based services such as primary care; personal care services including Meals on Wheels; assistance with transportation and housing; home, respite, and hospice care; assisted living; physical medicine and rehabilitation and other forms of subacute and chronic care which can be provided at a freestanding site, in a nursing home, or by a hospital; and secondary and tertiary care as provided by a hospital.

As a healthcare decision maker, what choices are available to you for capturing this market? The three major opportunities include:

1. **Offering à la carte services:** Provide contract services to an elder carve-out product, network of elder providers, and/or retirement community. Services might include ancillaries such as laboratory, X-ray, and pharmacy; primary care and/or specialty clinics; and emergency and acute care services.
2. **Managing the network:** Through your provider organization, secure risk contracts for elder services. Subcontract with other community providers to complete an elder network of services. Joint venture, purchase, and/or develop the case management feature to ensure appropriate service coordination and utilization.
3. **Develop an elder carve-out product:** Develop an organization that allows you to provide capitated elder care. The most important feature of this product is case management.

In exploring options for your institution, consider your response to the following questions:

- How does the proposed product fit with the organization's current vision, mission, and values?
- What is the maturity of the market? What share does the institution own or could it own?
- What degree of risk can the institution realistically assume? What impact would be incurred for assuming that risk?

So, how do we proceed? A client in the LTC industry once told us about a recent experience at a professional seminar. The speaker said to the audience, "*Define the need and fill it!*" Well that certainly says it all! A simple and straightforward statement full of opportunity. Our conversation continued with a review of the essential steps in crafting a service and/or product. These steps are not new. Indeed, they are readily found in the management literature. The difference, however, is that healthcare providers must understand *the importance of using information* for timely business decisions. Skipping steps or negating information will result in lost revenue. The steps are:

1. **Analyze demographic and psychographic analysis information.** Complete a demographic and psychographic analysis of the elder market in your community.
2. **Conduct phone surveys and/or focus groups.** Conduct phone surveys and/or focus groups with the target population to fully understand purchasing behavior and service requirements.
3. **Take an inventory of existing providers of service.** Identify the breadth and depth of the competition. It is important to look beyond the traditional healthcare arena to understand your market. What is the target service and segment of each competitor? What is the financial condition of the service and how does the public and the professional community view its value?
4. **Fill the demand.** Define the opportunities based upon consumer needs and competitor analysis.
5. **Evaluate the environment.** Develop or secure knowledge of service reimbursement, and national, state, and local regulatory requirements.
6. **Clarify the role:** Clarify the role your organization will play in providing the service. Is your organization the hub or a spoke of service delivery? What relationships are important to the success of the service?
7. **Verify assumptions and do it.** Verify demand and fiscal assumptions. Secure the necessary operating relationships. Establish service and outcome standards that reflect customer requirements. Relentlessly pursue delivering on those standards.

In conclusion, the long-term care market continues to change, moving well beyond the traditional medical model. Healthcare providers must be flexible and innovative in developing relationships, accepting risk, and securing expertise. These crucial skills will dictate who wins the market.

ENDNOTES

1. U.S. Bureau of Census. *1990 Census of Population* (CPH-L–1137) (Washington, D.C.: U.S. Bureau of Census, Population Division.
2. U.S. Senate Special Committee on Aging, AARP, Federal Council on the Aging, and U.S. Administration on Aging. *Aging America: Trends and Projections.* Washington, D.C.: American Association of Retired Persons, 1991. Washington, D.C.
3. Dychtwald, Ken and Joe Flower. *Age Wave: How The Most Important Trend of Our Time Will Change Your Future* (New York: Bantam Books, 1990).

4. Chopra, Deepak. *Ageless Body, Timeless Mind* (New York: Harmony Books, 1993), p. 134.
5. ibid., p. 82.
6. U.S. Bureau of Census. *1990 Census of Population* (CPH-L–1137) (Washington, D.C.: U.S. Bureau of Census, Population Division).
7. Aburdene, Patricia, and John Naisbitt. *Megatrends for Women: From Liberation to Leadership* (1992), p. 261.
8. Dychtwald, Ken, and Joe Flower. *Age Wave: How The Most Important Trend of Our Time Will Change Your Future* (New York: Bantam Books, 1990), p. 268.
9. U.S. Senate Special Committee on Aging, AARP, Federal Council on the Aging, and U.S. Administration on Aging. *Aging America: Trends and Projections.*
10. General Accounting Office, Washington, D.C. 1992, p. 6.
11. Maddox and Clark, 1992.
12. Guterman, S. et al. "The First Three Years of Medicare Prospective Payment: An Overview," *Health Care Financing Administration* (Santa Monica, CA: Rand Corp., 1988).
13. Leutz, Walter N., Merwyn R. Greenlick, and John A. Capitman. "Integrating Acute and Long-Term Care," *Health Affairs* (Fall 1994).
14. DuNah, Richard, Jr., et al. "Variations and Trends in State Nursing Facility Capacity: 1978–93," *Health Care Financing Review*. vol. 17, no. 1 (Fall 1995).
15. ibid.
16. Coopers & Lybrand. *An Overview of the Assisted Living Industry* (The Assisted Living Facilities Association of America, 1993).
17. Bowe, Jim. "Medicaid Takes the Plunge into Assisted Living," *Contemporary Long Term Care* (September 1993), pp. 33–35, 90.
18. Sloan, Frank A., May W. Shayne, and Christopher J. Conover. "Continuing Care Retirement Communities: Prospects for Reducing Institutional Long Term Care," *Journal of Health Politics, Policy, and Law* vol. 20, no. 1 (Spring 1995).
19. Zawadski, Rick T., and Catherine Eng. "Case Management in Capitated Long-Term Care," *Health Care Financing Review* (1988 Annual Supplement), p. 76.
20. Shen, John, and Ann Iverson, MPH. "PACE: A Capitated Model Towards Long-Term Care." *Henry Ford Hospital Medical Journal*. Vol. 40, Nos. 1 & 2, 1992, p. 42.
21. AARP Public Policy Institute. "Fact Sheet: Private Long-Term Care Insurance." (Washington, D.C.: American Association of Retired Persons, May 1, 1991).

PART SIX

ENABLING A NEW ORGANIZATIONAL ORDER

17 CHAPTER

Relationship Management and a New Organizational Order

If you are a hospital administrator, the CFO of a large health system, or a physician specialist, you are probably fed up with all this talk about paradigm shifting. To you, the reality of a new organizational order is most obvious when you look at your year-end financial report. If that isn't close enough to home, you are probably being faced with new responsibilities that include downsizing, streamlining, and reengineering. Those of you who still have jobs in healthcare can probably name a dozen or so friends who climbed with you to the top . . . and are now on the streets hawking themselves as "health-care consultants."

It's lonely at the top, you say? Today in the healthcare industry, that isolationist model of elite leadership is not only lonely, its *dangerous.* Success in the new millennium will require a new organizational order and those who rise to the top will recognize that *relationship management* will be the only way to win it all.

COPING WITH CULTURE SHOCK

In many healthcare systems today, the crisis of the marketplace has combined with internal crisis to create a toxic environment. Creativity and innovation have been suffocated. Downsizing means that some will win jobs while others will lose them. Fear and denial have too often turned convivial colleagues into venomous competitors. Today, all industry players must commit to new relationships by recognizing that competition can be the flint for collaboration. Healthcare systems require interdependence of all facets if quality care is to be the outcome.

Before any organization can move into a new future, it must allow time for very real grieving to occur. Letting go of old habits and ways of being in business can be very difficult. The tension of letting go is even more dramatic when doing so requires the acknowledgment that a lifestyle has ended. For instance, look at the CEO who states the need for more ancillary care but, on a day-to-day basis, spends most of his or her energy circling the wagons round the inpatient beds. Similarly, talk to the cardiovascular surgeon with five children, two ex-spouses, a boathouse, and a Jaguar—and see how easily he or she embraces the shift of financial incentives toward primary care medicine. In neither case has all this talk about "being vested in wellcare" been translated to a personal reformation. In most cases, measures of well-being parallel profitability.

Coping with culture shock means meeting head-on the cynicism and alienation that is becoming characteristic of an industry in chaos. It requires identifying the root causes of declining confidence in our leaders and institutions. For most healthcare employees, downsizing, massive layoffs, restructuring, and market share losses have all contributed to an environment of overall suspicion.

With the squeeze on profits and the pressure to get "lean and mean," some of our most grand, even mythical, corporations have experienced employee disillusionment of unprecedented proportions. As a consequence of all the scandal and broken promises, people feel betrayed. Although 93.8 percent of respondents to an *Industry Week* poll said that loyalty was an important factor in a company's success or failure, 75.6 percent said they thought their companies were less loyal to them than they were five years previously.[1]

Many more people now inquire if there is any leader who has the strength of character to sustain faith. People openly wonder if their health system leaders aren't just in it for themselves. Whatever happened to those who serve for the good of the community at large and the good of the company? Can any leader be trusted?

In America, top executive pay for health system leaders has gone through the roof at the same time that corporate performance has declined. Real or imagined, it appears that the average workers are suffering while the bosses are luxuriating. Their indulgence, say some, is costing people their jobs and companies their markets. Not only is there a perception that CEO pay is too high, scholars who have studied the subject conclude that "there are few, if any, meritocratic elements in the formulation of American CEOs' compensation."[2] In other words, for all the rhetoric about "pay for performance," there isn't much evidence to support a link between CEO salaries and their achievements. Recovery from the credibility recession may have to be linked to self-initiated reforms in executive pay.

A majority of line employees and managers believe that quality is very important. Espoused commitment to quality is understood as the first step in the improvement process. But embedded in the quality movement is a somewhat surprising issue. "Quality, quality, quality!" may be the new competitive war cry, but worker opinion suggests that companies aren't heeding it. In one survey of employee attitudes toward quality-improvement programs (conducted for the American Society for Quality Control by the Gallup Organization), 55 percent of employees reported that their companies said that it was extremely important to "show our customers we're committed to quality." However, only 36 percent stated that their companies considered "making quality everyone's top priority" extremely important. And only 35 percent said that the company was doing very well in that area.

Actions, say employees, are falling short in the quality-improvement game. But how can this be when so many dollars are being spent and so much effort expended to train every hospital employee in statistical process control and Pareto charts? How can this be when hospitals are competing vigorously to win the equivalent form of the Baldrige Award or the Deming prize? How can this happen when quality is at the top of nearly every organization's strategic agenda?

Perhaps the money, the training, and the prizes play a role. You can't pick up a local newspaper or a company newsletter without reading about the importance of quality. You can't miss the "quality is job one" ads on television. Expectations are raised. People come to believe that quality is the source of wealth and advantage. They expect the intensity of the actions—at a minimum—to match the force of the rhetoric. But when it comes to quality, apparently people have heard the talk but not seen the results.

And, as is often the case with rising expectations, even though more is accomplished it is not enough. People believe that what is being done is not enough to close the gap. Evidence supports this observation. For example, the quality of American automobiles has significantly improved in the last decade yet, relative to Japanese competition, they still lag behind. Perhaps American automobile industry leaders assumed that the competition would stand still while they caught up. When the perception is that leadership actions fall behind leadership promises, the credibility gap invariably widens. The message the workforce is sending, however, is a healthy one, one that enlightened leaders are heeding: Good is not enough when you dream of being great.[3]

USING BUSINESS DISCIPLINES

While the manner in which Columbia/HCA acquires hospitals has caused some concerns within the hospital industry, especially among not-for-profit hospital advocates, it is the manner in which the company operates hospitals that has made its competitors nervous and impressed financial analysts and investment bankers. With two major exceptions, Columbia/HCA is generally credited with running very strong and efficient operations that are redefining how health services are delivered in the markets they serve, and beyond.

The two exceptions are persistent criticisms that Columbia/HCA hospitals, at least in some markets (1) provide less charity care than not-for-profit hospitals and (2) take money out of the communities they serve to meet shareholder earnings requirements. The purpose of this section is to give an overview of how Columbia/HCA operates in the markets it currently serves.

Operational Organization

From the beginning, Columbia/HCA has been based on regional decentralization of decision making and operations. There are currently over 30 distinct market area "regions," each of which operates as a unit within the company. Within a region, all services and facilities are closely coordinated to function as a single healthcare provider with multiple locations. As a result, Columbia/HCA is able to achieve significant efficiencies and economies of scale, while minimizing duplication of services and capabilities within each region. This in turn helps the company achieve its goal of lowering the average cost per admission to what the company terms the "market leading position," meaning it is able to provide healthcare at the lowest cost in that market. This cost advantage is then used to attract exclusive contracts with managed care organizations.

Nationally, the regions are aggregated into five "groups." Florida, Eastern, Central, Western, and a "national" group which oversees individual hospitals and services that are not part of a fully formed regional network. For example, Capital Medical Center in Olympia, the only Columbia/HCA hospital in Washington, is part of the national group.

When Columbia/HCA acquires hospitals in an area, it consolidates senior management into an efficient regional organization, but it commonly keeps the most respected local administrators and other senior managers to the extent they are supportive of being part of the Columbia/HCA team. Further, the company places an emphasis on quality of care and puts its money where its mouth is by devoting financial resources to improve the appearance of hospitals and the public perception of quality at its institutions. As noted earlier, the company's regional strategy is to have a tertiary medical center as the regional "flagship"; increasingly, this includes seeking to align with academic medical centers in a number of regions.

Operational Characteristics

Seven key components distinguish Columbia/HCA operations from its competitors in most markets. The company emphasizes that it is merely applying management techniques and capital financing strategies that have proven successful in other industries. Many other hospitals and healthcare systems have also adopted one or several of these components. To date, however, Columbia/HCA seems to have done the best job of combining them into a synergistic and well-coordinated operational strategy. The components are:

- Vertical integration of all local medical services.
- Successful partnerships with physicians.
- Bottom-line management incentives.
- Significant upgrades of physical plants.
- State-of-the-art information systems.
- Exclusive managed care contracts.
- Aggressive cost cutting.

Columbia/HCA's approach to each of these operational components is outlined in the following sections.[4]

Vertical Integration of All Local Medical Services

As noted earlier, one of the features that distinguishes Columbia/HCA's operations from most other hospital-based systems is that it operates its holdings in each region as a single healthcare provider with multiple locations. This includes not only hospital inpatient and outpatient operations, but free-standing ambulatory surgical centers, home health agencies, outpatient diagnostic and imaging facilities, and in some markets, ownership of primary care physician practices (in Denver, for example). While achieving this integration is certainly an operational challenge, the bottom-line financial focus and the regional integration strategy help align mid-level management incentives and reduce internal empire-building.

Columbia/HCA also stresses that employees at all levels need to be team players. Those hospital administrators who in the past have been used to running their own show, acting independently, and engaging in "turf wars" internally and externally, have needed to change their ways when they become part of Columbia/HCA—or they do not last long.

This regional focus is often most visible when Columbia/HCA eliminates duplicative services in neighboring facilities or, in some cases, closes an entire facility. Decisions are made for the good of the region, where "good" is defined primarily on the basis of bottom-line financial performance and meeting the needs of local customers (patients and physicians). Depending on one's perspective, Columbia/HCA has been particularly effective (or ruthless) in applying strict economic criteria to overcome the "every little town has to have a hospital" phenomenon when nearby towns have Columbia/HCA facilities.

Successful Partnerships with Physicians

Columbia/HCA has repeatedly emphasized that cooperation and partnership with the physicians on its hospitals' medical staffs are key components of achieving longterm success. "Increase responsiveness to medical staffs to improve hospital operations" is at the top of the list on Columbia/HCA's stated operational strategies. Numerous anecdotes document the improvement of hospital/medical staff relationships once Columbia/HCA acquires a hospital.

It helps that the financial resources of Columbia/HCA can be brought to bear on investing in the latest technology. In large part, the emphasis on good physician relations stems from the realization that physicians are key customers and that positive relations can translate directly into increased admissions. Beyond that, however, senior managers at Columbia/HCA have often stressed the importance of aligning with the "best and brightest minds" in the healthcare business and usually identify physicians at the top of that list.

Under a program termed "syndication," Columbia/HCA encourages physician equity investment in the local subsidiary in developed markets. While paying scrupulous attention to state and especially federal regulations regarding physician investment in the delivery system that specify no more than 40 percent of revenues can come from physician-owner referrals, Columbia/HCA has offered hospital medical staffs and physicians in its clinics up to a combined total 20 percent ownership in the local subsidiary. This approach has been less common in the last several years, however, and company spokespersons say it is offered only if the physicians are interested; it is not a central component of their growth strategy.

A common approach is to offer units of shares (from 1,000 to 15,000 shares per unit) at $15 per share. Columbia/HCA also will buy back physician shares at any time for current market value, which to date has always resulted in a significant gain to investors. These investment arrangements have a non-compete requirement prohibiting the physician from investing in the competition.

Critics object to physicians shifting admissions to hospitals in which they have a financial interest. Empirical data are sparse, and Columbia/HCA responds that its physician partners are just investing in the hospitals where they already admit the majority of their patients.

Bottom-Line Management Incentives

Performance-based compensation is not a new concept in the private sector, especially among proprietary hospitals. What may be different at Columbia/HCA, however, is that the performance measures are strictly quantitative (such as financial performance and increased market share), focused on regional performance to minimize individual hospital suboptimization, extended further down the organization than is common, and can involve significant amounts of money.

Aligning managers' financial incentives to stress regional performance was credited by several interviewees as a key factor in Columbia/HCA's success in operating a region as a single provider with multiple locations. In addition to the regional presidents, hospital CEOs, chief financial officers, chief operating officers, and the chief nurse executive at each hospital are often included in incentive-based compensation arrangements. Performance-based compensation has yet to become widespread in not-for-profit hospitals, in part due to tax exempt considerations. As a result, Columbia/HCA has more tools available to help it achieve local area delivery system integration.

Physical Plant Upgrades

Columbia/HCA has a reputation for investing in significant upgrades of physical plants at many of its hospitals, in some cases remaking the image of the hospital in the process. Access to capital is a tremendous competitive advantage the company has stressed in negotiations and delivered after the deal closes. It has funded a $3 billion unsecured line of credit, with bankers competitively bidding lower interest rates to be part of the fund. In most instances, however, it uses its own commercial paper, at 3.3 percent to finance most of its capital improvements.

Additionally, each Columbia/HCA region, and most facilities within a region, have sizable "contingency funds" built into annual operating budgets to give administrators the ability to upgrade technology and improve performance without undue delays. The refrain that "it's not in this year's budget" is a far less common excuse for delay or an obstacle for making needed improvements in a timely manner.

State-of-the-Art Information Systems

Columbia/HCA is making a huge investment in state-of-the-art information systems. While the company spends less than one percent of revenues on information systems technology, that still amounts to over $150 million per year. Financial and clinical information are linked, and the system is accessible throughout the facility, in the physicians' offices, and even from their home computers. From a nationwide data center in Ft. Worth, Texas, the company is tying together health data in a manner that few competitors can match.

In some sites, nurses are using hand-held computers to record information as they deliver care. Optical scanners are used to input visual information such as an EKG result or an X-ray, thereby improving physicians' access to information beyond just a printed summary of the test result. Information is available much sooner than under conventional information dissemination methods, resulting in decreases in duplicative tests. Columbia/HCA even has a medical director for information systems, to increase physician acceptance and use.

Economies of scale are a significant factor in Columbia/HCA's ability to invest in the latest technology and push the limits of current development efforts. Using its purchasing clout to negotiate rock bottom prices on hardware and software, Columbia/HCA can also spread development costs across its entire system.

Uniform decisions and information system standards allow compatibility and easy information exchange throughout the information systems of Columbia/HCA hospitals and ambulatory care facilities. It also allows efficient roll-ups of performance data to the regional and group level, aiding in senior management decision making. At the moment, information system installation and training are the major bottleneck to having the entire hospital system using top-end technology. Hospitals acquired in 1995 may have to wait for over a year to obtain the newest systems.

Exclusive Managed Care Contracts

To the extend managed care involves patient channeling, either through benefits differentials or exclusive provider networks, Columbia/HCA is eager to negotiate exclusive managed care arrangements that increase its patient volumes in return for the lowest prices in the market. The growth of managed care arrangements in a market makes it increasingly attractive to Columbia/HCA, which believes it can out-perform competing delivery systems in every market. The clear purpose of Columbia/HCA's preferred provider networks is to steer patients to its facilities, and its negotiators are very explicit about the relationship between lower price and increased patient volumes. Its motto, according to the title of a recent *Forbes* article included in the Columbia/HCA investment brochure, seems to clearly be "more patients, please."

At the same time, Columbia/HCA is very clear at drawing a line between the delivery system and the insurance industry. The company contracts with managed care companies for patient volumes, but is not itself a managed care insurer. Bucking a trend toward integration of finance and delivery systems, the company's clearly stated mission is only to deliver needed medical care in the most efficient manner, not to take on the financial risk for improving the health of an enrolled population or of the community.

This clear delineation of their role in the healthcare system has struck a responsive chord in many hospital administrators and physicians. Consistent with this philosophy, Columbia/HCA is reluctant to enter into capitation arrangements, although it has done so in some markets in return for sizable guaranteed patient volumes or exclusive contracts. The company's goal is to offer one-stop shopping to HMOs and other managed care plans, creating a vehicle in which insurers "don't have to talk to as many people" to provide complete coverage.

Aggressive Cost-Cutting

Columbia/HCA applies a number of integrated cost cutting techniques, many of which are borrowed from other industries. Given the company's decentralized management structure, the relative emphasis of these techniques varies from region to region. It is the combination of these approaches, however, that makes Columbia/HCA the low price leader in many of its markets. There are six interrelated cost cutting strategies adopted in most markets:

- Volume purchasing, long-term supplier partnerships.
- Refinance hospital long-term debt at lower rates.
- Spend money to make money (invest in infrastructure).
- Local vertical integration, eliminating excess capacity.
- Align incentives for bottom-line performance.
- Innovate and streamline operations.

Each of these cost cutting strategies is briefly discussed below:

Volume purchasing, long-term supplier partnerships. Columbia/HCA is the largest purchaser of healthcare supplies in the world and uses its purchasing clout aggressively. One estimate is that Columbia/HCA is able to negotiate supply and equipment prices that are up to 12 percent lower than those available through other, voluntary purchasing cooperatives.

One reason for this larger discount is that most other group purchasing arrangements usually offer the hospital a choice among several vendors and only require that a certain percentage of total purchases (for example, 80%) come from these vendors. Columbia/HCA selects one vendor, and every hospital in its system buys 100 percent of its supplies from that vendor. Columbia/HCA may have saved as much as $300 million on the $2.5 billion in supplies and equipment it purchased in 1995.

Negotiating exclusive, long-term supply contracts with vendors has become a common practice for Columbia/HCA. In March 1995, General Electric (GE) and Columbia/HCA negotiated a five-year contract to have GE maintain and repair diagnostic equipment at all facilities and assist Columbia/HCA in selecting new equipment. In return, the company will buy all its primary imaging equipment (such as CT scanners and MRI units) only from GE.

Some have criticized having GE in a dual role as advisor and vendor, but few seem truly concerned that Columbia/HCA would be at a financial disadvantage in the arrangement. The arrangement is seen as unique in that, while exclusive supply contracts are common for routine items, exclusive contracts for high-end technology are rare. Other exclusive contracts have been negotiated for hospital pharmaceuticals, lab equipment, and supplies.

One of the first things Columbia/HCA does after acquiring a new hospital is to renegotiate the hospital's supply contracts, either converting them to the system-wide Columbia/HCA contracts immediately or getting equivalent prices from in-place contracts until the end of their term. This can result in big, one-time savings in hospital operating costs. For example, one hospital in Louisiana reduced its supply costs by 30 percent from what it had been paying under its VHA arrangements.

Refinance long-term debt. Columbia/HCA now has access to capital at a level never before seen in the healthcare industry. The company carries its own commercial paper at 3.3 percent. It is often able to achieve significant immediate savings at acquisition by retiring a hospital's long-term debt, frequently borrowed at interest rates more than double what Columbia/HCA can provide. In some instances, this one factor is the difference for a hospital between operating at a loss or having positive net income.

Spend money to make money. Because of its access to capital at very attractive interest rates and the economies of scale it can bring to development costs, Columbia/HCA can make investments in infrastructure, technology, and physical plant improvements that astound its competitors.

There is also continuing criticism that Columbia/HCA uses (or could use) its strong financial position to "buy business" by being able to price below cost to attract business. To date, this allegation remains unsubstantiated. It would certainly be possible for Columbia/HCA to allocate system-wide costs (for example, information system development costs) in such a way as to understate expenses in a region or for a specific hospital. However, since each region has shown increasing profitability under Columbia/HCA management over the years, there is little evidence that this approach has been adopted on a widespread basis from a national perspective. Internal cost shifting among purchasers based on volume does occur, but that is a fact of life for all hospital operations in these competitive times.

Local integration, eliminating excess capacity. A cornerstone of Columbia/HCA's philosophy is increasing operational efficiency. This includes reducing excess capacity and avoiding duplication or redundancy in service capability or provision. In many markets, particularly after the mergers with Galen, HCA, and HealthTrust, Columbia/HCA found itself with multiple facilities in close proximity to one another and closed one (or more) of the hospitals. A recent assessment by the Advisory Board Company of Washington, D.C., concluded that due to fixed costs, if Columbia/HCA has two hospitals in the same geographic area, it can close the marginal facility and "break even" financially if only *nine percent* of the patients treated formerly at the closed facility are treated in the future at the remaining facility. If the percentage is higher, Columbia/HCA achieves a proportional net gain.

Align incentives for bottom-line performance. One way in which redundancy and duplication are eliminated with minimal negative fallout is Columbia/HCA's emphasis on regionally aligned management incentives, including performance-based compensation. While turf battles still continue at times, there is both a strong corporate commitment to working as a team within a region and clear financial incentives to reward thinking and acting for the larger financial good.

Innovate and streamline operations. In the same vein, Columbia/HCA encourages local innovation and also sharing the "best administrative practices" on a systemwide basis. Among the cost cutting practices adopted by some or many of the regions are:

1. Reducing the payments under per case (DRG) reimbursement by opening specialized units that are reimbursed on a percent of charges or fee schedule basis.
2. Encouraging hospitals to follow a "best practices" approach of starting an IV for pneumonia patients in the emergency room, rather than waiting until after admission, resulting in a reduction in the length of stay for pneumonia patients.
3. Adopting consolidated, standardized administrative practices to reduce expenses (for example, consolidated accounting practices reduced audit costs from $3.6 million in 1993 to $500,000 in 1994).
4. Reengineering hospital processes, such as using less expensive people to do routine tasks (for example, using nurses aides to collect vital signs.
5. Consolidating similar services (for example, laboratory and pathology), or contracting out when it makes sense to do so (for example, laundry services).

6. Adopting electronic billing to all major clients to cut accounts receivable time.

Columbia/HCA's hospitals and its integrated healthcare system as a whole are on the leading edge of cost cutting practices. Critics have cited concerns that quality of care may suffer, but there is no hard evidence that this has occurred on a systematic basis. In 1994, over 14 percent of Columbia/HCA's hospitals were accredited "with commendation" by the Joint Commission on Accreditation of Healthcare Organizations (JCAHO), compared to under 5 percent for the nation as a whole. Columbia/HCA has linked executive compensation to JCAHO scores. On the other hand, after merging with HCA in 1994, the company did discontinue a quality improvement program initiated by HCA before the merger.

When the medical staff of a Florida hospital raised quality concerns about nursing reductions, Columbia/HCA management staff reviewed the situation with the physicians and nurses and reversed the change. Upper management has repeatedly told groups of employees to ask questions and be the squeaky wheel if they believe management is not doing things right.

ENDNOTES

1. Davis, B., and D. Milbank, "Employee Ennui," *Wall Street Journal* (February 7, 1992), p. A1.
2. Delacroix J., and S. M. Saudagaran, "Munificent Compensations as Disincentives: The Case of American CEOs," *Human Relations,* vol. 44, no. 7 (1991), p. 671.
3. Kouzes J., and B. Posner. *Credibility: How Leaders Gain and Lose It, Why People Demand It.* San Francisco: Jossey-Bass, pp. 37–40.
4. This section was adapted from Heineccius, Lance. "Report: Columbia/HCA: A National Profile," prepared for the Washington State Hospital Association, Seattle, WA (December 1, 1995), pp. 37–54, 73, 76.

18 CHAPTER

A Question of Ethics*

It has gradually become apparent that hospitals not only must adapt to radical changes in the healthcare delivery brought about by new technologies, medical advances, and payment structures, they must also consider organized ways of handling the myriad and complex ethical issues that such developments spark. Despite the fact that over the last three decades hospital ethics have focused primarily on the clinical interface between patients and hospitals and their staff, the American Hospital Association espouses that hospitals have ethical obligations to their *employees* and their *community* as well as their *patients*. Yet, there is still a wide range of ways in which the nation's hospitals and healthcare organizations allocate resources to handle organizational ethics. Outside of a patient bill of rights and a mission statement, organizational ethics has not risen to the top of the priority list in most hospitals.

For example, Kaiser Permanente in Oakland, California, contracts with a private group of bio-ethicists to ensure that ethical issues are managed appropriately at every level of the organization. Many hospitals have institutional review boards that provide approval and oversight for all research projects while ensuring compliance with federal standards. And, generally speaking, most hospitals have ethics committees that commonly address policies dealing with patient care issues such as life sustaining treatment.[1]

*Contributions to this chapter were made by Bruce White, JD, DO, Director, Center for Ethics, Saint Thomas Hospital, Nashville, TN.

GROUNDING PATIENT CARE

The role of ethics in clinical decision making is increasingly recognized as important by healthcare providers including physicians, nurses, clergy, pastoral care staff, and institutional ethics committee members. Many hospitals have formed, or are in the process of forming, ethics committees to deal with these issues. One of the important ethical dilemmas currently facing healthcare providers, ethics committees, patients, and patients' families is how managed care will impact the traditional physician–patient relationship.

Health systems must consider the import of clinical ethics both at the bedside and beyond the hospital walls. Physicians and nurses will need to be supported with ethics instruction as well as access to consultative services to aid in dealing with clinical ethics dilemmas associated with patient care.

Medicine is an inherently moral enterprise and cannot be carried out without physicians paying attention to the technical and ethical aspects of delivering quality care.[2] The development of clinical ethics in the United States over the past 30 years suggests that these basic ideas of medical practice are intertwined and that expertise in both medicine and ethics is desirable for the competent, caring physician to meet the demands of today's practice.[3] In addition, most physicians are aware of the fact that ethical dilemmas occur not only in difficult cases (for example, discontinuing life-support systems, writing a do-not-resuscitate [DNR] order, assessing a patient's decision-making capacity in stressful and fearful circumstances), but in everyday practice as well, and that they should be prepared to manage such problems to provide high-quality healthcare.[4]

Despite the fact that some physicians feel prepared to manage ethical dilemmas, others feel less capable in even recognizing moral problems in patient care.[5] Researchers have suggested that identifying many of the ethical issues in medical practice and developing strategies for resolving them requires special attention.[6] Furthermore, clinical medical ethics educators have recommended that medical training be grounded in patient care approaches by providing appropriate educational interventions, including practitioner mentoring and effective consultative assistance.[7]

In response to the need for competence in clinical medical ethics, medical schools and residency programs are beginning to offer formal ethics instruction to physicians-in-training, which has been recommended by educators, review committees, and practitioners.[8] In addition, some healthcare centers and institutions have established ethics committees[9] and consultation services[10] to allow for more direct and timely individualized assistance to physicians and patients and their families by offering collegial aid within the traditional medical model consultative context.[11]

The practitioner–patient relationship must take into account the following influences:

- What is the most appropriate medical intervention or treatment plan?
- Does the patient want to participate in the recommended treatment plan?
- Does the patient agree with (consent to) the recommended treatment plan?
- May the treatment plan be implemented within the institution?
- How is the treatment plan agreement obtained if the patient lacks decision-making capacity?
- How does the treatment plan impact quality of life?
- Who pays?
- Will any legal or quasi-legal standard be violated?
- Are religious concerns in the patient's care being addressed?
- How does any decision-making model meet the goals of the clinical ethics principles that theoretically guide patient care?

ORGANIZATIONAL DILEMMAS

The following hypothetical case studies are intended to illustrate the broad base of concerns inherent in a question of organizational ethics. Walk through these real-life scenarios as you begin to assess how and/or if your organization has internalized ethical standards throughout all business and medical operations.

Hypothetical #1

You are the chairman and CEO of a multi-hospital regional health system that includes three tertiary medical centers, eight community hospitals and an array of non-hospital organizations including home health agencies, outpatient centers, and a skilled nursing facility.

Your organization has been applauded for being proactive and initiating affiliation agreements with several local hospitals geographically placed for convenience to the patients in outlying market areas. These loose provider networks worked for a time to create a semblance of collaboration and to pacify a variety of health purchasers seeking "one-stop shop" contractual agreements negotiated on a discount or per diem basis. In the last year, however, lead HMOs/PPOs have begun to achieve a critical mass of covered lives and to consolidate into major purchasers interested in selective contracting. As the price window narrows, issues of quality and patient satisfaction are

The senior corporate officer for the hospital company is a regional vice president (RVP). The RVP reports to the corporate office over 1,000 miles away. The RVP is assisted by an associate regional vice president (ARVP).

Your CEO has asked you to serve as co-chair with the ARVP on a joint committee established by your hospital and the regional company hospitals. The committee's charge is to develop a draft shared values and mission statement for the joint venture.

Your hospital is only the second in the cooperative to begin networking activities of this type. Your hospital's national cooperative is very concerned about your institution's involvement with a for-profit organization. The values statement that is developed must reflect the values of a national cooperative and must be philosophically consistent with the cooperative's values and mission statement, which the cooperative uses widely in publicizing the work of its hospitals and the national organization. Similarly, the hospital company's executive management staff is very concerned about the wording of any joint document. They fear repercussions from the shareholders if the shared values and mission statement fail to reflect existing corporate goals and objectives.

At your first meeting with the ARVP, you both wish to plan a strategy for the initial committee meeting to maximize opportunities.

Questions:

- What additional information would you like to have?
- With copies of the national cooperative's values and mission statement and the company's statement of objectives, which of the following methods would you use to proceed?
    1. Use one document as the starting point for the joint venture statement.
    2. Select key words and phrases from both and use these as the starting point for the joint venture statement.
    3. Begin with key words and phrases from a document developed by another diverse group that garnered consensus.
    4. Ask the entire committee to brainstorm and develop a different approach.

During your meeting with the ARVP, you discover that you each hold different philosophies about "business ethics." You feel that

> there is and can be no divergence between the operation of a successful business organization and ethical behavior on the part of the organization. Such a

> divergence cannot exist because ethics is subsumed or totally contained in terms of marketplace performance. What is considered to be ethical is exactly the same as what is considered to be good business.

The ARVP, however, feels that this view is too narrow because it neglects how businesses, in their "quest for an efficient allocation of resources," impact their communities. He wants to see the values and mission statement reflect the broader view to "include the social aspects of corporate activities and encourage management to pay attention to the social impacts of corporate operations."

You would both prefer to settle this difference before the committee's first meeting—if the issue arises at the meeting, you would like to have a way of resolving it there without appearing to be at odds.

Questions:

- Does the difference have to be resolved or can a values and mission statement that combines both philosophies be written?
- If the difference is to be settled, how would you propose to resolve it?
    1. The philosophies are mutually exclusive; the values and mission statement cannot reflect both ideas.
    2. A values and mission statement can include both ideas.

EFFICACY AND ALLOCATION

An individual hospital seldom commissions a national survey on ethics issues in healthcare; in fact, it's rare that a single hospital would commission a national survey of any kind. Yet that's just what Saint Joseph's Hospital and Medical Center, in Phoenix, Arizona, did in 1992.[12] The results of that survey compare closely—perhaps for the first time—with the responses of the general public, physicians, and hospital administrators to sensitive questions on the ethics of allocating healthcare resources and treatment efficacy in an era of increasing scarcity. The results, based on a phone survey of 1,017 adult consumers and 200 healthcare professionals, also show a growing awareness among some consumers of the tough choices our society faces as it moves toward a consensus on healthcare reform.

"We are entering an era in which we will be requested to do less with less; although we all avoid the word 'rationing,' we as providers will be reimbursed less and will be forced to provide fewer services," says Joseph L. DeSilva, Saint Joseph's president and CEO. "With that on the horizon, we wanted to look at the ethical issues in resource allocation in the future."

While the Saint Joseph's survey, conducted by the Wirthlin Group, a NewYork based research firm, covers a range of ethics issues in healthcare—from biomedical ethics to the ethics of philanthropy—questions surrounding resource-allocation dilemmas were at the survey's core. In the survey, respondents were asked the intriguing question, "Should a heart bypass be conducted regardless of age or chance of survival?" While 54 percent of the general public said yes, only 11 percent of physicians and 8 percent of administrators answered affirmatively. Within the general public, a yes or no response was strongly correlated with level of education, with 64 percent of those with less than a high school education agreeing, and only 30 percent of those with postgraduate education agreeing.

To CEO DeSilva, that points up an important fact. "I don't think the public is terribly informed on resource-allocation issues," he says "And that's because the healthcare community fails to provide information that can be understood. It's been a question of providers protecting their turf, though it should be an issue of understanding the limitations placed on our resources and how they affect the public."

In general, providers are more willing than the public to grapple with the ethical issues of rationing and efficacy. Why? Perhaps it is because providers often examine these issues in the abstract, where numbers—not faces—govern their decisions. On a practical level, the question of ethics becomes blurred when one is personally connected with the health issues of an elderly parent or an at-risk infant. The response discrepancies do not mean that one group holds the "right" answer, while the other is "wrong." The question of resource allocation, that is, rationing, is a complex, sensitive, and potentially divisive policy question.

In 1990, Edward J. Connors, president of Mercy Health Services in Farmington Mills, Michigan, and chairman of the board of trustees of the American Hospital Association, stated: "Accept the reality of limits, that the open-ended era of uncontrolled expenditure is gone, and that all people can't have all they want or what physicians may want to provide." Noting that rationing is never a comfortable issue for those who care for the nation's ill, Connors nonetheless stressed the point that there is too much at stake for the hospital field to shunt such questions aside for others to decide by default.[13]

A BROADER QUESTION

Hospitals operating in an environment of change are challenged to examine the role that organizational ethics will play in their future. The contextual features that will determine how a philosophy of ethics is operationalized include: delivery system considerations, economic considerations, legal

CASE STUDY

CONSOLIDATION IN EL PASO, TEXAS

Columbia Hospital Corporation began its growth with the purchase of two ailing hospitals (Sun Tower and Vista Hills) in El Paso, Texas, in 1988. In the past seven years, Columbia/HCA has consolidated its position and grown to become the dominant healthcare delivery system in this West Texas city of nearly 700,000 people (currently the 21st largest city in the nation).

In 1988, the El Paso market had a very fragmented healthcare delivery system, low occupancy rates, a high percentage of low income families, and a history of poor relationships between hospitals and their medical staffs. The three dominant hospitals in the city were Sierra Medical Center (an American Medical International flagship hospital), Providence Medical Center, and E. V. Thomason Memorial Hospital, a public hospital system that treated the majority of the city's poor (about 30% of the population). At least five other acute care hospitals struggled for a share of the market. In 1988, there was no indication that the city's healthcare system was on the verge of a complete transformation.

In mid-1988, Columbia Hospital Corporation purchased two minor, struggling acute care hospitals (each with about 250 beds) and two outpatient diagnostic centers for $60 million. In the next five years, the company spent $140 million upgrading these facilities. Later in 1988, it bought Landmark Medical Center, a 355-bed acute care hospital that had an average daily census of only

considerations, and theological considerations. The issues of access and cost can create burdensome moral problems at the local level.

From a strictly ethical viewpoint, however, there seems to be no justification for cutting healthcare services that have proved to be beneficial to anyone before the following structural problems are corrected:[14]

1. We need to reduce administrative costs. The United States spends up to 24 percent of its healthcare resources on administration and paperwork, compared with around 11 percent in the Canadian system.[15] Substantial reduction of such costs—for example, to 14 percent—could be a major source of healthcare savings. Moreover, more than money is squandered by the distorted healthcare system; with such an overbearing load of administrative work, healthcare personnel end up pushing paper instead of attending to the ill.
2. We must enact tort reform to reduce dramatically malpractice insurance fees and defensive medicine. Limited benefits for pain and suffering, arbitration, and mediation are among the mechanisms that should be considered.

Concluded

54 patients. The purchase price was $11 million. The company immediately shut it down, transferring the patients and most of the equipment to its other facilities. This move reduced the number of inpatient hospital beds in El Paso by 16 percent. The company recouped its $11 million investment within one year due to increased patient volumes and the reuse of excess equipment.

Columbia Hospital Corporation later bought and closed a second, smaller facility, with a similar consolidation of patients and equipment. In El Paso, Columbia/HCA now owns two acute care hospitals, a psychiatric hospital, a regional cancer center, three outpatient diagnostic centers, a skilled nursing facility, two physical therapy centers, and a home health service. It has also created strong physician relationships through syndication.

The El Paso market has now consolidated into two competing proprietary networks (Columbia/HCA and Tenet) and a public hospital (E. V. Thomason). The two struggle to survive as for-profit networks aggressively competing for Medicaid managed care contracts. Local officials are concerned that if E. V. Thomason fails, the for-profit hospitals will not step in to fill the charity care void. The largest local employer, El Paso Natural Gas, fueled hospital consolidation in 1993 when it signed an exclusive hospital contract for its employees with Sierra, a contract since moved to the Providence system in return for an even lower price.

3. We must also stop performing procedures that are unnecessary or have no proven benefit. Some studies suggest that they amount to more than 20 percent of all procedures.[16]
4. We could save billions of dollars a year by insisting that drug companies stop promoting their wares by unsavory means, such as granting individual physicians and members of hospital pharmacies free entertainment, meals, and travel expenses, as well as other high pressure sales tactics and undue lobbying.
5. We must reduce the profiteering by suppliers, insurers, and healthcare professionals that drives up costs and undermines the public's trust in the system.
6. Above all, we must call society's attention, in the strongest possible terms, to other sectors that impose huge costs on the healthcare system. For instance, it makes no sense to bind the wounds of gun shots but disregard the guns. We should not remove the lead only from the bodies of children, but also from the walls of the apartments in which they live. We should not only provide chemotherapy and

CASE STUDY

COMPETITION IN LEE COUNTY, FLORIDA

Aggressive competition for managed care contracts has fueled an increasingly bitter struggle in Southwest Florida between Columbia/HCA and a not-for-profit hospital system. The battle began in late 1993 when the two systems went head-to-head in competition for county government employees, an exclusive contract valued at $9 million per year for the winner. Columbia/HCA won the one-year exclusive contract to treat the county's 3,100 employees and their dependents, saving the county an estimated $4 million over expected costs.

As part of its bid process, the West Florida region of Columbia/HCA commissioned a study comparing the charity care provided by the not-for-profit hospitals to the tax revenues Lee County was foregoing by treating these hospitals as tax-exempt. For six of the seven hospitals, their tax exemption far exceeded their provision of charity care. Lee Memorial, cornerstone of the not-for-profit bid, received a $100 million "tax break," but only delivered $4 million in charity care in 1992. Columbia/HCA's report suggested that the county ought to reconsider the tax exempt status of the not-for-profit hospitals. Spokespersons for the not-for-profit hospitals called Columbia/HCA's study methodology "massively flawed" (claiming Lee Memorial delivered

radiation treatment, we should also reduce the carcinogenic elements in the environment. Such steps would do wonders for healthcare costs and for the overall well-being of the public. The same holds true for enhancing care safety and pollution controls, and for providing meaningful jobs to persons often shut out of the economic system. Together such changes may do more to reduce healthcare costs than any changes within the health system itself.

SUMMARY

The question of ethics means coming clean when defining the mission and purpose of a healthcare business. Is it to make a profit? If so, go to it. Is it to serve the community? If the answer is yes, be prepared to measure success in terms of health status improvement, not dollars in the bank.

From the perspective of a patient, Joseph Cardinal Bernardin, Archbishop of Chicago, delivered a no-nonsense message to attendees at the American Medical Association's House of Delegates meeting in Washington, D.C., on December 5, 1995. Cardinal Bernardin said healthcare providers have too often succumbed to the "siren songs of scientific triumph, financial success

Concluded

$11 million in charity in 1992) and commissioned their own study of the four Columbia/HCA hospitals. Things have gone downhill ever since.

The open battle has drawn the attention of regulators and other state agencies in Florida, which are currently conducting statewide research into the issue of tax exemptions versus charity care. In addition, the Florida Agency for Health Care Administration investigated whether physician investment resulted in differential admission patterns based on patients' ability to pay (the draft report was never released). Florida's Attorney General pressured Columbia/HCA into dropping its non-compete requirement for physician syndication. The attorney general is now exploring whether Columbia/HCA uses revenues generated in some Florida markets to give deep managed care discounts in other markets.

This struggle has hurt the credibility of hospitals with the public, according to the director of the Tampa Bay Hospital Association. While the public may not understand the nuances of tax exemption and charity care calculations, it does understand that huge amounts of money are involved and that both sides of the battle are focused on financial gains. Columbia/HCA learns from its mistakes; the type of tax exemption/charity care analysis it did in Lee County has not been repeated in any other Columbia/HCA market region to date.

and political power." The Catholic leader, who was recently treated for pancreatic cancer, emphasized that healthcare should be evaluated by means other than success in the marketplace. The Cardinal also suggested that healthcare providers affirm their Hippocratic oath by showing a "willingness to affirm and incorporate in their lives the ancient virtues of benevolence, compassion, competence, intellectual honesty, humility and suspension of self-interest."[17]

Providers are being challenged morally, as well as fiscally. Health status assessments identify root causes of illness and injury. When faced with issues like the need for safer streets, and better sewage systems, nutritional habits, housing opportunities, or employment opportunities, healthcare leaders must feel the urge to toss up their hands and say: "That's not my job!" However, if these concerns impact utilization, then capitation may be the catalyst for some unusual investments. For the healthcare industry, developing a new organizational order lies at the point of intersection between a positive mission statement and a positive balance sheet. (See Figure 18–1.)

Columbia/HCA brings a different approach to addressing the challenges that confront hospitals and the healthcare delivery system as a whole. The company has embraced market competition rather than bemoaning it. It is applying bottom line financial accountability and aggressive business

CASE STUDY

TURNAROUND IN TAMARAC, FLORIDA

University Hospital is a 269-bed acute care hospital in Tamarac, Florida (near Ft. Lauderdale), creatively named for its University Drive address, not a teaching affiliation. In 1990, Columbia/HCA purchased the facility from its previous investor/owner and offered the medical staff an opportunity to invest in the ownership through its syndication program. Roughly 75 physicians on the medical staff, some initially skeptical, contributed $1.35 million of the $20 million acquisition cost in return for a limited equity interest in the venture.

The hospital lost money in 1989 and 1990, but under Columbia/HCA has made a "striking turnaround." Hospital operations made over $3 million in 1993 and over $4 million in 1994. Admissions jumped 33 percent from 1990 to 1992. Physicians have more than doubled the value of their investment, and are receiving a 25 percent annual return on their equity. Most physicians, however, say their biggest return is from improvements in the quality of the hospital.

Before the purchase, the hospital's physical plant had been neglected for years: the roof leaked, the wards were dirty, and the equipment was old and in disrepair. Columbia/HCA has made a significant investment in renovating the hospital. It is now, in the words of a non-investor physician, a top-notch facility with a professional, first-class support system. Information technology is

FIGURE 18-1

Are there grounds for *philosophic* and *practical* intersection?

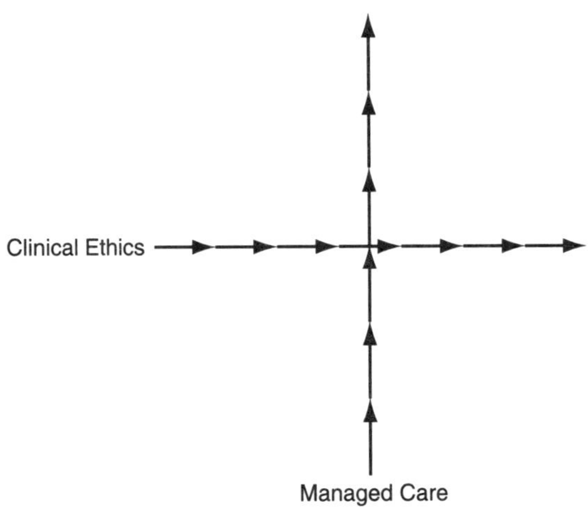

Concluded

state-of-the-art, nursing turnaround is practically zero, and in the words of one physician, "the whole staff has gotten the feeling that the hospital administration and ownership is more responsive to (the medical staff's) needs and the patient's needs." The hospital administrator has formed a physician advisory committee of about a dozen investor–physicians, and the medical staff in general has become more accepting of the advantages of effective utilization management in improving the hospital's bottom line.

Despite the physician syndication (now transferred from the single hospital to Columbia/HCA's regional South Florida division), the company does not negotiate managed care contracts involving physician services in Broward County. Columbia/HCA bargains solely for its facilities, leaving physicians to negotiate their own arrangements with HMOs and PPOs.

As of mid-1994, Columbia/HCA hospitals in south Florida were also not interested in forming physician–hospital organizations. When physician groups receive global capitation from managed care organizations, the company aggressively goes after the hospital business and attempts to offer the lowest prices for inpatient and other services on a fee-for-service basis. In south Florida, as elsewhere in the nation, Columbia/HCA has no interest in taking on financial risk.

practices in a manner not seen before in the American healthcare system. Columbia/HCA has become a catalyst for change, even in markets where the company as yet has no presence.

Competitors must articulate an alternate vision—It is insufficient and irresponsible for competitors to merely worry and complain about the damage Columbia/HCA might do to the healthcare system and the communities it serves. Competitors that disagree with the company's vision of the future, and who believe that healthcare should be more than just a business, must develop a strong vision of an alternative approach. They must also be able to articulate that vision clearly, and (most challenging) demonstrate that it is as financially viable as the Columbia/HCA approach. The alternative vision must be able to thrive in a competitive market environment, in order to capture the patient volumes that are essential to success.

CREATING AN ALTERNATE VISION

This book speaks to an audience that is faced with the dilemma of defining a new way of being in business. It has been said many times and in many ways that first defining a mission and vision is of jugular importance. The intent here is *not* to convince anyone that they must take the author's perspective and jump on the community health and integrated medicine bandwagons. The intent *is* to force you to understand that you must decide for yourself what your vision is, state it clearly so that others understand, and act accordingly.

Lots of people today point a negative finger at Columbia. Many deride them for "being in the business of making money off of sick people." Hey! Someone's got to be in the acute care business. From an investor's eye, Columbia has been a bull's-eye. At least up until now, Columbia has not confused its ways of being in business with useless rhetoric or pacifying platitudes to community action groups. The company has simply entered markets with the vision of running a very efficient acute care shop. It has rarely strayed from the objective of streamlining operations in order to maximize economies of scale. It is pretty common to read about Columbia entering a market, acquiring four hospitals and then closing two of them. Although some criticize the organization for its cutthroat approach to market dominance, in the author's opinion, Columbia can be heralded for reducing service duplication within markets.

Columbia's way of being in business is not bad. It is one choice of a vision. The Catholic Hospital Association has committed to another vision, one that embraces health status improvement, the needs of the underserved and enhanced patient responsibility for well-being. With a clear vision and a commitment to strong business, some of the health systems within the Catholic Hospital Association are proving that it is possible to make a difference and also make a profit. The tough part is staying true to this vision and leading into the future.

It takes the right leader, willing to do the right thing, to transform relationships into partnerships, opportunities into achievements, and plans into actions. Is that you? Transformational leadership is about creating a new organization that results from the alignment of personal, organizational, and community goals. These concepts are explored in the book, *Transformational Leadership: Renewing Fundamental Values and Achieving New Relationships in Health Care,* by Mary K. Kohles, William G. Baker, Jr., and Barbara A. Donaho. "When accomplished," writes Barbara Donaho, "everyone has achieved recognition as a valued individual, everyone has learned the skills of challenging and questioning the present reality, and everyone has the opportunity to take their place as leaders in order to build a stronger, more humanistic health care delivery system."

Transformational leaders are individuals who identify and achieve opportunities for improved consumer value and for building collegial relationships in partnerships. They inspire others in their quest for personal and organizational fulfillment by asking questions, setting direction, and managing the boundaries of the organization's business while liberating caregivers and other stakeholders to do their work. In his book, *Leadership Is,* Owen writes: "To manage is to control: to lead is to liberate." Creativity, imagination, and a participative management style that models and encourages collaborative staff behavior throughout the organization are skills used by transformational leaders. These individuals are achievers, yet place the well-being of others and the organization above personal endeavors.

Aggregated comments from healthcare executives show similar characteristics and values attributed to true transformational leaders. They indicate that transformational leaders:

- **Are proactive and prospective:** Prospective organizations and their leaders respond rapidly to early signals of market needs and opportunities, and consistently attempt to be the first to provide service to meet those needs.
- **Are charismatic and passionate:** Transformational leaders are dynamic individuals who use their creativity and imagination to achieve positive change by developing the skills and talents of others who have the passion to move the organization toward a defined future.
- **Use noncensored communication:** Managers who want employees to be truthful, open, and candid should role-model the behavior they expect from their employees.
- **Are stewards:** *Stewardship* is a spiritual dimension built on the core of a personal value system; it inspires commitment and a sense of common ownership by every stakeholder in the organization. Within the patient-centered care philosophy, a steward maintains a focus on providing the best value for meeting the needs of the patient in the most appropriate care settings.
- **Are contemplative:** A *contemplative* is an individual who is disciplined to set aside time for regular quietness and solitude to examine his or her life, relationships with others, efforts within the organization, and contribution to the community and society at large.
- **Care for the souls of individuals and the organization:** Dominick Flarey, administrator and COO, Youngstown Osteopathic Hospital, sums it up: "A leader who is faith-filled displays a strong faith in the ability of the people, the organization, and the healthcare system to change and grow."
- **Have integrity and respect colleagues:** Transformational leaders "walk the walk" rather than just "talk the talk." Transformational

leaders demonstrate their integrity through their actions; they are highly ethical and communicate their message consistently and directly during the change process.

- **Are catalysts for creativity and innovation:** Creativity is needed to generate alternative approaches to problem and issue resolution.
- **Are facilitators:** The transformational leader's ability to achieve consensus among diverse constituencies is critical to the success of any change process.
- **Function as team members:** The ability of the transformational leader to function as a team member, whether on the executive team or a small task force, is critical to innovation and improvement processes.
- **Empower others:** Another important characteristic of transformational leaders is their willingness to empower employees.
- **Recognize that relationships are vital to restructuring and transition:** Relationship-building is key to the success of restructuring in and outside the organization. Skills in collaboration, interdependence, and co-creation are the outgrowths of effective and meaningful relationships.
- **Often are cantadoras, or tellers of stories:** Visionary leaders often use stories as tools to break resistant behaviors, build trust, achieve new attitudes, and direct collective energy toward a desired outcome.

Today is your opportunity to be a leader. Are there risks? Absolutely, but what is the alternative? You can either choose to commit to a new organizational order or look for a middle manager's role in a new industry. If you stay in healthcare, you will need to build relationships, awaken greater self-realization in others, and give up a *piece* of the pie in order to *win it all.*

ENDNOTES

1. "Hospital Ethics: Broadening Obligations," *Society for Healthcare Planning & Marketing Newsletter*, (February, 1995), pg. 1.
2. Pelligrino, E. D. *Humanism and the Physician* (Knoxville, TN: University of Tennessee Press, 1984).
3. Pelligrino, E. D., M. Siegler, P. A. Singer. "Teaching Clinical Ethics," *Journal of Clinical Ethics* vol. 1 (1990), pp. 175–180.
4. Connelly J. E., and C. Campbell. "Patients Who Refuse Medical Treatment in Medical Offices," *Arch Intern Med*, vol. 147 (1987), pp. 1829–1833.

5. Jonsen, A. R., M. Siegler, and W. J. Winslade. *Clinical Ethics,* 2nd ed. (New York: Macmillan, 1986).
6. Perl, M. and E. E. Shelp. "Psychiatric Consultation Masking Moral Dilemmas in Medicine," *New England Journal of Medicine,* vol. 307 (1982), pp. 618–621.
7. Meisel, A. "Legal Myths About Terminating Life Support," *Arch Intern Med,* vol 151 (1991), p. 1502; White B. D., et al.: "A Medical Ethics Issues Survey of Five Pediatric Training Programs," *Am J. Dis Child* vol. 154 (1991), pp. 628–632.
8. Pelligrino, E. D. "Clinical Ethics: Biomedical Ethics at the Bedside," *JAMA* vol. 260 (1988), pp. 837–839; Fost, N., and R. E. Cranford. "Hospital Ethics Committees: Administrative Aspects," *JAMA* vol. 253 (1985), pp. 2687–2692; and Rosner, F. "Hospital Medical Ethics Committees: A Review of Their Development," *JAMA,* vol. 253 (1985), pp. 2693–2697.
9. Cranford R. E., and A. E. Doudera. *Institutional Ethics Committees and Health Care Decision Making* (Ann Arbor, MI: Health Administration Press, 1983).
10. White, M., J. C. Fletcher, and P. Foubert. "Biomedical Ethics and an Ethics Consultation Service at the University of Virginia," *HEC Forum* vol. 2 (1990), pp. 89–99.
11. LaPuma, J., and S. Toulmin. "Ethics Committees and Consultants," *Arch Intern Med* vol. 149 (1989) pp. 1109–1112.
12. Hagland, Mark M. "New National Survey Finds MDs, Administrators, Public at Odds," *Hospitals* (September 5, 1992), p. 44.
13. "Finding Agreement Between Public Relations, Marketing, and Rationing," *Hospital Ethics* (January/February 1990), p. 44.
14. Etzioni, Amitai, et al. "Core Values in Health Care Reform: A Communitarian Approach," *Health Care Management: State of the Art Reviews,* vol. 1, no. 1 (August 1994), p. 118.
15. United States General Accounting Office: "Canadian Health Insurance: Lessons for the United States" (Washington, D.C.: General Accounting Office, 1991); Woolhandler, S. and D. U. Himmelstein. "The Deteriorating Administrative Efficiency of the U.S. Health Care System." *New England Journal of Medicine,* vol. 324 (1991), pp. 1253–1258.
16. Brook, R. H., and K. N. Lohr. "Will We Need to Ration Effective Health Care?" *Issues Sci Technol* vol. 3 (1986), pp. 68–77; Eddy, D. M. "Medicine, Money and Mathematics," *Am Coll Surg Bull,* vol. 77 (1992), pp. 36–49; and Siu, A. L., W. E. Manning, and B. Benjamin. "Patient, Provider and Hospital Characteristics Associated with Inappropriate Hospitalization," *American Journal of Public Health,* vol. 80 (1990), pp. 1253–1256.
17. "Cardinal Questions Doctors' Focus," *Hospitals and Health Networks* (December 20, 1995), p. 18.

19 CHAPTER

Choosing to Lead

What does it mean to be a leader? It means recognizing the adversary, understanding the risks, and choosing to make an irretrievable leap into the unknown. Because there are no overt or tried-and-true answers to healthcare's immediate dilemma, leaders must be willing to own the problems and take risks to solve them.

Healthcare leaders must conceive a vision, share it throughout the organization, and then—with agreement—develop systems for pursuing it together. Leaders will be challenged to put in place managers with sophisticated skills in order to be relieved of day-to-day operational responsibilities. Though difficult, it is far more important for leaders to intertwine the most significant aspects of their organization: its mission, its people, and its future.

THE ESSENTIAL LEADERSHIP RIGHTS

In his book, *Leadership is an Art,* Max DePree outlines eight essential leadership rights.[1] Their application to the business of healthcare is synthesized as follows:

1. **The right to use individual talents/skills/abilities** in relationship to the organization's goals.
2. **The right to be involved.**
   - We need a system of *input*—leaders must arrange for involvement with both internal and external customers.

- We need a system of *response*—leaders must make that involvement genuine. It is a great error to invite people to be involved and contribute their ideas, then exclude them from the evaluation, the decision-making process, and the implementation.
- We need to take *action*—together we must translate our interaction into products and services on behalf of our customers.

3. **The right to a covenantal relationship.**
   - Contractual relationships, whether written or understood, are normal in business and industry. The contractual relationship tends to be legal and is based on reciprocity. *Covenantal relationships* fill deep needs, and enable work to have meaning and be fulfilling. They make possible relationships that can manage conflict and change.
4. **The right to understand.**
   - Together, we need to understand our *mission.* We have the right to understand the strategy and the direction of the group.
   - Everyone has the right to understand his or her *personal career path.* We all need to know the opportunities in this group and how we can realize them. Inherent in this is the right to enlarge one's competence through study and new experiences.
   - We need to understand our *competition.* By knowing the quality and closeness of our competition, we can work more effectively.
   - We have the right to understand the elements of our *contract*—covering compensation, working conditions, shared benefits, incentive opportunities, expectations, and normal constraints. We have the right to understand the motivation and philosophy around reengineering. We have the right to know when our job is at risk before a "pink slip" arrives.
   - It is essential to good understanding that leaders clarify the responsibility of each member of the group. These and other elements of the right to understanding obligate leaders to communicate, to educate, and to evaluate.
5. **The right to affect one's own destiny.**
   - Few elements in the work process are as important to personal dignity as the opportunity to influence one's own future. The processes of performance evaluation, promotion, and transfer should always take place with the person's involvement.
6. **The right to be accountable.**
   - To be accountable, we need to have the opportunity to contribute to the group's goals. We need the opportunity to share in both the

ownership of the group's problems and also the inherent risk. We need to have our contributions measured according to previously understood and accepted standards of performance, and this transaction needs to take place in an adult-to-adult relationship.

- At the heart of being accountable is the matter of caring. In many areas of business, sadly, "to care" is an innovation.

7. **The right to appeal.**
   - We need to build into our group structures a non-threatening avenue of appeal. One of the most important responsibilities of leaders is to work hard at offering these rights to those we lead.
8. **The right to make a commitment.**
   - To make a commitment, any employee should be able to answer yes to the following question: Is this a place where they will let me do my best? How can leaders expect a commitment from the people they lead if those people feel thwarted and hindered? And believe me, there are many obstacles constructed by unthinking leaders.
   - One of the key inhibitors to the right commitment in corporations today occurs when, in the perception of those who follow, the leadership is not rational. One of the key responsibilities of leadership is the obligation to be rational.
   - Teaching and learning underlie business literacy and action. Business literacy is the "why" of what corporations do, and action is "what" they do. Only through good communication can we convey and preserve a common corporate vision. To liberate people, communication must be based on logic, compassion, and sound reasoning.

Sounds good, doesn't it? Unfortunately, for those of you now functioning in organizations eaten up with fear and crisis management, it probably sounds like goody-two-shoes, pie-in-the-sky thinking. You might believe that such a philosophy could be espoused by the Catholic Health Association, but you would probably doubt that it would ever hit the streets with the momentum brought by a for-profit entity. Well, you are wrong.

The truth is that the organizations that are converging leadership abilities with a commitment to a vision and mission are the ones that are rising to the top. PhyCor, Inc., is one recognized emerging industry leader in the physician practice management industry. Its broad geographic reach extends through the West, Southwest, Southeast, Mid-Atlantic, and Northeast United States. PhyCor currently operates 31 multi-specialty clinics in 20 states, and has management agreements with nearly 1,900 physicians—approximately half of whom are primary care physicians. In addition, PhyCor manages independent associations (IPAs) with approximately 5,000 physicians in 14 markets. PhyCor's market success can be attributed to a strong, deep management team with a unique commitment to principled leadership. Read PhyCor's leadership statement and ask yourself: Could this kind of commitment add value to—and pay off for—my organization as well?

SUCCEEDING IN A RESTRUCTURED HEALTH SYSTEM: PHYCOR, INC.

Leadership is not a right that can be purchased or conferred; it must be earned. It is not permanent; it must be continually re-earned. It is a position held as long as those choosing to follow believe in the direction and course of action of the leader.

All purchasers of healthcare—government, business, and consumers—are seeking solutions which will limit their financial exposure. The Federal Government cannot afford for the Medicare system to continue as is; the system's financial viability is at risk and its beneficiaries are unwilling to bear additional personal expense. State by state, Medicaid is problematic and unacceptable to all involved—and moving toward managed care contracting. Increasing healthcare costs are threatening the economic future of businesses—employees and retirees, in turn, resist costs being shifted to them.

The debate on healthcare reform was publicly aired in Congress and the media during the mid-1990s. Legislative consensus was not reached and reform was not governmentally mandated. However, there is a mandate; market forces have accelerated, and it is clear that market-driven healthcare reform is now underway.

Market by market, leadership roles are being assumed by those who are willing and capable of leading. Unaligned physicians are ready to join with those who demonstrate leadership. Purchasers will choose providers based upon their ability to deliver healthcare cost-effectively while achieving superior clinical outcomes and maintaining exceptional levels of patient satisfaction.

Those who meet these criteria will be rewarded with increased market share, which, if managed effectively, will produce superior professional and economic rewards. To respond and position for the future, insurers, hospitals, and physician organizations are coming together through alliances, relationships, and networks.

However, it is increasingly clear that the success of these networks—based upon cost, clinical results, and patient satisfaction—is dependent upon physician performance. Thus, the manner in which physicians organize themselves, the degree of empowerment they possess, and their ability to set the tone for medical delivery is pivotal to any competitive managed care strategy.[2]

Today, uncertainty reigns concerning the future of healthcare delivery and the various roles that will be played. Only strong leadership can align the market forces and resources necessary to create a successfully restructured healthcare system.

ABOUT LEADERSHIP: THE AUTHOR'S PERSPECTIVE

> Courage does not mean conquering fear as much as it means integrating real passion into our lives. Courage gives us inner strength to enter the fray and to choose to live passionately. Living passionately gives deeper meaning to our work. But when we care deeply, fear can become our biggest obstacle. When we have fears of losing a job, of decreasing prestige, of not having a place, we know we are touching the crux of our life's passion. Courage is acknowledging the fear, choosing to learn knowledge and wisdom and then acting with a prayer.
>
> *Ausculta, 1996*

As I was driving to Atlanta recently, I listened for the first time to a Stephen Covey tape. Of course, I had heard about his "seven steps" but either my conceit or my busy schedule had kept me from an intimate exploration of their value and worth. I listened with the ears of a child and I heard true wisdom.

I was first struck by the phrase, "Build your security on the integrity of your actions and mission statement." Isn't that the essence of the challenge we face today as individuals, communities, and health systems?

I was then fascinated by Dr. Covey's description of the four quadrants for time management. (See Table 19–1.) As a consultant, I recognized that for many years my activities could have been categorized into quadrants #1 and #3: When you are working with clients in a reactive managed care environment, everything is *urgent,* whether it is important or not. Only since I have begun to work in community health, wellness, and integrated delivery network development have I been able to move out of urgent/crisis management and into quadrant #2, Not Urgent/Important. With my energies focused here, I am working with others to address the needs that will make the greatest difference. The effort is not flashy, but it is of substance and can be sustained

TABLE 19–1

The Four Quadrants of Time Management

#1: Urgent Important	#2: Not Urgent Important
#3: Urgent Not Important	#4: Not Urgent Not Important

over time. Listening to Dr. Covey's tape, I became more convinced than ever that the future of our healthcare industry will be shaped by those working in quadrant #2.

This leads into the final awakening offered to me from that voice in my dashboard: We need leaders *and* managers. Neither is more important in function, but the leaders will be fewer in number. According to Dr. Covey, leaders must remove themselves from the day-to-day urgent crisis management and commit their energies to leading, to holding forth the mission and intention of the organization. As I have said in earlier chapters, it is this mission that must inform all activities; it must be the original image in the holograph.

I have personally grappled with the fact that I am a leader. For a long time, I tried to deny it and attempted to fit into top-down, hierarchal structures. That didn't work. When I realized that I had no choice but to follow my inner voice, I built up some pretty strong emotional callouses so as not to be hurt by my colleagues who laughed at the notions of health status management, and holistic care, and told me I was "too academic"—or worse—"too idealistic" for the pragmatic world of business. Still, going my own way alone wasn't my answer. Leadership has no purpose when it exists in isolation.

I made a commitment to take a risk, to share my ideas, to take a stand. I wrote a vision statement. (See Figure 19–1.) I found that I began to be regarded as an educator and as a strategist. I found myself contributing to and deriving strength from a virtual organization of professionals. I have been both celebrated and humbled. However, my personal measure of success has not been determined by either circumstance; it has been defined by the opportunities and the persons who have allowed me to put my vision statement to work. Instead of working in isolation, I have found that I function in rich, interactive, and highly productive relationships.

My intention here is not to inflate myself or my accomplishments. My goal is to share with you a part of my own deep learning. Today my work is a vocation, a consequence of a voice within me that defines meaning and identity. My purpose is not to excel as a managed care business development specialist by copying surface strategies; my purpose is to enrich the communities and organizations in which I operate by grounding my activities in my own moral sensibility and not just in my intellect.

My work now comes easier and is more satisfying. If I were in danger of letting my ego succumb to narcissism, I would be saved by the great leaders from whom I am privileged to learn. I have discovered the joy of interdependence and displaced the fragile fear associated with individual accomplishment. I am finding that my community is increasing.

What must be done will require the gifts of many—not the talents of a few. I stand in awe of the leaders I meet every day, many of whom are profiled

FIGURE 19–1

Ausculta

Vision Statement

Managed care and healthcare reform are fostering a great deal of change in a very "sick" industry. The motivation for change exists in the face of the reality that survival is the issue for most healthcare providers. The opportunity now exists for transformation.

The possibilities around the metamorphosis of healthcare services are endless. Those of us within the industry today can contribute or dissipate energies to the opportunity. For some, momentum is building toward a new vision of how we can sculpt the architecture for **care-giving communities**. The opportunity now exists to craft an industry that will be vested in well-being vs. disease. I am committed to contributing my talents and energies to this vision.

The pragmatics of this transformation are critical. Each of us must accept the challenge to move out of the current paradigm and begin to maximize our innovative and creative problem-solving skills. I am interested in combining the best of my analytical thinking and process management skills with a passion for crafting change within the healthcare environment. The following areas are ones in which I believe my contributions would be of greatest value.

Transforming the delivery of care from an autocratic/antiseptic disease-oriented system, to one that is shaped by the needs of those it serves. Some movement toward this vision can be accomplished via:

- Reengineering healthcare services so that the patient is the "driver" and education and informed decision making become the central themes.
- Designing spectrums of care that bring services to the patients.
- Restructuring the hospital environment to reflect a focus on "healing" vs. "sickness."
- Shifting from a high-tech focus on treatment to one that emphasizes a multidisciplinary and complementary approach to well-being.

Identifying opportunities for community collaboration. Find ways to work together to:

- Prioritize healthcare needs.
- Make "living well" an available and visible theme wherever people work, eat, play, and worship.
- Share accountability for prevention and education with existing organizations that already "touch" people, i.e., health departments, schools, churches, community service organizations. (Note: This can become the new face of hospital marketing.)

Addressing the need for congruence in a vision for community-based care, managed care strategies, and strategic partnerships/alliances.

Documenting outcomes:

- Tracking opportunities for increased operational efficiency.
- Measuring impact on cost of care, both short and long term.
- Evaluating patient satisfaction with regard to the healthcare environment in their community, their experience with episodes of care, and their perception of the impact of both on their quality of life.

in this book. We are united by mission and vision: When the soul is involved, the work is not carried out by the ego alone; it arises from a deeper place and therefore is not deprived of passion, spontaneity, and grace. We may get to the point where our external labors and the *opus* of the soul are one and the same, inseparable. Then the satisfactions of our work will be deep and long-lasting, undone neither by failures nor by flashes of success.[3]

Won't you join us? Won't *you* be a leader?

ENDNOTES

1. DePree, Max. *Leadership is an Art* (New York: Bantam Doubleday Dell, 1989).
2. "Choosing to Lead," PhyCor® The Physicians' Corporation. 30 Burton Hills Blvd., Suite 400, Nashville, TN (615/665–9066).
3. Moore, Thomas. *Care of the Soul: A Guide for Cultivating Depth and Sacredness in Everyday Life* (New York: Walker & Company), pp. 283, 300.

INDEX

ABOUT THE AUTHOR

Over the last fifteen years, Genie James—a leading healthcare strategist—has independently consulted across the gamut of healthcare business: metropolitan health systems, rural community hospitals, physician groups, and venture capital start-ups.

In 1990, Ms. James formally organized a consulting agency to focus on community health issues and integrated models of care. She named her company *Ausculta,* which literally means "listening with the heart." Her work over the next six years demonstrated that fiscal realities and philosophical intentions can reside on the same balance sheet.

Today, Ms. James holds a position with Quorum Health Resources as Director of Integration Strategies. She works with Quorum hospitals to develop regional delivery systems and community partnerships.